International Students

Strengthening a Critical Resource

Maureen S. Andrade and Norman W. Evans

AMERICAN COUNCIL ON EDUCATION
® The Unifying Voice for Higher Education

ROWMAN & LITTLEFIELD EDUCATION
Lanham • New York • Toronto • Plymouth, UK

378.1982691 INTERNA 2009s

International students

Published in the United States of America
by Rowman & Littlefield Education
A Division of Rowman & Littlefield Publishers, Inc.
A wholly owned subsidiary of The Rowman & Littlefield Publishing Group, Inc.
4501 Forbes Boulevard, Suite 200, Lanham, Maryland 20706
www.rowmaneducation.com

Estover Road
Plymouth PL6 7PY
United Kingdom

British Library Cataloguing in Publication Information Available

Library of Congress Cataloging-in-Publication Data

Andrade, Maureen S., 1961–
  International students : strengthening a critical resource / Maureen S. Andrade
and Norman W. Evans.
    p. cm.
  Includes index.
  ISBN 978-1-60709-175-2 (cloth : alk. paper) — ISBN 978-1-60709-177-6
(electronic)
    1. Students, Foreign—United States 2. College student orientation—United
States. 3. Cross-cultural counseling—United States. 4. English language—Study
and teaching—Foreign speakers. 5. Intercultural communication—United States.
I. Evans, Norman W. II. Title.
  LB2376.A65 2009
  378.1'9826910973—dc22   2009004959

∞™ The paper used in this publication meets the minimum requirements of
American National Standard for Information Sciences—Permanence of Paper
for Printed Library Materials, ANSI/NISO Z39.48-1992.
Manufactured in the United States of America.

To and for the many thousands of international
students who have enriched our lives.

Contents

Figures and Tables

FIGURES

TABLES

1

The International Student Picture

Some might argue that as less than 4 percent of students at colleges and universities in the United States are international students (Bhandari & Chow, 2007), expending ever-decreasing resources on their support is inadvisable. Others may observe that international students are typically well prepared, representing the educated elite of their nations, and they are generally well funded through personal means or government sources and thus unlikely to need academic or financial assistance. Their academic preparation is an indicator that they are likely to succeed in American institutions of higher education.

To support this view, one could consider that first-year persistence rates for international students are comparable to those for all students—80.1 percent compared to 80.2 percent (Hayes, 2007). Six-year graduation rates show the same trend with persistence rates of 58.7 percent for international students compared to 57.8 percent for domestic students (Hayes, 2007). Another factor that seemingly points to the conclusion that international students are not due much notice is that, by definition, they are in the United States on student visas for purposes of short-term study and thus have little impact on the future of the nation.

What this picture omits is the contributions of international students to institutions of higher education in the United States and to national interests. It also ignores the substantial educational and cultural adjustment needs of international students in spite of their academic accomplishments in their own nations. This adjustment is complicated by the fact that many international students are nonnative speakers of English (NNES),

1

and although they may have attained some degree of English proficiency in their own countries, often experience considerable challenges when faced with the demands of academic English in their course work. Similarly, weaknesses in English proficiency can affect social interaction, which may result in isolation, impede cultural learning and exchange, and negatively impact overall adjustment (e.g., see Chapdelaine & Alexitch, 2004; Lewthwaite, 1996; Lin & Yi, 1997; Rajapaksa & Dundes, 2003; Schutz & Richards, 2003). Even international students who speak English natively or have high proficiency levels may experience cultural dissonance or be unprepared for educational differences.

Those who suggest that international students have always sought educational opportunities in the United States and will continue to do so must consider the impact of increasing global competition in the international student market, a key reason higher educational institutions cannot overlook international student adjustment issues. Although the United States historically has enjoyed an advantage over other nations and continues to attract the larger share of the market—22 percent of all internationally mobile students and 30 percent of the share of the eight leading host countries—this percentage has been declining since 1997 (Chin & Bhandari, 2006; Bhandari & Chow, 2007). In fact, one source reports that the market share has decreased from a high of 40 percent in the past decade (Schneider, 2002).

Another factor to consider is that the United States also has the lowest overall percentage of international student higher education enrollments in comparison to its main competitors—less than 4 percent compared to approximately 20 percent for Australia, 15 percent for the United Kingdom, 14 percent in Germany, and 12 percent in France (Bhandari & Chow, 2007). Other countries have formed national strategies to recruit international students, including ways to provide needed information, simplify the application process, and deliver attractive degree programs, while the United States currently has no such marketing plan (NAFSA, 2006c).

The purpose of this book is to provide an in-depth, comprehensive treatment of international students in the United States to inform institutions about how they can most effectively benefit from international student enrollment and offer the kind of support needed to create an unparalleled educational experience. Given the current global competition for international students and the funding they provide to resource-strapped institutions of higher education, increased familiarity with international student issues and effective programming practices is critical. This familiarity supports a greater understanding of the largely undiscovered educational resource represented by international students, a rethinking of the role of these students on campuses in the United States, and effective strategic planning.

This book reflects a variety of voices and contexts representing different institutional types and student populations, thereby offering an array of possibilities for how institutions can best benefit from and support international students. It establishes a foundation of general principles on which those working with international students can base initiatives appropriate to their own contexts. When considering a response, on a national or an institutional level, to the recruitment, support, and success of international students, an understanding of international student diversity in terms of socioeconomic status, cultural and linguistic backgrounds, home country educational systems, academic and professional goals, and academic level (i.e., undergraduate or graduate) is critical to understanding their needs. International student populations vary across institutions, and a successful strategy or program at one university may not be equally successful at another. However, the practices described in this volume demonstrate that many successful programs share similar foundational principles that are broadly applicable.

This chapter provides an overview of international students in the United States that serves as the basis for subsequent chapters. The chapter first discusses demographic information about international students—enrollment numbers, sources of origin, geographical locations of international students in the United States, host institutions, areas of study, sources of financing, and retention statistics. It then presents a compelling case for the importance of international students to the United States on a variety of levels—educational, financial, and political. The chapter reviews threats to international student enrollments, such as global competition, the strengthening of higher education infrastructures in sending countries, and complacency. International students are critical to American higher education goals. Further insights about this group of students are necessary to help them have a successful educational experience and enable U.S. institutions of higher education to continue to benefit from a long history of attracting and welcoming international students.

DEMOGRAPHICS

This section provides a snapshot of international students in the United States—their enrollment patterns, preferred types of host institutions, geographical locations in the nation, chosen areas of study, sources of financing, and persistence. While it is recognized that the specific figures cited are current at the time of publication and will not be completely accurate even in a year's time, they are presented as a means of demonstrating overall trends in the area of international student education in the United States. Although these trends are expected to remain fairly constant and are based on several years of data and information known to affect enrollments, unforeseen circumstances are possible. The data is based on the most recent information from Open Doors (Bhandari & Chow, 2007), published by the Institute of International Education, unless otherwise referenced.

Approximately 583,000 international students are enrolled in higher educational institutions in the United States. Following a period of enrollment declines, the nation has recently experienced more positive trends, as indicated by the percentage change of international student enrollments provided in table 1.1. This pattern holds true for total numbers of international students as well as for new students arriving in the country. The former increased by 8 percent in 2005/2006 and by 10 percent in 2006/2007. The gender of international students is fairly balanced at the undergraduate level, but at the graduate level, males comprise the majority at 59 percent. Similarly, only 4 percent of undergraduate international students are married as compared to 21 percent of graduate students.

The top sending countries for the United States in descending order are India, China, Korea, Japan, and Taiwan, together accounting for nearly half of all international students. India has the largest portion of enrollments (14.4 percent), reflecting a recent and apparently short-term reversal of declining numbers. Enrollments from Japan, however, continue to decrease. Shifts in the composition of sending countries tend to occur gradually due to economic, political, or academic factors within the country itself or in the United States.

Certainly, the September 11 terrorist attacks are an example of a factor that impacted international student enrollments, with lingering effects. Enormous decreases in the number of applications to graduate programs occurred, for example. In spite of recent positive trends in the number of

Table 1.1.   Annual Percentage Change of International Student Enrollments

Year	Percentage Change
2000/01	+6.4%
2001/02	+6.4%
2002/03	+0.6%
2003/04	−2.4%
2004/05	−1.3%
2005/06	−0.05%
2006/07	+3.2%

first-time graduate enrollments of international students, applications in 2007 were still 27 percent below those of 2004 (Redd, 2007b).

International students tend to be concentrated in metropolitan areas, with approximately 90 percent living in large or mid-sized cities or their suburbs. New York, Los Angeles, Boston, Washington D.C., and Chicago host the largest numbers. Table 1.2 indicates approximate geographical distributions of international students within the country. Forty-three percent of all international students live and study in California, New York, Texas, Massachusetts, and Florida. Similar to the data on sending countries cited earlier, although population fluctuations occur from year to year and actual numbers and rankings of various cities or states change, the general picture of where international students live and study remains fairly constant.

The majority of international students study at the graduate level (45.4 percent) as opposed to the undergraduate level (40.8 percent). Approximately 11 percent of the latter group is at the associate's level, predominantly at community colleges. Others are enrolled in nondegree educational programs (6.7 percent) or are participating in optional practical training (7.1 percent) to gain experience in their field of study before returning home. International students represent a substantial percentage of overall enrollments in U.S. graduate schools (12 percent). Although the nation has almost two thousand higher education institutions, more than half of all international students (60 percent) are studying at only 156 of these institutions with doctoral/research institutions being the most popular choice. Once again, enrollments tend to fluctuate somewhat among doctoral/research, master's, baccalaureate, and associate's institutions. For example, in a given year, enrollments at doctoral institutions may decline by 1 percent but increase by 2 percent at master's institutions and 1 percent at baccalaureate institutions.

Similarly, the most popular fields of study for international students remain generally constant with slight variations from year to year. Business/management and engineering are the most in demand, with approximately 18 percent and 15 percent of the total enrollment respectively. Physical and

Table 1.2. Geographical Distribution of International Student Enrollments

Geographical Area			
West	Midwest	South	Northeast
23%	22%	30%	25%

Note. Rounded to the nearest full percentage point.

life sciences, social sciences, and mathematics and computer sciences are the next most popular areas of study, each comprising approximately between 8 and 9 percent of the total international student enrollment. Growth in enrollments of international scholars (those at doctoral institutions who are conducting research or teaching) has recently slowed from an 8 percent increase in 2005/2006 to a 1.3 percent increase in 2006/2007. Forty-five percent of these scholars are from China, Korea, India, and Japan with the majority (73 percent) conducting research and a smaller number (8 percent) both teaching and doing research. Of these, 68 percent are studying in four areas: life and biological sciences, health sciences, physical sciences, and engineering.

Other types of educational programs that attract international students to the United States are intensive English programs (IEPs), which are sponsored by colleges and universities nationwide, sometimes as part of a continuing education unit and at other times housed in an academic department. IEPs may also operate as independent private schools. The American Association of Intensive English Programs (AAIEP) has nearly 300 members, providing some estimate of the widespread nature of these programs. Some university programs, however, may not be classified as IEPs as they do not enroll students in English courses for a minimum of 18 hours per week. The latter generally focus on matriculated students who may be concurrently enrolled in other university courses while IEPs are for nonmatriculated students who want to learn English for a variety of purposes—personal or cultural enrichment or university admission in the United States. Students may enroll in IEPs for only a few weeks or for a year or more preparatory to admission to an institution of higher education. IEPs are most often considered revenue sources for their sponsoring institutions as English language proficiency is viewed by many as a means of providing greater employment opportunities and economic stability, and learning English in an English-speaking environment is much sought after by learners.

Although only about 3 percent of international students in the United States are enrolled in IEPs, they represent a significant source of income for some institutions and also serve as a means of recruiting students into the institution. IEPs suffered the greatest losses following September 11, which started a period of declining enrollments. Because many IEPs offer educational programs of short duration, they are more sensitive to economic, political, and educational changes (Chin & Bhandari, 2006). The difficulty of getting visas to study English after the terrorist attacks contributed to declining enrollments and forced many IEPs to close (NAFSA, 2006c). In fact, enrollments are less than half of what they were in the year 2000. Korea and Japan represent the largest portion of international students in IEPs with Saudi Arabian students in third place. In 2006, IEP enrollments increased by

3.6 percent, largely due to an enormous increase (227.7 percent) of Saudi Arabian students on home government scholarships. (See chapter 8 for information about the adjustment of Saudi students.)

Not only IEPs value international students for the funding they bring to the institution, but so do other academic programs, institutions as a whole, and the cities and states that host them. The approximately $14.5 billion contributed annually by international students and their dependents for living expenses is significant. California benefits from approximately $2 billion annually and New York, $1.8 billion. This is one of the key reasons for global competition for international students. Sources of international student funding are indicated in figure 1.1. Much of it is from outside the United States. International students at the undergraduate level fund a greater portion of their expenses from personal sources— close to 82 percent of the cost of their education—compared to graduate students, who contribute approximately 46 percent of their educational costs from personal and family funds. For undergraduates, only about 11 percent of their education expenses are provided by U.S. universities in contrast to graduate students who receive 46.6 percent of their funding from this source.

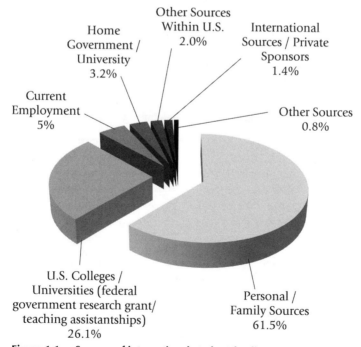

Figure 1.1.   Sources of international student funding. 2006/07.

Retention statistics for international students are not readily available, demonstrating some lack of interest in this population. Two organizations that do track persistence and/or graduation rates for nonresident aliens (i.e., international students) are the National Collegiate Athletic Association (NCAA) and the Consortium for Student Retention Data Exchange (CSRDE). CSRDE rates are based on data from a consortium of 440 colleges and universities rather than on national figures. As reported earlier, first-year persistence rates and six-year graduation rates for international students are no worse, and even slightly better, than those of American students, as indicated in table 1.3. (NCAA does not track first-year persistence.)

Considering that international students are at least as successful as American students, why be concerned about their success? Numerous first-year programs have been developed to support domestic students. These are typically based on persistence theories such as those of Tinto (1993) and Astin (1984) as well as research about nontraditional and minority students, discussed in more detail in chapter 2. Programs specifically developed for international students are highlighted in chapters 5–9. These programs demonstrate that institutions recognize the adjustment needs of international students and also value their contributions, wanting them to succeed so that future international students will seek educational opportunities at their institutions. Research into what specifically affects international student withdrawal or persistence is nearly nonexistent, however. A case study of one institution's research with two specific international student populations is examined in chapter 3 and provides insights into how traditional persistence theories may or may not account for the behaviors of a very different group of students.

Table 1.3. Persistence and Graduation Rates—International Students and All Students

	International Students	All Students
First-Year Persistence 2006/07 (Hayes, 2007)	80.2%	80.1%
Six-Year Graduation 1999 Freshman Cohort (NCAA, 2006)	59% (average across all divisions; range of 49%–66%)	57% (average across all divisions; range of 46%–63%)
Six-Year Graduation 1999 Freshman Cohort (Hayes, 2007)	58.7%	57.8%

In sum, although the actual figures quoted in this chapter vary from year to year, some generalizations are possible. Most international students in the United States are from Asia, specifically India, China, Korea, and Japan, and most study at the graduate level. Business, mathematics and computer science, engineering, life and biological sciences, health sciences, and physical sciences are the most popular fields of study. International students live predominantly in metropolitan areas and fund most of their own educational expenses from sources outside the United States, although this is truer of students at the undergraduate level than of those at the graduate level. Persistence and graduation rates for international students are comparable to those of domestic students although numerical indicators may mask transition challenges.

International student enrollment patterns demonstrate some consistencies as represented by the figures cited; however, they are subject to a number of factors that may be difficult to predict; thus, institutional leaders must be constantly aware of possible threats to current patterns and plan strategically. The United States has recently experienced declines in overall enrollments and in enrollments from its top sending countries. Although these seem to have leveled off, constant scrutiny is needed to analyze and predict political, economic, and educational shifts within the United States and globally that may affect enrollments. While the recent rebound in enrollments is positive, it only restores enrollments to the 2002 level (Redden, 2007) and should not be viewed as a reason to relax. Internal institutional factors and decisions regarding academic programs, support programs, recruitment and admissions, and institutional missions also have effects. Factors impacting the United States generally are addressed later in the chapter. First, we examine why international students are a critical resource.

INTERNATIONAL STUDENTS AS A CRITICAL RESOURCE

As mentioned previously, international students comprise approximately 4 percent of the entire higher education enrollment in the United States. While this number appears relatively low, it masks the fact that individual universities and programs may have large percentages of international students, particularly if institutional missions focus on educational goals associated with international studies, intercultural learning, diversity, or globalization or if they are located in areas of the country that attract international students. Similarly, some fields of study host significant numbers of international students. Many campuses recognize the benefits of international student enrollments. Even those whose main motivation for admitting international students is financial (viewing them as "cash cows") are best served by supporting their source of revenue. Institutions with low international student enrollments also have the potential to benefit.

National interests are promoted when higher education produces graduates with the intercultural sensitivity and competence to be effective in a global workforce. International students can be significant contributors to this goal. They enrich institutions by enabling American students to have direct contact with those from outside their national borders, thereby preparing them to be global citizens (NAFSA, 2003). Survey findings representing a broad spectrum of Americans indicate that they recognize the importance of preparing future generations with the ability to participate in an interconnected world (NAFSA, 2006a). Americans believe that this goal can be accomplished through gaining knowledge about world cultures and developing the skills to operate in an interconnected society through interaction with people from other cultures. Rapid technological changes and communication advances are impacting the lives of people worldwide and creating a global society. As this society emerges, those possessing world knowledge and international capabilities will have the advantage.

Diversity in the classroom and on campus accompanied by meaningful interaction, both structured and unstructured, encourages understanding across borders and advances global preparedness. Global competence can be developed through classroom discussions and assignments, which are broadened by international student perspectives. International students should be viewed as resources that add educational value. Faculty can internationalize the content of their courses through lectures, readings, and assignments and ask international students to contribute with case studies or related information from their own countries (Coleman, 1997), thus preparing American students for situations different from those they would typically encounter. Faculty can also encourage group projects requiring American and international students to collaborate. This prepares students for real-world situations in which they may need to work with those different from themselves, balance each other's strengths and weaknesses, and practice principles of conflict resolution (Coleman, 1997).

Outside the classroom, international students are also a resource for intercultural learning (see chapter 8). As with classroom exchanges, programs or events organized for the purpose of cultural exchange help American students broaden their understanding of international students and international students learn more about American ways. Universities may sponsor international education programs involving local schools and communities, service learning, internships, workshops and discussions on American ways, international festivals or culture clubs, workshops for faculty and departments working with international students, visits to American families, learning communities, and peer partnerships (e.g., see Abe, Talbot, & Geelhoed, 1998; Peterson, Briggs, Dreasher, Horner, & Nelson, 1999; Shigaki & Smith, 1997). Work opportunities such as internships provide international students with greater exposure to American life, help them financially, and benefit the economy (NAFSA, 2006b). These opportunities also allow employers to increase their intercultural expertise and knowledge of practices in other countries. Support programming may focus on assistance for students' families to help them adjust to daily life and integrate better with the local community. Counseling services may be a key for mediating successful cultural adjustment (e.g., see Jacob & Greggo, 2001).

These programs may be based on intercultural adjustment or learning theories such as the U-curve theory (Adler, 1975; Lysgaard, 1955; Oberg, 1960), which posits that newcomers to a culture progress through several stages: initial enthusiasm, feelings of alienation and rejection, increased ability to adapt, and finally, acceptance of differences and the ability to function comfortably in the new culture. Another theory that serves as the basis for intercultural programs is Furnham and Bochner's (1986) Social Skills and Culture Learning Model, which emphasizes the importance of social interaction in cultural adjustment. Bennett's Development of Intercultural Sensitivity Model (1998) provides insight into intercultural growth for both international and American students, describing the development of intercultural sensitivity on a scale ranging from ethnocentric to ethnorelative thinking.

These scales demonstrate the value of how one's world view is expanded through intercultural experiences, and specifically the potential for rich educational growth through in-class and out-of-class cultural exchanges among international students and their professors and peers. They also emphasize the importance of guiding and supporting cultural interaction as understanding and empathy may not develop unaided. In the educational realm, international students benefit American higher educational institutions in very practical ways. A shortage of American students enrolled in some graduate programs, especially in scientific fields, has resulted in universities depending on international teaching assistants to provide undergraduate courses in these areas, which otherwise could not be offered (NAFSA, 2003; Peterson et al., 1999). Having international graduate students teach American undergraduates expands their viewpoints as they are exposed to different educational approaches, knowledge bases, and world views. Teaching assistantships provide financial support to graduate students, help them develop teaching skills, as many will become faculty themselves, and fill a need in the institution.

Teaching American undergraduates also exposes international graduate students to American culture as represented by these students. This practice presents a unique opportunity for reciprocal cultural learning (chapter 8 showcases an example of how this goal can be supported by partnering international teaching assistants with undergraduate cultural/linguistic "guides"). Additionally, by attracting the top international students to its graduate programs, the nation builds its knowledge economy, resulting in the development of cutting-edge jobs, new knowledge and skills, and an environment that encourages leadership, innovation, and creativity (Gray, 2003; NAFSA, 2006c). In fact, advocates of greater national support for international students suggest looking at their output in terms of contributions to research (Jacobs, 2005). Professors at American universities train international graduate students to be researchers. The research of individual professors is enhanced by the assistance of these students, and the status of the university is enhanced by the reputation of its faculty.

The results of research—the creation of new knowledge, technology, innovation, and products—allow the United States to be academically competitive worldwide and enjoy a strong economy and standard of living. Collaborative research is needed to address world problems (NAFSA, 2006b). Collaboration begun in U.S. institutions between faculty and international students may be extended to opportunities for international research through these students and their connections.

Some international students remain legally in the country to contribute needed skills after they graduate (NAFSA, 2003), especially in scientific fields. The nation relies on scientists born outside the United States but trained in the United States (Gray, 2003). Former international students also frequently become faculty members at American universities where they enhance institutional research reputations.

Another way of measuring the output of international students is to determine how many of the nation's graduate faculty were once international students in the United States and how many have their names on patent applications for new inventions, which not only demonstrates evidence of expert research skills but is a source of institutional revenue (Jacobs, 2005). The nation should consider how many international graduate students are hired as graduate faculty in the top universities in the nation, particularly in fields that strengthen the economy, such as science, technology, engineering, math, and business (Jacobs, 2005). In their capacity as faculty, they continue to give back by training the next top students to be researchers and contribute to society.

In addition to educational benefits—those that enrich learning, those that focus on more practical areas of need, and those with long-term positive impact on society—the influence of international students extends beyond the institution to areas of national interest. American higher education institutions have a reputation for educating world leaders. The U.S.

Department of State (n.d.) accounts for a total of 216 world leaders in 81 countries who received their education in the United States. The experience of living in the United States and associating with Americans increases appreciation of political values and organizations and lays a foundation for positive relations (NAFSA, 2003). Personal connections are made to the United States as a country and between future leaders from the United States and other countries, which leads to the facilitation of foreign policy (NAFSA, 2003, 2006c). Associating with those from different countries helps dissolve stereotypes on both sides, open minds, create friendships, and develop appreciation for different world views. International alumni of the United States have fond memories of their educational experience (Peterson et al., 1999) and become ambassadors and supporters of the United States (Gray, 2003) as they fill positions of influence in politics, business, and education, guiding and shaping the policies of other nations. International education is an investment in helping the world be secure (NAFSA, 2006c). This goal is realized as international students interact on campus and in the community, and intercultural understanding is increased for all involved. Higher education is positioned to fill a strong role in supporting American interests abroad through the alliances and loyalties of its international students.

The economic benefits of admitting international students to institutions of higher education have already been mentioned. These benefits impact institutions, communities, states, and the nation. Additionally, upon their return home, international students often continue to purchase and support U.S. goods and services (NAFSA, 2003). Connections among international and American students may lead to business and trade ventures of a global nature that benefit the United States as well as other countries. Fundraising from international alumni who have become prominent is also an important source of institutional revenue (Coleman, 1997).

In sum, today's college student must be prepared for the effects of globalization. Those who enter the work force need the skills to appreciate and communicate with those different from themselves. They need to understand diverse perspectives and the world beyond the borders of the United States. International students can assist higher education institutions in preparing students for these future roles. The admission of international students provides opportunities for greater exposure to and understanding of varied experiences and intercultural learning within and outside the classroom. Communities can also be involved in intercultural learning programs. International students contribute on a practical level by teaching undergraduate classes, aiding research, developing new knowledge, and filling employment needs in the United States, particularly in scientific fields and at top research universities. They are assets to foreign policy through the friendships they form and their understanding of American values, particularly as many become future leaders who will influence the politics and economies of their own and other nations. The financial benefits of international students while in the United States and upon returning home are significant.

The contributions of international students cannot be realized unaided. Chapter 2 addresses the adjustment factors of international students. Transitions into the American higher educational system and into American culture must be smooth so that international students feel comfortable and have a positive experience. Effective intercultural learning initiatives are shared in chapter 8, demonstrating that simply placing diverse students together with no structuring or training does not automatically result in greater understanding. Opportunities for intercultural development must be created. The final section of this chapter addresses challenges affecting national interests in the international student market.

THE GLOBAL COMPETITION FOR INTERNATIONAL STUDENTS

As noted in the discussion of demographics, international student enrollments in the United States experience fluctuations. These upward and downward movements reflect the degree of the nation's competitiveness with other nations (Johnson, 2006). The general trend since the 1950s has been upward; however, a number of factors have recently created concerns. Visa issues such as mandatory face-to-face interviews, extended processing time, employment restrictions, the intent-to-return-home condition, and impressions of high refusal rates contribute to perceptions of closed doors and declining or stagnating enrollment figures (U.S. Government Accountability Office [USGAO], 2007). Although recent declines have stabilized, aggressive competition from other countries for a larger share of the international student market and the increased ability of top sending countries to provide quality higher education and job opportunities in their own countries continue to threaten the U.S. position. These issues are discussed next.

The global mobility of international students in the near future is potentially enormous (Schneider, 2002). Other nations besides the United States recognize the contributions of these students. Global competitors are equipped with strategies to attract them so as to benefit from educating the next world leaders and the elite in the fields of science and technology (NAFSA, 2006c). The United Kingdom has a new immigration policy to attract international students and highly skilled workers (Coun-

cil of Graduate Schools [CGS], 2006d) and has, in fact, increased enrollments by 118,000 since 1999 with the goal of recruiting an additional
one hundred thousand in the next five years (NAFSA, 2006c). Some believe that "America's tradition of world dominance in doctoral education,
which has fueled research and innovation since the first PhDs were
awarded in the United States in the 1880s" (Strauss, 2006, p. A06) is in
danger due to high attrition rates of 50 to 60 percent and competition
from China, India, and the European Union. Others believe U.S. graduate degrees and research opportunities are the nation's key advantage
(Schneider, 2002).

In a survey of graduate deans, 40 percent expressed concern with international student issues, particularly the Bologna Process (Brown,
2006), a reform movement involving 46 European nations cooperating
to create a seamless higher education system with transferable credit and
degrees in English to encourage mobility and attract students (Council of
Europe Higher Education and Research, n.d.; Foley, 2007; NAFSA,
2006c). This process has been compared to higher education reforms in
the United States after World War II in that it democratizes higher education by providing the necessary funding to make it accessible (Foley,
2007) and by allowing open access. However, it extends to one-quarter
of the countries in the world, creating an enormous global impact: "The
Bologna Process may force the entire world to redefine higher education
in the twenty-first century" (Foley, 2007, p. 3). Discussions regarding the
impact of Bologna on U.S. higher education are increasing in momentum. Some believe that the process will result in more European students
seeking master's degrees in the United States after completing their three-
year degrees at home while others predict that more American and non-
European students will be attracted to European higher education institutions than to those in the United States (Bologna Isn't Coming to the
United States—It's Here, 2007). Chapter 6 provides a possible approach
to competing with European institutions with regard to English language
requirements.

In addition to the Bologna Process in Europe, other nations outside the
United States are offering a variety of study programs involving on-site,
satellite sites, and distance education and have made attracting international students a national priority with increased outreach, simplified administrative procedures, and cooperation among stakeholders beginning at
the national level (Schneider, 2002). Scholarships, informative and inviting
websites, central planning, and enhanced budgets are also characteristic.
Overall, international student concerns ranked sixth for graduate school
deans in 2007 (Redd, 2007a), demonstrating the importance of this population to U.S. higher education.

The economic advantage of international student enrollments has been addressed. This is a primary motivating factor behind global competition. In Canada, revenues from international students are essential to higher education (Lee & Wesche, 2000). International student recruitment in the United Kingdom is driven by the need to increase cash flow and be competitive as fundraising is not practiced and the government caps tuition fees (Marshall, 2005). Some Australians are concerned that English standards are being overlooked so as to attract international students to educational institutions (Coley, 1999). The careful planning and recruiting efforts of these countries is producing results. U.S. competitors have much larger international student enrollment percentages—consider Australia at 20 percent and the United Kingdom at 15 percent compared to less than 4 percent for the United States. "Compared with major Anglophone host countries, the United States has a large untapped capacity to absorb significant future growth in international student enrollment" (Chin & Bhandari, 2006, p. 24).

Other countries are also more liberal in allowing international students greater work opportunities during and after their studies (see chapter 9 for a discussion of how work restrictions in the United States affect international scholars). In Australia, international graduates contribute needed expertise to the workforce in the areas of information and communications technology and engineering (Colebatch, 2005). Competitors also permit international students to work both on and off campus, thereby giving them a fuller educational and cultural experience. The U.S. requirement for international students to state their intent to return home after graduation is perhaps one of the most criticized government policies in relation to international students (e.g., see Johnson, 2006; USGAO, 2007; NAFSA, 2006c). By all accounts, the United States needs highly skilled workers from around the world to maintain global competitiveness and contribute in technology, scientific fields, and research industries. In fact, the possibility of employment in the country is one of the attractions of a U.S. degree, along with the quality of education, research opportunities, foreign-born faculty, English learning opportunities, and democracy (USGAO, 2007).

These advantages are being eroded. Policies restricting international students from research and lab access and requiring them to state their intention not to immigrate are two examples. Foreign-born faculty could be an advantage of the past if top research institutions are restricted from hiring the products of U.S. graduate programs. Intensive English programs have been seriously affected by immigration policies that have made obtaining a visa difficult or at least created the perception that getting a visa to study short-term in the United States is simply too much trouble. These challenges have led to fewer students coming to the United States to learn English and contributed to closures of many IEPs. "One would be hard pressed to think of another major power in the world that discouraged the study of its language" (NAFSA, 2006c, p. 5). Recent rebounds in IEP enrollments have only begun to restore the nation to former levels and are predominantly attributed to a government scholarship program for Saudi Arabian students (see more on adjustment challenges for Saudi Arabian students in chapter 6). In an attempt to maintain security and protect national interests, the United States is restricting its opportunities to gain full advantage of the talents and skills of international students. It is also losing potential allies. In addition to competition from other nations, developments in students' home countries may also have an impact. India and China, two primary sources of international students for the United States, account for 25 percent of all international students (NAFSA, 2006c). Both countries have developed sufficient educational systems and national economies to enable their citizens to pursue American-based tertiary education (Brown, 2006). Improvements and growth in higher education within these countries, however, suggests the possibility of students staying in their home countries to pursue graduate studies, and indeed, some reports indicate that China and India are encouraging students to remain home (NAFSA, 2006c). High tuition at American institutions may also be incentive for students to study at home or pursue their educations in other countries (International Institute of Education [IIE], 2005). These students may also be attracted to European universities due to the advantages offered by the Bologna Process, including three-year degrees (Impact on U.S. Competitiveness, 2007).

A review of national data demonstrates the dependency of U.S. research institutions on international students. Over half of all international students in the United States are enrolled at doctoral degree–granting and research universities. In fall 2006, survey responses from universities granting 75 percent of all master's degrees and 89 percent of all doctorate degrees indicated that 16 percent of the total graduate enrollment consisted of non-U.S. citizens (Redd, 2007c). International students account for 48 percent of all enrollments in engineering, 40 percent in the physical sciences, and 27 percent in the biological sciences. Only 16 percent of U.S. graduate students are enrolled in these fields. These figures clearly demonstrate reliance of graduate programs in these fields of studies on international students and the wisdom to allow them to be recruited into the American workforce upon graduation.

In spite of these factors, the nation remains disengaged and complacent, unable to recognize the competition for international graduate students (NAFSA, 2006c). "What is most alarming is that, for the first time, the United States seems to be losing its status as the destination of choice for

international students" (NAFSA, 2006c, p. 2). The United States is not competing for a declining resource but for the expanding possibilities of an increasingly mobile population of international students (Schneider, 2002).
The nation has not yet adjusted its thinking related to security and immigration and lacks an overall national strategy (NAFSA, 2006c). The U.S. portion of the international student market decreased from 25 percent to 22
percent between 2000 and 2004 (CGS, 2006c). Although the 9 percent and
12 percent increases in international graduate applications in 2006/2007
and 2005/2006 are promising, they do not compensate for the 5 percent
decrease in 2004/2005 and the 28 percent decrease in 2003/2004 (CGS,
2006a, 2007b). In fact, applications are down significantly since 2003.

Recent application increases are attributed to immigration changes, particularly reduced time for obtaining visas (CGS, 2006a; IIE, 2005), and institutional improvements, specifically more efficient admission processes;
use of information technologies, call centers, new staff and resources; increased recruitment; and greater awareness of global trends (CGS, 2006c).
The U.S. Department of State reports issuing more student visas in 2007
than in 2006, and they are attempting to streamline visa processing, including some instances of waiving the interview for those renewing their
visas (Redden, 2008).

Although some improvements have been made in visa procedures, the
various entities in the federal government responsible for international
student oversight, such as the Departments of State, Education, and Homeland Security, do not coordinate their efforts. For example, policies restricting international students' access to research and labs and their ability to get social security numbers and driver's licenses and to stay in the
country and work after graduation counteract the progress made in sim-
plifying the visa application process (Johnson, 2006). Although individual
government agencies make policies they consider in the nation's best interest, their goals are dissimilar (Johnson, 2006). Participants in a forum
sponsored by the U.S. Government Accountability Office (USGAO) noted
that the United States lacks an integrated approach and recommended the
government develop a coordinated plan, change immigration policies (especially to allow international students to stay in the country and work),
and recruit new sources of international students from developing nations
(USGAO, 2007).

Forum participants suggested a number of reasons the United States may
be in danger of losing its share of the market. In addition to those already
discussed (i.e., the recruitment strategies of other countries, more educational options within students' own countries, and the effects of U.S. government policies—both real and perceived), high costs of tuition and en-
trance exams such as the TOEFL and GRE and challenges with bolstering

recruitment budgets to remain competitive were also cited. One difficulty with declining or flat enrollments is that because enrollment numbers do not provide information regarding the quality of international students coming to the United States, the nation remains uninformed as to whether it is still attracting the best and brightest international students or maintaining its numbers but losing these students (USGAO, 2007). U.S. graduate schools perceive the quality of applicants as being maintained or increasing overall, but this could vary by program (CGS, 2006b). Similarly, enrollment decreases impact some institutions more than others. Those with the largest international student enrollments tend to have the greatest gains in applications (CGS, 2007a). The ability to maintain or increase recruitment budgets contributes to competitiveness.

Common criticisms related to the topic of global competition for international students are the lack of a national strategic plan, coordination, communication, and integration. These themes are pervasive in the discussion of the nation's response to the issue. Coordination must occur among government departments, nongovernment agencies, and higher education institutions. The USGAO forum, which brings together leaders from government, universities, higher education organizations, research institutions, and industry to discuss the problem and make recommendations, is a crucial first step. Some of the more common suggestions for addressing prevailing conditions are proactive recruitment, particularly in untapped areas of the world; better advising and outreach with information pertaining to visa procedures, study opportunities, advantages of the United States as an education destination, and how to locate an appropriate university. In addition, modification of immigration law to encourage global mobility through internships, allowing employment off campus, lengthening optional practical training (OPT), recruiting needed expertise to the workforce, permitting study at IEPs on a tourist visa, and eliminating restrictions on research involvements would do much to encourage international student enrollments in the United States. Other suggestions include expanding distance education and offshore programs, addressing education costs, increasing joint funding efforts, forming international education partnerships, and greater understanding of current and future trends based on a historical analysis (e.g., see USGAO, 2007; NAFSA, 2006c).

Certainly changes that eliminate barriers at the national level are critical. Coordinated efforts should be a top priority. However, institutions must examine their own strategies for attracting and supporting international students and coordinate efforts within their own campuses. This involves having a clearly stated objective related to the rationale for admitting international students, which will shape strategies for their recruitment, admission, and support. Institutions must collect data related to international student persistence and adjustment patterns in order to identify appropriate academic, social, and support programming. Institutions must also consider international student interests and find ways to offer incentives, capitalizing on the advantages that attract international students. Analyzing new educational trends and the recruitment campaigns of competitors is also essential. Some evidence indicates that U.S. institutions are being proactive, particularly at the graduate level where 79 percent of institutions reported implementing one outreach intervention and one-third indicated initiating more than one (CGS, 2006b). These included new programs, collaboration with international agencies, student funding, recruitment travel, increased marketing budgets, and the dedication of new admissions staff to international students.

Threats to international student enrollments in the United States include global competition, the strengthening of higher education infrastructures in sending countries, and complacency, which prevents a proactive approach. Constant enrollment fluctuations, although seemingly subtle, can gradually erode the position of the United States in hosting international students. Although it is difficult to predict which sending countries, programs of study, institutions, or areas of the country will be primarily affected, examining the strategies of competitors and the educational, political, and economic movements of sending countries are useful in predicting and preparing for change. Communication and collaboration among organizations supportive of international education to effect change in government policy is key. Finally, institutions must address areas over which they have internal control to ensure they fully understand the vital resource they have on their campuses.

CONCLUSION

Given the significance of international students to U.S. higher education and the current arena of global competition, an in-depth understanding of these students is critical. Chapter 1 has reviewed the current status of international students in the United States including demographics, the benefits of international student enrollments, and threats to American market dominance. Creative and effective ideas for addressing challenges at an institutional level from a broad array of perspectives are addressed in subsequent chapters. First, however, we explore the international student experience in terms of their transition and success in U.S. higher education.

REFERENCES

Abe, J., Talbot, D. M., & Geelhoed, R. J. (1998). Effects of a peer program on international student adjustment. *Journal of College Student Development, 39*(6), 539–547.

Adler, P. S. (1975). The transitional experience: An alternative view of culture shock. *Journal of Humanistic Psychology, 15*(4), 13–23.

Astin, A. (1984). Student involvement: A developmental theory for higher education. *Journal of College Student Personnel 25,* 297–308.

Bennett, M. J. (1998). Intercultural communication: A current perspective. In M. J. Bennett (Ed.), *Basic concepts of intercultural communication. Selected readings* (pp. 1–34). Yarmouth, MI: Intercultural Press.

Bhandari, R., & Chow, P. (2007). *Open doors: Report on international educational exchange.* New York: Institute of International Education.

Bologna Isn't Coming to the United States—It's Here. (2007). In C. Murphy (Ed.), *The Bologna Process, International Educator supplement* (pp. 12–13). NAFSA: Association of International Educators. Retrieved November 16, 2007, from http://www .nafsa.org/_/Document/_/bolognaprocess_ie_supp.pdf

Brown, H. (2006). Data sources: 2006 international applications. *Communicator, 39*(4), 3–4.

Chapdelaine, R. F., & Alexitch, L. R. (2004). Social skills difficulty: Model of culture shock for international graduate students. *Journal of College Student Development, 45*(2), 167–184.

Chin, H. K. K., & Bhandari, R. (2006). *Open doors: Report on international educational exchange.* New York: Institute of International Education.

Colebatch, T. (2005, January 22). *Foreign students settle.* Retrieved December 1, 2005, from http://www.theage.com.au/news/Immigration/Foreign-students-settle/2005/ 01/21/1106110942999.html?oneclick=true

Coleman, S. (1997). International students in the classroom: A resource and an opportunity. *International Education, 26,* 52–61.

Coley, M. (1999). The English language entry requirements of Australian universities for students of non-English speaking background. *Higher Education Research & Development 18*(1), 7–17.

Council of Europe Higher Education and Research. (n.d.). What is the Bologna process? Retrieved July 3, 2006, from http://www.coe.int/T/DG4/HigherEducation/ EHEA2010/BolognaPedestrians_en.asp

Council of Graduate Schools. (2006a, March). Findings from 2006 CGS international graduate admissions survey phase I: Applications. Retrieved July 4, 2006, from http://www.cgsnet.org/portals/0/pdf/R_intlapps06_1.pdf

———. (2006b, August). Findings from 2006 CGS international graduate admissions survey phase II: Final applications and offers of admission. Retrieved June 12, 2007, from http://www.cgsnet.org/portals/0/pdf/R_intladm06_II.pdf.

———. (2006c, October). Findings from the 2006 CGS international graduate admissions survey phase III: Admissions and enrollment. Retrieved November 23, 2006, from http://www.cgsnet.org/portals/0/pdf/R_Intlenrl06_III.pdf

————. (2006d, March 23). Graduate applications from international students increase significantly but numbers remain below 2003 levels. Retrieved July 4, 2006, from http://www.cgsnet.org/portals/0/pdf/N_pr_intlapps06_1.pdf

————. (2007a, April). Findings from the 2007 CGS international graduate admissions survey phase I: Applications. Retrieved June 12, 2007, from http://www.cgsnet.org/portals/0/pdf/R_IntlApps07_I.pdf

————. (2007b, August). Findings from the 2007 CGS international graduate admissions survey phase II: Final applications and initial offers of admission. Retrieved April 10, 2008, from http://www.cgsnet.org/Default.aspx?tabid=172

Foley, C. J. (2007). Bologna: An opportunity for international cooperation. In C. Murphy (Ed.), *The Bologna Process, International Educator supplement* (pp. 3–4). NAFSA: Association of International Educators. Retrieved November 16, 2007, from http://www.nafsa.org/_/Document/_/bolognaprocess_ie_supp.pdf

Furnham, A., & Bochner, S. (1986). *Culture shock.* New York: Methuen.

Gray, P. E. (2003). Security versus openness: The case of universities. *Issues in Science and Technology, 19*(4), 89–90.

Hayes, R. (2007). *2006–07 CSRDE Retention Report: The retention and graduation rates of 1999–2005 entering baccalaureate degree-seeking freshman cohorts in 438 colleges and universities.* Norman: The University of Oklahoma Center for Institutional Data Exchange and Analysis.

Impact on U.S. Competitiveness. (2007). In C. Murphy (Ed.), *The Bologna Process, International Educator supplement* (p. 16). NAFSA: Association of International Educators. Retrieved November 16, 2007, from http://www.nafsa.org/_/Document/_/bolognaprocess_ie_supp.pdf

International Institute of Education. (2005). International student and total U.S. enrollment. Retrieved July 4, 2006, from http://opendoors.iienetwork.org/?p=69692

Jacob, E. J., & Greggo, J. W. (2001). Using counselor training and collaborative programming strategies in working with international students. *Journal of Multicultural Counseling and Development, 29*(1), 73–88.

Jacobs, B. (2005). The tangible contributions of international graduate students: An alternative approach and some evidence from the University of Rochester. *Communicator, 38*(4), 1–3.

Johnson, M. M. (2006, July 28). Toward a new foreign-student strategy. *The Chronicle of Higher Education, 52*(47), B16. Retrieved June 12, 2007, from http://chronicle.com/temp/reprint.php?id=vjrnw1qdw4nld9jc8d12z6jkp1zlxpxr

Lee, K., & Wesche, M. (2000). Korean students' adaptation to post-secondary studies in Canada: A case study. *The Canadian Modern Language Review, 56*(4), 637–689.

Lewthwaite, M. (1996). A study of international students' perspectives on cross-cultural adaptation. *International Journal for the Advancement of Counselling, 19*(2), 167–185.

Lin, J. G., & Yi, J. K. (1997). Asian international students' adjustment: Issues and program suggestions. *College Student Journal, 31*(4), 473–479.

Lysgaard, S. (1955). Adjustment in a foreign society: Norwegian Fulbright grantees visiting the United States. *International Social Science Bulletin, 7*, 45–51.

Marshall, E. (2005, February 4). Cash-short schools aim to raise fees, recruit foreign students. *Science, 307,* 656.

NAFSA: Association of International Educators. (2003, January). In America's interest: Welcoming international students. Retrieved July 4, 2006, from http://www.nafsa.org/_/Document/_/in_america_s_interest.pdf

———. (2006a). Americans call for leadership on international education. A national survey on preparation for a global society. Retrieved June 12, 2007, from http://www.nafsa.org/_/Document/_/americans_call_for_leadership.pdf

———. (2006b, March). An international education policy for U.S. leadership, competitiveness, and security. Retrieved June 12, 2007, from http://www.nafsa.org/_/Document/_/toward_an_international_1.pdf

———. (2006c, June). Restoring U.S. competitiveness for international students and scholars. Retrieved July 4, 2006, from http://www.nafsa.org/_/Document/_/restoring_u.s.pdf

Oberg, K. (1960). Culture shock: Adjustment to new cultural environments. *Practical Anthropology, 7,* 177–182.

Peterson, D. M., Briggs, P., Dreasher, L., Horner, D. D., & Nelson, T. (1999). Contributions of international students and programs to campus diversity. *New Directions for Student Services, 86,* 67–77.

Rajapaksa, S., & Dundes, L. (2003). It's a long way home: International student adjustment to living in the United States. *Journal of College Student Retention, 4*(10), 15–28.

Redd, K. E. (2007a). Data sources: Results for the CGS pressing issues survey. *Communicator, 40*(5), 3–4.

———. (2007b). Data sources: Trends in international graduate student enrollments. *Communicator, 40*(4), 3–4.

———. (2007c). Graduate enrollment and degrees: 1996 to 2006. Retrieved April 11, 2008, from http://www.cgsnet.org/Default.aspx?tabid=168

Redden, E. (2007, November 12). More foreign students—everywhere. *Inside Higher Ed.* Retrieved November 16, 2007, from http://www.insidehighered.com/news/2007/11/12/opendoors

———. (2008, February 8). Any advice about visas? *Inside Higher Ed.* Retrieved April 11, 2008, from http://www.insidehighered.com/news/2008/02/08/visas

Schneider, M. (2002, November 25). Others' open doors: How other nations attract international students. Implications for U.S. educational exchange. Washington, DC: U.S. State Department Bureau of Educational and Cultural Affairs. Retrieved June 15, 2007, from http://exchanges.state.gov/iep/execsummary.pdf

Schutz, A., & Richards, M. (2003). International students' experience of graduate study in Canada. *Journal of the International Society for Teacher Education, 7*(1), 10–23).

Shigaki, I. S., & Smith, S. A. (1997). A cultural sharing model: American buddies for international students. *International Education, 27,* 5–21.

Strauss, V. (2006, April 18). Competition worries graduate programs. *Washington Post,* A06. Retrieved July 4, 2006, from http://www.cgsnet.org/portals/0/pdf/N_Post_0406_Competition.pdf

Tinto, V. (1993). *Leaving college: Rethinking the causes and cures of student attrition* (2nd ed.). Chicago: University of Chicago Press.

U.S. Department of State. (n.d.). Foreign students yesterday, world leaders today. Retrieved July 27, 2004, from http://exchanges.state.gov/education/educationusa/leaders.htm#top

U.S. Government Accountability Office. (2007, January 23). Global competitiveness: Implications for the nation's higher education system (Report No. GAO-07-135SP). Retrieved June 12, 2007, from http://www.gao.gov/new.items/d07135sp.pdf

2

Adjustment Issues

If quantity of research is any measure of an issue's importance, then international student retention does not seem to matter much. Research undertaken nearly a decade ago on international student issues in higher education revealed just how very little, almost nothing, had been written about international student retention (Altbach, Kelly, & Lulat, 1985; Evans, 2001). This is particularly surprising since retention was arguably the most researched topic in higher education at the time. Perhaps even more amazing is how little has changed in the last ten years. Retention still tops the list of most-studied higher educational issues (Braxton, 2002; Braxton & Hirschy, 2005; Seidman, 2005; Tinto, 2005), but scholarship on international student retention is limited to a few doctoral dissertations and a handful of journal articles (Altbach et al., 1985; Altbach & Wang,1989; Andrade, 2003; Brawner Bevis & Lucas, 2007; Evans, 2001).

At least two lines of reasoning can be used to explain this inert state of inquiry. First, one might conclude from the scarcity of research that international student retention is not important since international students represent only 4 percent of the entire student population. A second and somewhat related explanation is that we seem to take international students for granted. Because they are not citizens, their attainment does not matter to us, but it should. As noted in chapter 1, international students contribute to our campuses and society in many significant and often inestimable ways. Their success and progress is an issue with far-reaching consequences for students, institutions, and even nations.

Student achievement, regardless of whether the students are domestic or international, should be and often is the core of an institution's mission, and as such, knowing how to measure and facilitate that success becomes an institutional priority. While student success is a complex construct, it can be measured to some degree of certainty with such metrics as retention and graduation rates. While not exact indicators, they provide a general sense of student achievement. On the other hand, ensuring and enabling student persistence to graduation has proved to be a daunting task. Many institutions go to considerable lengths to provide support services and programming to ease student transitions into higher education and increase retention rates. These services include orientations, academic support centers, tutors, and counselors to name a few.

While support services can be helpful, not all efforts assist students equally, and not all students have the same support needs. One of the most salient findings from retention research is that student persistence in higher education can be linked to such student background characteristics as socioeconomic status, ethnic minority, and parents with limited education (Astin, 1982; Attinasi, 1989; Andrade, 2003; Braxton, 2002; Evans, 2001; Hagedorn & Tierney, 2002; Rendon, Romero, & Nora, 2002; Seidman, 2005). Such a conclusion suggests that effective retention programming should be based on student limitations, not on institutional convenience. In other words, the more focused services and programming are on identified student needs, the greater the probability that students will attain their educational objectives. Expanding support services to accommodate for students' background characteristics has significant implications on how well an institution facilitates international student success.

All students who transition into a new environment face adjustment issues; a university can be an intimidating place for any new student. However, international students come to U.S. campuses with vastly dissimilar backgrounds and frames of reference from those of U.S. students. Their uncertainties about university life are magnified because they have to undertake university challenges often in a second language and almost always in a culture that is both literally and figuratively thousands of miles from the familiar. When we consider the obstacles they have to overcome, the odds against their success seem almost overwhelming. An institution's responses to international student adjustment needs can also be daunting. Helping students with diverse backgrounds succeed is a complex matter that requires support services and programming based on a firm understanding of students' distinctive needs.

With these issues in mind, this chapter provides an overview of student retention research in higher education and what it tells us about students' transitional experiences with the aim of improving our understanding of factors that can facilitate international students' transition into the U.S.

higher educational system. The overview begins with a brief chronological review of student retention in U.S. higher education and then leads to the most current thinking on the subject. This exploration provides a foundation on which to build a discussion central to this book; namely what we know about the adjustment issues international students encounter and how research can inform programming efforts for these students. An important aspect to this discussion is the presentation of Seidman's (2005) retention formula that has considerable practical application in an international student context. The overview in this chapter provides a backdrop for the two retention studies discussed in chapter 3 and the programming presented in chapters 4 through 9, which universities and colleges across the country are using to help international students.

RETENTION: PAST AND PRESENT

The three-hundred-year history of higher education in the United States has a relatively short chapter on student retention, without even a footnote on international students. Prior to the 1950s, student retention was a matter of little importance. In many ways the attitude was survival of the fittest and so much the better for the institution. It was common for students to drop out of school without completing a degree. However, retention became a matter of considerable importance as higher education entered its golden era of expansion immediately following World War II, and as university diplomas gained greater currency in a job market fueled by expanding industry and technology (Berger & Lyon, 2005).

A direct consequence of expanding enrollments and increased student diversity was declining student preparation for university studies. More students were enrolling, but many were also leaving without completing a degree. Furthermore, students from certain groups were dropping out of college at much higher rates than others. As awareness of the attrition problem grew, the need to understand root causes and find solutions increased. Retention research became both institutional and national priorities in the late sixties, and has continued unabated ever since.

Early Retention Studies

Most student retention research before the 1970s was limited in at least three ways. It tended to be descriptive (Tinto, 1993), it was hampered by the lack of clear and consistent terminology (Hagedorn, 2005), and it did not provide an explanatory model that could account for the complexities of student retention. Pascarella (1982) summarized the situation: "Until recently, most attrition research was descriptive and atheoretical, resulting in a large number of individual investigations that were difficult to synthesize into a meaningful body of knowledge on which to base policy" (p. 89).

Current Retention Research

Retention scholarship has advanced considerably in the past thirty years to the credit of many researchers. Few, however, have contributed more to current understanding of student persistence than Alexander Astin and Vincent Tinto. Their work has influenced nearly every aspect of retention research, programming, and policy. Furthermore, in recent years, important research on minority students has clarified how minority students differ from traditional students with regard to matters of retention (Rendon et al., 2002, p. 130). Since these lines of research have implications for international student retention, each shall be briefly considered.

Astin: Impact of college on students. Astin's work primarily focuses on how college experiences influence student development and by extension how that factor affects student retention. His research, which is based on an enormous data set collected over thirty-five years from hundreds of institutions and thousands of students, suggests that student involvement is central to student retention (Astin, 1975, 1993). By this he means, "It is not so much what the individual thinks or feels, but what the individual does, how he or she behaves, that defines and identifies involvement" (1984, p. 298). Astin (1984) further suggests two important points that ought to be considered when designing educational programs for students, namely that the degree of student involvement will affect the quality and quantity of student learning and development and that "the effectiveness of any educational policy or practice is directly related to the capacity of that policy or practice to increase involvement" (1984, p. 298).

Tinto's interactional model of departure. Many have researched the complexities of student retention; however, none has received the level of attention given to Tinto and his interactional theory of college student departure. Braxton and Hirschy (2005) note that Tinto's theory "enjoys paradigmatic stature" (p. 61). It is beyond the scope of this overview to explicate the model; however, a summary of several key points will be helpful. Tinto (1975, 1987, 1993) supports Astin's position that involvement is central to positive educational outcomes and persistence. At the same time, he suggests that integration is essential to student persistence. Integration must occur both socially and academically. Without some measure of social and intellectual integration, a student's chances of continued persistence in higher education dramatically decrease (Tinto, 1993).

Despite years of extensive research on Tinto's model, compelling arguments suggest that it has failed to provide a valid, reliable explanation for student retention (Braxton, Sullivan, & Johnson 1997, 2002; Braxton, Tierney,

1992a). The model's greatest limitation is that it is based on traditional, mainstream students' experiences, and nontraditional, minority, or international student's experiences in and preparation for higher education are different from those of traditional students. Considerable research suggests that the less traditional the student, the less predictive and applicable Tinto's model seems to be (Attinasi, 1989; Evans, 2001; Makuakane-Drechsel, 1999; Nora, Attinasi, & Matonak, 1990; Rendon et al., 2002; Tierney, 1992a; Zea, Reisen, & Beil, 1997).

Minority student retention. Because Tinto's model is so prevalent but is limited in its applicability to nontraditional student populations, a sizeable research base on minority student experiences in higher education has emerged in recent years (Rendon et al., 2002). While this line of research is still relatively new and questions far exceed answers, several pertinent points from the research suggest that programming ought to meet the specific needs of the students and that adjustments need to be made by students and institutions (Evans, 2001; Rendon et al., 2002; Tierney, 1992b; Tinto, 1993). In this regard, Rendon et al. (2002) note that research on American Indians, Asians, Pacific Islander, Filipinos, Puerto Ricans, Cubans, and immigrant students is "especially fertile territory" (p. 130). While Rendon et al. stop short of identifying international students in their list, it is not beyond reason to suggest that international students share many adjustment issues with minority students, and much can be gained by the comparison.

Current State of Student Retention

Despite decades of research, causes for student departure from higher education are far from conclusive. What most can agree to, however, is that it is a complex problem that will require multifaceted explanations, and even then the root causes may never be completely explained (Braxton, 2002; Hagedorn, 2005). Regardless of the complexities, several themes applicable to international students have surfaced from the voluminous literature on student retention.

Tinto (2005), for instance, acknowledges that while there may be some disagreement over the details of different theories, "the broad dimensions of a theory of student retention are starting to emerge" (p. ix). Among other things, he says "we can say with a good deal of confidence that academic preparation, commitments, and involvement matter" (p. ix). Bean (2005) provides a detailed summary of nine retention themes found in retention research, many of which echo Tinto's observations. The nine themes are intentions, institutional fit and commitment, psychological processes and key attitudes, academics, social factors, bureaucratic factors, external environment, student background, and finances.

Research suggests that many of these factors have a direct impact on non-traditional student populations. For example, certain minority students, for instance, may come to a university from a low socioeconomic background and have limited finances, poor academic training, and little if any prior exposure to higher education. All of these components can be used to predict the potential for success in post-secondary institutions (Attinasi, 1989; Rendon et al., 2002; Andrade, 2003; Evans, 2001; Dougherty, 1994; Makuakane-Drechsel, 1999; Noel et al., 1987; Tierney, 1992a; Tinto, 1987, 1993). A recent retention model that accounts for student variables affecting retention is Seidman's retention formula (2005). Because of its practical approach to retention and its applicability to nontraditional student populations, the framework of the formula will be used for the discussion of international student retention and adjustment issues in this chapter.

Seidman's Retention Formula

Seidman's formula is based on two key elements: identification and intervention. Specifically the formula states, "retention = early identification + (early + intensive + continuous) intervention" (p. 296). *Early identification* means that an institution attempts to identify a student's needs and at-risk potential as early as possible. Such identification can be done as part of the admission process or earlier if feasible. The sooner potential difficulties are identified, the sooner intervention can begin and the more focused it can be. *Early intervention* begins at the "earliest time possible after identification of a problem" (p. 298). Early intervention can begin even before a student enrolls at the university. *Intensive intervention* is "strong enough to effect the desired change" (p. 298). This may mean that a student is involved in an intervention program until the academic or social skill is mastered. Coupled with this idea is that intervention must also be *continuous*, in other words "intervention that persists until the change is effected" (p. 298).

Based on these principles, an institution needs to identify, with specificity, new students' needs and then develop programming accordingly. For instance, new-student orientations would have to be much more dynamic than most currently are. The typical new-student orientation—generally limited to one or two days—is a good example of what early, intensive, and continuous interventions are not. Content and themes presented in orientation programming would need to be reviewed and adapted to each incoming class of new students.

The applicability of this formula in an international student context is promising. Knowing precisely what issues international students may face when they arrive on campus allows institutions to focus the type, intensity, and duration of support that they provide. As Astin (1970) suggested, we cannot measure the degree of success we have had helping students unless we know with certainty the abilities and characteristics with which students entered our institutions.

Summary

The current literature base on student retention in higher education is extensive. Few have contributed more to our understanding of the "departure puzzle" than Tinto and Astin (Braxton, 2002). Their scholarship is both thorough and highly studied. In particular, Tinto provides a comprehensive student-departure model, which has been researched extensively. The research suggests that the model is less than adequate for nontraditional student populations. Recent research on minority student retention in higher education has attempted to counter this defect. Seidman's retention formula, while designed to improve retention in general, shows significant utility and applicability to minority, nontraditional, and international student populations.

To this point in the chapter, little has been said about international student retention primarily because little has been written on the subject. The remainder of the chapter focuses on what we know about international student retention, the adjustment issues that these students face, and how Seidman's (2005) formula might be applicable in an international student context. To facilitate comparisons and provide insight, this discussion begins with an overview of what we know about minority student retention in higher education.

INTERNATIONAL STUDENT RETENTION
AND ADJUSTMENT ISSUES

For the sake of consistency and accounting accuracy, U.S. agencies such as the National Center for Educational Statistics (NCES) do not classify international students as minorities. However, international students, especially those from developing countries, have much in common with minority students. For example, many of the factors that make persistence in higher education a significant challenge for minority students also affect certain international students. Several definitions may help clarify this point.

A definition of *minority* can be as straightforward as a percentage of the total. However, the term also bears the connotation of being disadvantaged, of lacking access to and attainment in higher education (Astin, 1982). In addition, minority is typically defined along ethnic lines. For example, the U.S. Office of Management and Budget's definition of minority includes blacks (or African Americans), Hispanics, American Indians/Alaskan Natives, and

Asians/Pacific Islanders. Furthermore, minority students are often defined by at-risk qualities. These traits fall into several categories, namely, the specially admitted, first generation, disadvantaged, and ethnic minorities (Ting, 1998). Others suggest that at-risk students "possess a collage of academic, social, and economic problems that challenge their success in college" (Roueche & Roueche, 1994, p. 4).

These at-risk factors can be categorized in three groups: academic, social, and personal. Academic issues include English as a second language, poor academic preparation, first-generation college student, and a limited world view. Social factors include not being part of the dominant culture, having few college role models or mentors, and, once again, having English as a second language. Personal factors consist of low self-esteem, extensive family responsibilities, financial concerns, employment, and low socio-economic status.

An important point that may already be apparent to those who have worked with international students from developing countries is that many of the at-risk factors shown to affect minority student retention may also affect international students. Certain populations of international students have limited access to higher education; they may also come from educational systems that are lacking; financial resources can be limited. In addition, they are often first-generation college students.

Several points made earlier in this chapter warrant repetition here. First, as Astin (1970) has proposed, we cannot begin to measure our level of success in helping students achieve their goals until we are certain of their abilities and limitations from the time they enter the university. Similarly, Seidman (2005) suggests, we must identify student needs and at-risk factors before we can offer meaningful intervention. The balance of this chapter focuses on retention patterns and identifies adjustment issues for international students.

International Student Retention

International student retention statistics are not typically provided in government higher education reports. The major concern seems to be how many international students are coming to study and not how successful they are once they arrive. Not even the Institute of International Education's *Open Doors* provides information on international student achievement. This lack of data makes it difficult to offer any kind of historical perspective of retention and graduation rates for international students. However, as reported in chapter 1, some data suggest that international students seem to persist through the first year in college at about the same rate as the general university population—80.2 percent, and six-year graduation rates are also similar to those of the general population—58.7 percent.

In spite of these comparable statistics for international and domestic students, room for improvement is substantial. Numbers can mask the challenges that students face. Seidman's formula for retention offers a viable approach for improvement in the area of international student support: Identify the needs (the at-risk factors) and apply appropriate, focused intervention (programming).

International Student Adjustment Issues

An important point that often gets overlooked in the busy academic shuffle of higher education is that international students are, in many ways, strangers in a strange land with numerous adjustment concerns. A brief example of students from Micronesia illustrates what it may be like to come to the U.S. higher education system for the first time. This brief example also highlights some common adjustment categories that will be discussed in more detail.

A small undergraduate university that has a long history of educating international students from the Pacific islands enrolled a cohort of nine students from the Micronesian nation of Kiribati. Some of the students had been out of high school for as long as five years. Most, however, were recent high school graduates. All of the students had completed their high school education in the government and private schools on the main atoll of Tarawa prior to departing for the United States. It should be noted that these high schools were lacking in many significant ways. The students had very little exposure to computers, and even less experience with computers in high school. Textbooks used in the schools were often outdated when they were available, and because they were expensive and hard to replace, students were often not allowed to take them home. Library facilities were severely lacking according to U.S. standards. The only teaching credential earned by some of the high school teachers was a high school diploma.

Average annual income of most families was US$500. None of the students had ever traveled more than a few hundred miles from their home atoll, and English was their second language. In short, these students had a number of at-risk factors working against them before they ever boarded their first airplane bound for the United States. Within two years, six of the nine students had dropped out of school; only two had graduated from the university.

This example serves as a good beginning for a discussion of the issues international students face on U.S. campuses. These adjustment challenges of Micronesian students were many, and perhaps quite pronounced because of the students' background, yet all students who come from different cultures and backgrounds are likely to have some difficulty adjusting to academic and social life in the United States. Each group, whether from Kiribati or

France, from Mexico or Korea, encounters different and often difficult adjustment issues. Regardless of a student's origins, however, most international student adjustment issues fall into three categories: academic, social, and personal (Altbach et al., 1985). We now consider international adjustment issues as they relate to academic, social, and personal matters.

Before considering the academic, social, and personal issues, a note about their interrelatedness is in order. While adjustment issues can be categorized as academic, social, and personal, such groupings tend to simplify extremely complex matters. Student adjustment issues overlap and interact extensively. For instance, English language skills have a profound impact on a student's academic achievement. Language skills also influence a student's ability to socialize in meaningful ways with other students and community members, which in turn affects a student's personal life. Furthermore, when a student's social life is upset, it stands to reason that academic performance will be affected. Research suggests that international students' academic success "flows from the confluence of a number of factors, including language proficiency, learning strategies, and classroom dynamics" (Able, 2002, p. 18). Bundling adjustment issues into categories in this section is for ease of reference only.

Academic issues. As noted before, international students face many challenges similar to those facing domestic students; their impact, however, is often amplified for international students because of cultural and linguistic differences. In addition, international students face academic challenges unique only to them. For example, most domestic students do not have to attempt university studies in a second language, nor do they have to adjust to an entirely new educational system (Schutz & Richards, 2003). A student educated in the United States has some sense of how students and teachers there interact; international students typically do not have such insight (Jiang Bresnahan & Cai, 2000; Schutz & Richards, 2003).

Establishing cohort support takes effort for any student, but international students generally have very little idea how to accomplish this, or even whether this should be done. Practically everything about the learning environment in the United States is new to international students: the grading system, the type and quantity of work that is required, and expected classroom behavior to name a few. It stands to reason that the greater the number of variables a student must manage, the more difficult the adjustment will be.

Language is frequently identified as the most prominent adjustment issue with which international students contend (Altbach & Wang, 1989; Holmes, 2004; Kim, 2006; Lindemann, 2005). The less proficient a student is in English, the more the university experience diminishes (Fletcher & Stren, 1989). This is not to suggest that strong English language skills guarantee that adjustments will be easy. Correlations between language skills and adjustment issues do, however, suggest that the less skilled a student is in English, the more difficult the university experience will be (Abadzi, 1984; Senyshyn, Warford, & Zhan, 2000).

Language skills affect every aspect of a student's academic life: the ability to write, participate in class, study in groups, and read assignments. Reading assignments alone can keep students up late into the night and away from social activities common to university life. When faculty were asked to identify the most common factors affecting the success of international graduate students, the ability to function in the English language was identified as the single most common academic factor (Trice, 2003). Similarly, students identify language as their most common academic stressor (Lin & Yi, 1997).

In addition to language concerns, international students come to U.S. campuses with many apprehensions and uncertainties. Over the years, international students' academic concerns have included language, teacher–student relationships, coursework and grades, institutional expectations, self-esteem, stress and time management, and integration with domestic students (Altbach & Wang, 1989; Yi, Lin, & Kishimoto, 2002). Because the academic environment is usually new to these students, they are often unsure of the academic expectations and academic life in general (Shutz & Richards, 2003). For instance, students express uncertainty about what a student–faculty relationship should be like (Jiang Bresnahan & Cai, 2000). When one considers the almost absolute respect teachers receive in certain cultures, it should come as no surprise that international students are confused by the seemingly collegial relationships they observe between students and teachers in this country.

When students are left to their own devices to sort through the many academic adjustments they face, stress, tension, and even various forms of withdrawal can result (Ryan & Ogilvie, 2001). A more reasonable approach is for the institution to provide these students with orientation and insight that are relevant to their unique view of university experience. Furthermore, too often, international students receive their orientation in short one- or two-day sessions that are often intended for all new students, domestic and international alike. The scope and sequence of orientation programs should reflect the extensity of information students must process as they adapt to their new surroundings. Adapting to a new academic system can be complex and requires time and resources.

Social and personal issues. The importance of social integration and support is well documented and clearly conceptualized in Astin's developmental theory of student involvement (1984). According to Astin, an "involved" student is one who devotes energy to academics, spends time on campus, interacts often with faculty, and participates in student organizations or other cocurricular activities. Involvement, he says, "refers to the quantity and quality of the physical and psychological energy that students invest in the college experience" (p. 528). Increased involvement translates into increased success.

What varies in the case of international students is the level of consciousness to which these pieces of the success puzzle often rise. As noted in this chapter and as well as in chapter 6, language proficiency is a major piece of the puzzle that most native students need not think much about except in relation to writing skills or mastery of new discipline-specific vocabulary and the more natural, almost unconscious, acquisition of new vocabulary used in new social contexts. For the international student operating in an entirely new linguistic context, however, language proficiency is an intensely conscious concern. Slang, colloquialisms, and popular culture references simply do not translate even if the words are understood. No dictionary or phrase book will help with understanding the context and intent of fellow students' or professors' use of such language. Not only does a student not understand the intent, the student may also miss out on the "joke" and subsequently not feel like a part of a class or a social situation.

Cultural differences can have a huge impact on the social and personal adjustments of international students. Becoming integrated into a culture requires language proficiency but also cultural awareness, and the two are closely related. Edward T. Hall's classic work, *The Silent Language*, proposed to treat culture in its entirety as a form of communication (1959). Whatever shortcomings Hall's approach holds, international students today clearly identify their own "perceived social and linguistic incompetence" as a barrier to their participation and success in a foreign classroom, and such perceptions affect self-esteem and morale (Lewthwaite, 1996, p. 182). For the graduate student whose language proficiency is often used as an explanation for a student's poor performance in a class, the impact becomes more than a morale issue and may create anxiety about a number of other factors.

Students who are living and working in new cultural contexts often do not fully understand what is taking place or how they should respond. Thus, it is important to provide ample opportunity for social interactions with members of the host culture that allow international students to learn and refine the culture-specific assumptions, social skills, and nonverbal cues that help them to function effectively in cross-cultural situations (Furnham & Bochner, 1982). In short, involvement with host nationals outside the classroom translates into success inside it. Such interactions also serve the purpose of providing opportunities for American hosts to "understand" English with an accent.

As international students find that they are understood in social settings, they will gain confidence in their language skills that will carry over into the classroom. Programs that match international students with domestic students as roommates, conversation partners in English language centers, or as partners in social activities organized through an international office provide a means for international students to be exposed to idioms, test their English language skills as both a speaker and a listener, and become exposed to the host culture.

Involvement for international students, however, is a more complex phenomenon than it is for domestic students. Although far from home and the social networks that supported them there, many internationals have access to campus groups of co-nationals—other students from the home country and either their dependent family members or other students' dependents. The home culture for such students, at least in a limited sense, is close at hand. Mental health professionals who work with international students have observed that conational friendships or communities can be an important resource, allowing opportunity for cultural values to be enforced and expressed and providing some softening of the loneliness and homesickness that is an inevitable part of life abroad (Lin & Yi, 1997). For international students that have access to large or clearly defined conational groups, other international students may become an important source of empathy and refuge.

Despite these benefits, research has also consistently shown that larger conational communities often correlate with less host culture involvement, which in turn can produce greater levels of culture shock. Social interaction with the host culture is known to correlate with successful cultural adjustment (Al-Sharideh & Goe, 1998; Chapdelaine & Alexitch, 2004; Mallinckrodt & Leong, 1992). To succeed, then, international students must somehow find time outside the classroom for involvement in two worlds. They need a "bicultural network" comprised of bonds with other internationals and with host nationals. The latter group needs to include not only peers but also teaching faculty and college officials (Lin & Yi, 1997). Unfortunately, not all faculty, staff, and administrators are aware of the special needs of international students, and this may be especially true at the graduate level, where opportunities for interaction outside a classroom or lab are more limited.

Many international students come from educational contexts where cocurricular involvement is not seen as a contributing factor in academic success. The number and kind of opportunities for such involvement available on U.S. campuses is, in itself, a source of bewilderment for many international students. Student services personnel in the United States, and a growing cadre of their academic colleagues, understand the research of Astin and others and try to structure university environments and programs accordingly (Kuh et al., 1991). Graduate schools have taken on more student services in recent years because social support does not end with an undergraduate degree. In fact, the pressures and adjustments may be greater for graduate students, and being an international student adds one more layer. International students, however, often arrive on campus assuming that time commitments they make outside of attending class will reduce the time they have to study, therefore reducing their likelihood of academic success.

CONCLUSION

Domestic student retention has been and continues to be a matter of great importance in higher education. Research on the subject is extensive, spanning decades. The level of attention and depth of inquiry can be attributed to a variety of factors, not the least of which is the complexity of the issues and the consequences to individuals and institutions if students do not persist. Despite the extreme attention given to student retention, to date, international student retention has had very little consideration, yet the stakes are no less significant for this student population than they are for domestic students. The relatively small enrollment numbers of international students may in part account for the lack of attention given to the subject. This should not minimize, however, the need to understand adjustment issues faced by international students and to provide support services accordingly.

This chapter has reviewed a number of key issues related to domestic student retention and has suggested that certain factors affecting domestic student retention may also be applicable to an international student population. Similarities notwithstanding, international students come to our universities with many adjustment issues distinctive to their backgrounds. While these issues are extremely complex and interrelated, they can generally be classified as being academic, social, and personal in nature.

Current retention research suggests that a clear understanding of academic, social, and personal issues is a prerequisite to offering meaningful support. For instance, Seidman's (2005) retention formula stipulates that early identification of student adjustment issues should be followed by early, intensive, and continuous intervention. Chapter 3 presents several studies that focus on international students who persisted in a U.S. university and those that did not. The issues that contributed to their persistence or departure offer further insight into international student adjustment issues. Subsequent chapters focus on the intervention aspect of Seidman's formula.

REFERENCES

Abadzi, J. (1984). Evaluation of foreign students' admission procedures used at the University of Alabama. In B. Hale, C. Stansfield, and R. Duran (Eds.), *Summaries of studies involving the test of English as foreign language, 1963–1982*. Princeton, NJ: Educational Testing Services, 1984.

Able, C. F. (2002). Academic success and the international student: Research and recommendations. *New Directions for Higher Education, 117,* Spring.

Al-Sharideh, K. A., & Goe, W. R. (1998). Ethnic communities within the university: An examination of factors influencing the personal adjustment of international students. *Research in Higher Education, 39*(6), 699–725.

Altbach, P. G., Kelly, D. H., & Lulat, Y. G.-M. (1985). *Research on foreign students and international study.* New York: Praeger.

Altbach, P. G., & Wang, J. (1989). *Foreign students and international study.* New York: University Press of America.

Andrade, M. S. (2003). *International students: Patterns of success.* Unpublished doctoral dissertation, University of Southern California.

Astin, A. W. (1970). The methodology of research on college impact, part one. *Sociology of Education, 43,* 223–254.

———. (1975). *Preventing students from dropping out.* San Francisco: Jossey-Bass.

———. (1982). *Minorities in American higher education.* San Francisco: Jossey-Bass.

———. (1984). Student involvement: A developmental theory for higher education. *Journal of College Student Personnel, 25,* 297–308.

———. (1993). *What matters in college? Four critical years revisited.* San Francisco: Jossey-Bass.

Attinasi, L. C. J. (1989). Getting in: Mexican Americans' perceptions of university attendance and the implications for freshman year persistence. *Journal of Higher Education, 60*(3), 247–277.

Bean, J. P. (2005). Nine themes of college student retention. In A. Seidman (Ed.), *College student retention: Formula for student success.* Westport, CT: American Council on Education/Praeger.

Berger, J. B., & Lyon, S. C. (2005). Past to present: A historical look at retention. In A. Seidman (Ed.), *College student retention: Formula for student success.* Westport, CT: American Council on Education/Praeger.

Brawner Bevis, T., & Lucas, C. J. (2007). *International students in American colleges and universities: A history.* New York: Palgrave Macmillan.

Braxton, J. M. (2002). *Reworking the student departure puzzle.* Nashville, TN: Vanderbilt University Press.

Braxton, J. M., & Hirschy, A. S. (2005). Theoretical developments in the study of college student departure. In A. Seidman (Ed.), *College student retention: Formula for student success.* Westport, CT: American Council on Education/Praeger.

Braxton, J. M., Sullivan, A. V. S., & Johnson, R. M. J. (1997). Appraising Tinto's theory of college student departure. In C. J. Smart (Ed.), *Higher education: Handbook of theory and research* (Vol. 12, pp. 107–164). New York: Agathon Press.

Chapdelaine, R., & Alexitch, L. (2004). Social skills difficulty: Model of culture shock for international graduate students. *Journal of College Student Development 45*(2), 167–184.

Dougherty, K. (1994). *The contradictory college: The conflicting origins, impacts, and futures of the community college.* Albany: State University of New York Press.

Evans, N. (2001). *In their own words: Polynesian students' perspectives on persistence in an American university.* Unpublished doctoral dissertation, University of Southern California.

Fletcher, J. F., & Stren, R. E. (1989). Language skills and adaptation: A study of foreign students in a Canadian university. *Curriculum Inquiry, 19*(3), 293–308.

Furnham, A., & Bochner, S. (1982). Social difficulty in a foreign culture: An empirical analysis of culture shock. In S. Bochner (Ed.), *Cultures in contact: Studies in cross-cultural interaction* (pp. 161–198). Elmsford, NY: Pergamon.

Hagedorn, L. S. (2005). How to define retention: A new look at an old problem. In A. Seidman (Ed.), *College student retention: Formula for student success.* Westport, CT: American Council on Education/Praeger.

Hagedorn, L. S., & Tierney, W. G. (2002). Cultural capital and the struggle for educational equity. In W. G. Tierney & L. S. Hagedorn (Eds.), *Increasing access to college* (pp. 1–8). New York: State University of New York Press.

Hall, E. T. (1959). *The silent language.* New York: Anchor Books.

Holmes, P. (2004). Negotiating differences in learning and intercultural communication. *Business Communication Quarterly, 67*(3), 294–307.

Jiang Bresnahan, M., & Cai, D. H. (2000). From the other side of the desk: Conversations with international students about teaching in the U.S. *Qualitative Research Reports in Communication, 1*(4), 65–75.

Kim, S. (2006). Academic oral communication needs of East Asian international graduate students in non-science and non-engineering fields. *English for Specific Purposes, 25*(4), 479–489.

Kuh, G. D., Schuh, J., Whitt, E., & Associates. (1991). *Involving colleges.* San Francisco: Jossey-Bass.

Lewthwaite, M. (1996). A study on international students' perspectives on cross-cultural adaptation. *International Journal for the Advancement of Counseling, 19,* 167–185.

Lin, J. G., & Yi, J. K. (1997). Asian international students' adjustment: Issues and program suggestions. *College Student Journal, 3,* 473–479.

Lindemann, S. (2005). Who speaks broken English? U.S. undergraduates' perceptions of non-native English. *International Journal of Applied Linguistics, 15*(2), 187–212.

Makuakane-Drechsel, T. H. (1999). *Factors affecting Hawaiian student persistence at four community colleges on the island of Oahu, Hawaii.* Unpublished doctoral dissertation, University of Southern California.

Mallinckrodt, B., & Leong, F. T. L. (1992). International graduate students, stress, and social support. *Journal of College Student Development, 33,* 71–78.

Noel, L., Levitz, R., Saluri, D., & Associates. (1987). *Increasing student retention.* San Francisco: Jossey-Bass.

Nora, A., Attinasi, L. C., & Matonak, A. (1990). Testing qualitative indicators of precollege factors in Tinto's attrition model. *Review of Higher Education, 13*(3), 337–355.

Pascarella, E. T. (Ed.). (1982). *Studying student attrition, 36.* San Francisco: Jossey-Bass.

Rendon, L. I., Romero, E. J., & Nora, A. (2002). Theoretical considerations in the study of minority student retention in higher education. In J. Braxton (Ed.), *Reworking the student departure puzzle.* Nashville, TN: Vanderbilt University Press.

Roueche, J. E., & Roueche, S. D. (1994). Responding to the challenge of the at-risk student. *Community College Journal of Research and Practice, 18,* 1–11.

Ryan, M. M., & Ogilvie, M. (2001). Examining the effects of environmental interchangeability with overseas students: A cross-cultural comparison. *Asia Pacific Journal of Marketing and Logistics, 13*(3), 63–74.

Schutz, A., & Richards, M. (2003). International students' experiences of graduate study in Canada. *Journal of the International Society for Teacher Education, 7*(1), 10–22.

Seidman, A. (2005). *College student retention: Formula for student success.* Westport, CT: American Council on Education/Praeger.

Senyshyn, R. M., Warford, M. K., & Zhan, J. (2000). Issues of adjustment to higher education: International students' perspectives. *International Education, 30*(1), 17–35.

Tierney, W. G. (1992a). An anthropological analysis of student participation in college. *Journal of Higher Education, 63*(6), 603–618.

———. (1992b). *Official encouragement, institutional discouragement: Minorities in academe-the Native American experience.* Norwood, NJ: Ablex.

Ting, S. M. R. (1998). Predicting first-year grades and academic progress of college students of first-generation and low-income families. *Journal of College Admission, 158*(Winter), 14–23.

Tinto, V. (1975). Dropout from higher education: A theoretical synthesis of recent research. *Review of Educational Research, 45,* 89–125.

———. (1987, 1993). *Leaving college: Rethinking the causes and cures of student attrition.* Chicago: University of Chicago Press.

———. (2005). College student retention: Formula for success. In A. Seidman (Ed.), *College student retention: Formula for student success.* Westport, CT: American Council on Education/Praeger.

Trice, A. (2003). Faculty perceptions of graduate international students: The benefits and challenges. *Journal of Studies in International Education, 7*(4), 379–403.

Yi, J. K., Lin, J. G., & Kishimoto, Y. (2002). Utilization of counseling services by international students. *Journal of Instructional Psychology, 30*(4), 333–342.

Zea, M. C., Reisen, C. A., & Beil, C. (1997). Predicting intention to remain in college among ethnic minority and non-minority. *The Journal of Social Psychology, 137*(April), 149–160.

3

Keys to Persistence—International Students in Higher Education

Persistence research has gone beyond a focus on traditional students to include the diverse populations now present on university campuses. Much of this research was reviewed in chapter 2. As access to higher education widens, institutions and faculty must be prepared to understand and address differing student needs for students to recognize success and for institutions to be effective in accomplishing their missions. As noted in chapter 1, the United States has historically been a country of choice for international students. However, compared to other nations, it may not fully recognize the benefits of international student enrollments. The nation enrolls a relatively small percentage of international students in relation to its total, whereas other countries such as Australia and the United Kingdom have actively recruited international students to the point that they comprise a sizable portion of overall enrollments.

The comparatively small percentages of international students in U.S. higher education (4 percent undergraduate; 12 percent graduate) may account for why these students have not been the focus of much retention research. Although the literature contains some studies related to international student adjustment and services (e.g., see Hechanova-Alampay, Beehr, Christiansen, & Van Horn, 2002; Jacob & Greggo, 2001; Mendelsohn, 2002; Rajapaksa & Dundes, 2002; Tompson & Tompson, 1996; Trice, 2003), few have examined persistence patterns or identified factors that affect the departure or persistence of international students.

The funding international students contribute to institutions and to local and state economies is one of several reasons to be concerned about the success and continued enrollment of international students. Supporting this population also ensures future enrollments of international students so that the educational experiences of both domestic and international students can be enhanced, and the United States can sustain its ability to remain globally competitive.

This chapter showcases two complementary studies conducted at the same institution—one examined the experiences of international students from the Pacific Islands and Asia who were near graduation, and the other examined the experiences of international students from the Pacific Islands who left the university without graduating. We discuss related literature and share the students' stories and insights to illustrate factors that led to students' persisting or departing. At times, similar factors resulted in persistence for some students and in departure for others. The chapter will identify the environmental, cultural, educational, and personal factors that affected students positively or negatively and explain why the same factors had differing effects on students.

Although international student populations vary, as do the institutions that host them, the chapter provides greater understanding of international students' experiences in the American higher education system and of factors that potentially affect their success. First, we provide information related to institutional context and student backgrounds. Then we discuss the factors affecting persistence for both groups of students—those who persisted and those who departed. Six factors played a critical role in the students' experiences: future vision, relationships, family, the institution, spirituality, and structure.

THE CONTEXT

The institution where these studies took place is uniquely positioned to expand the knowledge base of international student persistence issues. The institution is a small, private, religiously affiliated undergraduate university with an international student population of close to 50 percent of the student body. Most of these international students speak English as a second language, as do many of those on campuses throughout the nation. In contrast to international students in general, these students come from low socioeconomic backgrounds. They are financially sponsored by the institution through a work–study program. Many would not have the opportunity for higher education in their own countries due to lack of access or finances. Many come to the university for this reason and also because of their shared religious affiliation.

International student enrollment is comprised as follows: Asia: 29 percent, Pacific Islands: 15 percent, and Other International: 5 percent. At the institution generally, approximately 31 percent of students are over twenty-five, 42.3 percent are male, 92.3 percent are full-time, 95.1 percent are members of the sponsoring religious organization, and 30.7 percent are first-generation (neither father nor mother attended any college).

Given its mission to provide educational opportunities to those from Asia and the Pacific Islands, the university is committed to building students' intercultural understanding. It is also committed to ensuring that international students who are nonnative English speakers (NNESs) (the majority) have high levels of English proficiency. Were English skills to interfere with learning, professors would either need to adjust their course work to accommodate the students or allow them to fail. To ensure that international students who are NNESs have adequate academic English skills, they are tested upon arrival and required to enroll in credit-bearing English as a Second Language (ESL) courses as needed.

National retention and graduation figures were reviewed in chapter 1. Table 3.1 compares national and institutional rates for domestic and international students. Institutional rates are lower than national rates in all cases but one—six-year graduation rates for international students, and these are comparable. Among the two major groups of international students at the university—Asian and Pacific Islands—first-year retention rates are comparable; however, six-year graduation rates are quite different. Reasons for the lower rates for Pacific Island students will be shared later in the chapter. The lowest retention and graduation rates at the institution are for domestic students. These students are not the focus of the current discussion. Their lower persistence rates can be accounted for by the fact that they tend to come to the university due to its location and enjoy a one-year experience after which they transfer to other institutions. The university has addressed this issue by recruiting transfer students from community colleges who will be more likely to graduate.

Table 3.1.   Retention and Graduation Rates—National and Institutional Comparisons

	First-year Retention	*6-year Graduation*
Overall (national)	77%	57%
Overall (institutional)	58%	40%
International students (national)	80%	53%
International students (institutional)	72%	55%
International students—Pacific Islands (institutional)	75%	57%
International students—Asian (institutional)	73%	71%
Domestic students (institutional)	48%	37%

Note. National data provided by the Consortium for Student Retention Data Exchange (CSRDE).

The factors discussed next are the result of qualitative research involving interviews and focus groups of international students—both those who persisted and those who departed, as well as the staff and administrators who work with them in various capacities. Students who persisted were in their senior year at the university and were asked questions about their adjustment experiences and factors that had contributed to their success. Those who had departed were tracked to their home countries or, in some cases, within the United States, and interviewed to determine for what reasons they had left the institution. Although the institutional context of the study has some unique features, as do the students, the findings provide insights into the applicability of existing persistence theories to this population and establish a foundation for international student persistence research upon which future studies can build.

FACTORS THAT INFLUENCE DEPARTURE AND RETENTION

The following section reviews the six key areas—vision, relationships, family, the institution, spirituality, and structure—that influenced students' experiences and their decisions to remain at the university or depart. In each section, we review related literature and then discuss the differences between the two groups.

Future Vision

One of the key components of Tinto's (1987, 1993) persistence model is student commitment to the goal of graduating and to the institution. For diverse students, such as minority students, this factor is also central although it takes a variety of forms. In studies examining persistence variables for minority students, for example, having high aspirations (Brown & Robinson Kurpius, 1997), motivation (Allen, 1999), the desire to succeed (Hernandez, 2000), and strong determination based on a personal vision (Hendricks, 1996) have been found to be strong persistence factors. In some cases, these characteristics have applied only to minority students (e.g., see Allen, 1999) or were much stronger for minority students than for non-minority students (e.g., see Brown & Robinson Kurpius, 1997).

Although international students are not American minority students, they may share similar characteristics such as not being academically prepared or having been accustomed to different academic expectations, being first-generation college students, feeling like a minority in a majority environment, experiencing dissonance between home and university cultures, and encountering discrimination.

The desire to succeed was also central in the experiences of the international students who were interviewed. The students who persisted had a clear vision of the future—they knew why they wanted an education and were committed to doing what was necessary to be successful. A number of factors contributed to this vision, and these factors sometimes contradicted each other. Those who departed lacked focus or a clear purpose for attending the university. First, we examine the experiences of students who persisted and then those of students who departed.

Students who persisted. International students in their senior year who were interviewed about their backgrounds and experiences at the university shared a strong belief in the value of education. This was a key factor in their experiences. They recognized that to be able to support themselves and their future families financially and to enjoy a comfortable life, they would need an education. The source of this vision differed, however. In some cases, having humble beginnings was an incentive.

A student from Hong Kong, for example, explained that her parents were factory workers with little education. They worked hard to provide her with educational opportunities outside of school so that she could do well academically and be accepted to a university. From this environment, she understood the importance of having an education to get a good job and worked hard to qualify for university admittance. Although she encountered challenges at the university, she overcame these by reminding herself of her goal to graduate. "There are times when I was really stressed, that I felt like I wasn't able to accomplish what I want here, and I almost quit, and I felt like after reviewing your goals that reminds me why am I here."

In other cases, students' desires for education were unsupported by their parents, but this served as a motivating factor. One senior from the Pacific Islands was needed at home after she finished high school to help with younger siblings while her parents worked. Although she also enrolled in several classes at a local community college, the demands of helping at home and going to school were too much, so she did not continue her studies. Due to the emphasis on education that she received through her religious involvements, however, she was determined to pursue an education. Eventually, she went back to the community college and then to university in the United States, although her parents told her to get married and let her husband take care of her. She said, "I never expected when I went back to school to come this far, and I cannot give it up just to have fun. I cannot afford to be distracted."

Although the motivating factors for pursuing an education differed among the students—the encouragement or discouragement of parents, religious teachings, or humble beginnings—having a goal to graduate was a strong factor in helping students overcome challenges. Few of the students had parents with experiences in higher education, yet this appeared to motivate them to strive for further education to better their own lives. Obtaining a degree was something that each student valued. One of the most pervasive factors that influenced students to persist was having a future perspective. This perspective was generally evident prior to enrollment, suggesting that initial commitment to the goal of graduating positively affected persistence; thus, the current findings support this aspect of Tinto's (1987, 1993) interactional model.

Students who departed. Nearly every student who departed the university without graduating expressed a clear understanding of the positive impact a university education could have on his or her future. Their thoughts, however, were retrospective. A common theme in these students' comments was when they entered the university as new students they lacked a clear vision for why they were going to university. Lack of vision is not a problem unique to international students. Many first-year students enter school unsure of what they want to major in or if they want to be in college at all (Astin, 1993; Pascarella & Terenzini, 1991, 2005; Tinto, 1993). International students share similar uncertainties. At the same time, participants in the research that focused on Polynesians frequently articulated two reasons for their lack of vision that seem to be uniquely descriptive of this population of students: they went to school as a way out (off the island) and to obey their parents' wishes.

Students expressed a variety of reasons for wanting to have a way off the island. One student described how as the oldest child, she was responsible for many household chores such as caring for her five younger siblings, preparing meals, and cleaning around the house in addition to her responsibilities as a high school student. A university education was never a thought, much less a goal, until a teacher asked her if she would be interested in studying in the United States. "I never thought about university until a high school teacher asked me if I wanted to go to the U.S. to study. Of course I said yes. Just to get away from home—to get out of [name of her country]." By her own admission, she entered university for the wrong reason.

Similarly, another student said he jumped at the chance to go to college to "get away from a stern father." One student actually enrolled in the university out of spite. "A family member told me I could not make it in school. I decided that I was going to come to school so I could show her she was wrong. I really did not want to come [to the university]; I was just angry with her." Many of these students went to the university not for what the university offered, but because of what the islands did not offer.

Other students chose to study abroad not because they wanted a way out but because they felt obligated to obey their parents. Strict obedience to elders, especially parents, is a strong value in Polynesia. Many students had parents who never completed high school. Very few parents had any post-secondary education, and only a few of those ever graduated from a university. Despite this, many parents could see that having a college education would economically benefit their children, so they insisted that their children attend university. One student from American Samoa speaks for many in a similar situation when he said, "My father said I had to get a college education. There was no negotiating an education in my family. I had no choice but to do what my father said."

Much can be learned from these examples of students who lack vision and did not persist in college. Lack of internal motivation is a common variable among these students. Current retention research suggests that the lack of incentive or a clear intention can have a pivotal role in a student leaving college without a diploma (Bean, 2005; Tinto, 2005). Such was the case with many of these students.

The Power of Relationships

Involvement with peers is a central factor to persistence. Astin's (1984) theory of student involvement, based on the identification of student characteristics and institutional factors that influence academic success, argues that students who are involved socially and academically within the institution have a tendency to persist; those who are less involved are more likely to depart. The theory emphasizes involvement with academics, peers, and faculty, and specifically the behavioral aspects of involvement such as participation in curricular and cocurricular activities.

Tinto's model has a similar component—social and academic integration. Students who integrate socially and academically into the institution are more likely to form the commitment necessary to persist to graduation. This aspect of Tinto's model has been criticized (Tierney, 1992) because it implies that students are expected to sever ties with their past communities, particularly if they are unsupportive or detract from academic success, and integrate into the mainstream culture, values, and attitudes of the institution.

Indeed, research has shown that students who reported receiving strong support for college attendance and those who perceived the need to reject the attitudes and values of their former communities were less likely to leave college (Elkins, Braxton, & James, 2000). Members of racial and ethnic minority groups reported less community and family support. Encouragement from family, friends (both old and new), and significant others positively affects integration and the decision to persist to graduation (Nora, 2002). Particularly in cases in which students are physically separated from their families or families are unsupportive, peers and faculty at the institution can provide new systems of support.

In addition to retention theories, cultural adjustment research also provides insights into the importance of relationships in international student adjustment and persistence. Interaction with hosts lessens culture shock (Chapdelaine & Alexitch, 2004). However, if cultural differences are great or if students have a large conational group or are accompanied by partners or children, social interaction with hosts decreases and greater levels of culture shock are experienced. When interaction fails to occur, students are less likely to learn appropriate cultural behaviors and therefore are less likely to adjust to the new environment. The kind of interaction needed to alleviate culture shock and increase cultural learning occurs through social involvement and integration.

The acts of observing, participating, and developing long-term relationships in the host culture are examples of behavioral learning strategies that are a component of cultural learning (Taylor, 1994). The learner adapts these strategies to balance disequilibrium, or feelings of stress and heightened emotions caused by cultural dissonance. As international students interact with others in academic and social contexts, they become familiar with American culture. The deeper the level of their interactions (i.e., forming relationships vs. simply observing), the more successful they will be in overcoming cultural dissonance.

The power of relationships, involving both coculturals and American peers, had differing effects on those who persisted and those who departed. Students who persisted reported that making friends within and outside their own cultures had a critical positive effect on their experiences at the university. They also benefited from the example of students from their own cultures who were succeeding and from professors, staff, and religious leaders who took an interest in them and supported them. For those who departed, relationships interfered with their academic progress. These students put friends before study, and this often led to poor academic performance. We next examine the experiences of these two groups of students.

Students who persisted. International students who persisted reported that making friends within and outside their own cultures served different but equally important purposes. Some students, for example, felt that associating with native English speakers helped them learn English and become familiar with the American culture but that it was also important to maintain contact with students from their own countries. A student from Asia said,

My roommates . . . we spent a lot of time together doing things. . . . I have chance to practice my English. And then, of course I joined the [name of country] club. . . . That helps because sometimes if you just have American groups, it's just so hard because some thing they won't be able to understand you fully.

Students especially benefited from the good examples of peers from their own cultures. A Pacific Island student attributed some of his desire to excel to role models from his country. He saw them succeeding and wanted to be successful as well. He asked himself, "How can I be like that also?" and tried to emulate them.

Professors, staff, and religious leaders who took an interest in students played a critical role. A student from the Pacific Islands explained: "The same kind of teachers that we have here, they make you feel special. I come from a background where the teachers [sic] is right, that's it. Here . . . the teachers help you feel appreciated." A few students expressed particular appreciation for professors or staff who were from their own countries as they felt these people understood their adjustment needs. For most students, relationships of this type stood out as being stronger than the others, but all of the students emphasized at least one of these sources as being critical in their experiences. Overall, networks of personal support had an enormous impact.

Students who departed. In most cases, for students who departed, relationships interfered with their academic progress. As we shall see in this and the next section, relationships with family and friends were powerful influences in the lives of students who departed from the university. In both cases, these relationships were two-edged swords. As has been noted, on one side, friends set good examples, act as confidants, and provide solace through the hard, homesick adjustment days. On the other side, they present a great temptation to go see the sights of their new surroundings and culture, or as one Pacific Island student said, "Just hang out with instead of doing school work." Nearly every student who departed acknowledged the strong influence friends had on pulling them away from their studies.

Many of the participants who did not persist to graduation, all of whom were Pacific Islanders, noted how difficult it was to say no to a friend and how this distracted them from their responsibilities as students. A student from Fiji acknowledged this fact. "It is not in our blood to say no to someone when they invite you to go with them. It would be considered rude. We just can't say no." One student recalls her father frequently telling her that her biggest problem when she went to university would be not being able to say no when she had to. Another student told of the time he was placed on nonacademic warning for allowing friends to stay in his room for several nights. "I knew I wasn't supposed to. But what could I tell my friends?" A high school principal in Tonga summarized this challenge nicely: "Our students feel great embarrassment saying no to their friends. Here we teach our children that not sharing is mean, and that friends and relationships are more important than personal needs." With such an upbringing, he said, "Polynesians find it nearly impossible to say no when they have to."

The need for and the influence of social support on a university student's success is well documented in retention literature (Astin, 1993; Attinasi, 1989; Furnham & Bochner, 1982; Tinto, 1993: Tierney, 1992). This social support can come from a variety of sources and can influence a student both positively and negatively. However, one point is quite clear from this research: relationships with conationals are powerful. Those who associated with focused, successful students seemed to benefit as research suggests they will. On the other hand, associations with less focused students had detrimental effects. A student from Tonga articulates this point eloquently:

> When my friends came by my room and wanted to head into town or something, I couldn't say no. If I stayed back to study I would be mocked and made fun of for making school more important than being Tongan. I couldn't do that.

The Role of Family

Tinto's theory suggests that students may need to separate from their past associations and integrate into the new environment to be successful. A number of studies have examined this separation aspect with regard to the role of family. Although some findings demonstrate that students who persist do not have stronger levels of family encouragement than those who depart (e.g., in the case of American Indian students; Brown & Robinson Kurpius, 1997), most research has found positive links between family encouragement and persistence (e.g., see Cabrera, Nora, Terenzini, Pascarella, & Hagedorn, 1999; Eimers & Pike, 1997; Hendricks, 1996; Hernandez, 2000; Nora & Cabrera, 1996). This finding is true for students from a wide variety of home backgrounds. Parental encouragement positively influences the transition into the institution, the commitment to graduation, and persistence. This support sometimes takes the form of pressure on students to succeed for fear of disappointing loved ones (Hernandez, 2000).

The finding that continued family encouragement contributes to persistence does not contradict Tinto's separation concept. Tinto does not say that all relationships with family must be severed; only those that are unsupportive of higher educational goals. It may be necessary for students to reject some beliefs, values, and associations if they counter the student's goals or newly learned viewpoints, but such rejection is not always necessary.

Family support can be viewed as a form of cultural or social capital (e.g., see Bourdieu, 1986; Coleman, 1988), providing students with a support network. National survey findings indicate that the majority (78.6 percent) of freshmen enjoyed family support in the first year; only 20.9 percent reported family responsibilities that frequently or occasionally interfered with course work (Hurtado et al., 2007). In these cases, encouragement and support from faculty or teaching assistants has been found to neutralize the negative effects of family obligations (either caring for a family member or working to provide financial support for family) on persistence (Nora, 2002).

In the case of the international students who were interviewed, family relationships both supported and distracted students from their educational goals. For those who persisted, families exerted a strong influence on the desire to pursue an education and to be successful. Sometimes parental opposition was as motivating as parental encouragement in that some students were determined to get an education even though their parents preferred them to stay home, get married, or seek employment. Students who left the university were often distracted from their educational pursuits due to family problems in their home country or parents who missed them and wanted them to come home. In these cases, Tinto would say that separation from students' past communities is needed for successful integration and persistence to be realized. Next, we gain insights into the differing experiences of these two groups of students.

Students who persisted. The influence of family had positive effects on international students who persisted. This often began in the home before students came to the university, helping them form a desire to pursue an education. The example of older siblings, a family commitment to education, and the home environment influenced the educational vision of a student from the Pacific Islands. She explains: "I would say a tradition in my family was to graduate from high school, [and] go to [name of university]. . . . Because of the positive influences of my older brothers and sisters . . . I decided that I wanted that in my life, too."

Negative or mixed parental attitudes toward higher education also served as a motivating factor. An Asian student commented: "My mother doesn't encourage [further studies] a lot. Just go out to work. Earn money." A Pacific Island student said that his parents liked the idea of him going to university, "but they didn't like it, too. . . . They're gonna miss me. . . . My dad would say, 'Ahh, that's a good career right there. You can stay here and work'. . . . And I see something he doesn't see." These students had formed a commitment to education based on their vision of the future, as discussed in the first theme, and due to other sources of influence.

Family continued to influence students while at the university. One Pacific Island student explained that her mother always reminded her about the importance of school, to do her homework, and listen to her teachers. The belief her mother had in her, that she would complete her studies, motivated her to graduate. She commented: "I think it's my parents' support. My siblings' influence, everybody graduates, so it's kind of expected of me."

In contrast, she said that some of her friends' parents made them feel homesick by expressing how much they missed them, sometimes causing the student to return home.

For most of the students who persisted, an expectation that they would attend university was apparent early in life, and this was primarily the result of their home environments. This expectation kept them motivated as did the examples of older siblings who had been successful in obtaining a degree. Words of encouragement from home helped students focus and commit themselves to their studies. For those whose families were not supportive, their own desires to be successful were sufficiently strong to overcome any influence keeping them from their goal.

Students who departed. A strong family relationship, a common characteristic in Polynesian cultures, was both a blessing and a curse to first-year students trying to make adjustments in their new environment. In many instances, families are the very reason students went abroad to study. Students often included in their reasons for getting a university education the need to help family. Nearly every student who dropped out of university had parents or family members tell them something similar to what a student from the Cook Islands related: "My brother once told me 'Don't you dare give up. You owe it to the family to make them proud.'"

Despite such encouragement, many students did not persist. The reasons are multiple, but one theme frequently surfaced as the students told their stories: most family members had no idea what it meant to be a university student in a new culture. Parents would often tell students who were departing home for the United States to work hard, listen to their teachers, and do their best, but that was usually the extent of advice for success they were given.

Many of the students who did not persist came from homes where parents had very little education; many had not completed high school. The dynamic of parents wanting children to get more education and at the same time not fully understanding the strains and demands of university life often placed students in the impossible situation of being in two places at one time. A student from Samoa recalls, "My mom would write me letters telling me about problems back home; that dragged me down." Being in the United States but wanting to be back home to help family was hard on many of the students. Students frequently spoke of feeling the strain from a family crisis. For instance, a student from Fiji recalled her first real discouragement came when she received a letter from home telling her that her parents had been separated for over two months. "All the while I am trying to manage things here at school, I am trying to figure out what's going on at home and what am I trying to do here."

An administrator in Samoa summarized the issues in these terms: "Homesickness is a very real problem for our students, and parents here are not very helpful in getting their students over it. Their letters or phone calls telling the students about all the problems at home and how much they are missed make it hard for the students to adjust."

The parallels between family influences and relationships with friends are striking. Retention research indicates that these can be positive factors in helping students succeed. The reverse is also true. When friends or family do not offer positive influences, students tend to stray from their original goal even when that goal was, in part, shaped by the same individuals who pull students away from school. A French Polynesian student provides a clear example of this point. He reported that his reason for going abroad to study was to "get away from a stern father." When he discovered that his father was in serious financial difficulties, he immediately dropped out of school (he was in his third year) and went home to help in the family business. This student has not returned to school and does not see how he will ever be able to. His reason is revealing to the current discussion. "My family commitments are too great right now."

Institutional Factors

A variety of institutional factors have been studied to determine their impact on student persistence. The power of relationships, that is, support from peers and professors within the institution, is one institutional factor that has been identified as positively affecting persistence and was discussed earlier. Attinasi (1989, 1992) found that social integration, specifically peer- and faculty-mentoring relationships, helped students manage the university environment and negotiate the physical (size), social (number of people), and cognitive (choices of study, hard courses, complicated instruction) geographies. Persisters developed cognitive maps to help them scale down the environment or to simplify and organize it according to their needs and experiences. As explained previously, international students who persisted were positively affected by relationships with peers and professors while those who left the university had difficulty balancing the demands of relationships with their studies.

Institutional factors include social involvement in terms of participation in curricular and cocurricular activities, the use of support services, and programming such as orientation, learning communities, and first-year seminars. Much first-year programming has the goal to get students involved and integrated into the university and form relationships so that they will persist (e.g., see Astin, 1984; Tinto, 1987). This involvement might include internships, joint research projects with faculty, service learning, interactive classrooms, peer collaboration, and faculty mentoring. Cocurricular activities help students connect with each other, explore interests, and develop different talents and skills.

Students also need to become accustomed to the higher educational system, which may be different from their expectations. This includes program curricula, styles of teaching, academic expectations, and the day-to-day operations of the university. If these differ from what students are accustomed to or expect, transitional challenges will likely develop. National data indicate that the expectations of students about their college experiences (e.g., grades, satisfaction, participating in clubs, socializing with those from different ethnic groups) generally exceed the reality of what actually happens in their first year (Hurtado et al., 2007). As discussed in chapter 2, international students are particularly unfamiliar with many aspects of an American university. For them, expectations may vary greatly from reality.

Another element of the institution that potentially affects persistence is employment. Work responsibilities can act as a pull factor. At the end of their first year, only about one-quarter of the approximately 30 percent of first-year students who worked either on or off campus reported that job responsibilities interfered with their course work (Hurtado et al., 2007). In contrast, 25 percent of seniors reported having missed class due to work responsibilities, and 45 percent reported not having time to study due to work during their college experience (Hurtado et al., 2007). On-campus employment potentially helps students make connections with faculty, staff, and peers and strengthens their institutional commitment. Off-campus employment may not offer the same benefits in terms of aiding involvement and strengthening institutional commitment. Both may interfere with academic demands; however, as noted earlier, supportive relationships with faculty and significant others can compensate for this (Nora, 2002).

For international students, institutional factors contributed to their decisions to stay at the university or leave. These factors included participation in extracurricular activities, use of support centers, experiences with campus bureaucracy, the unfamiliar educational system, and employment. As could be expected, institutional factors had different effects on those who persisted and on those who departed, as we next discuss.

Students who persisted. Student success for international students who persisted was only weakly related to use of formal support services or participation in extracurricular activities. In general, students who used formal services found them helpful. English language classes were mentioned most frequently. A student from Asia commented: "I enjoy [ESL] classes because you go to the class with people that have the same level of language. . . . in the GE [general education] class . . . you just feel like, overwhelm [sic]." Students also indicated some involvement in student clubs, sports, or performing groups, but these were not emphasized as being a critical part of the transition process. Such participation does, however, indicate that students were actively making connections and were involved in campus life.

Two key areas had a significant positive impact on students' experiences. These were the diverse environment and employment. The diverse student population was helpful in promoting a sense of belonging, and students emphasized making friends from a variety of cultures. An Asian student observed that if she had stayed in her own country, she would not have had the opportunity to associate with and learn from people from so many different backgrounds. Of Polynesian students, she said, "Their life is totally different from ours. They are more giving, loving, more easy-going, which probably I needed to learn."

Most of the international students came from low socioeconomic backgrounds and were recipients of work–study scholarships, enabling them to study at the university. Employment was a new experience as working part-time while attending high school was not common in their countries. Although the students who persisted were unaccustomed to managing their time effectively to accommodate their new responsibilities, after an initial adjustment period, they felt their work experiences provided them with balance and the opportunity to gain real-life job skills. Their associates at work, both supervisors and peers, were also a source of support to them. A Pacific Island student commented: "It [work] helps me to adjust to my life and what life will be like in future." An Asian student said, "You work as a team with your coworkers and you have a closer relationship with them because you have to help each other."

Regarding the systems of the university—curricula, academic expectations, and infrastructure—students experienced challenges but were able to adjust by forming appropriate strategies as evidenced by a student from the Pacific Islands: "I learned that going for help is a perfect thing to do, especially to teachers." Similarly, although students had experienced frustration with campus bureaucracy at times, they were able to take it in stride and maintain a positive attitude toward the institution. A student from Asia exemplified this attitude: "I like to focus on the positive side, 'cause a lot of the school is not perfect." Students mentioned that various offices on campus (e.g., registrar, admissions, financial aid) seemed unorganized or that getting a response to a problem was sometimes difficult or delayed, but they had formed strategies for these situations. These included taking care of the problem immediately, persevering until it was resolved, or even simply complaining about it and then accepting that they could not change the system. An Asian student commented: "When I came here first, I bothered [sic] a lot, but now I just say, 'Yeah, that's the way it is.'"

For the most part, people—peers, faculty, religious leaders, and staff (as discussed here and in the previous themes)—were more influential than formal institutional support services. As students interacted with others in the classroom, social activities, and work situations, they built networks of support. Connecting with individuals who offered encouragement and support and served as role models had a positive effect on students' lives.

Students who departed. The students who departed were, in many cases, not able to manage the responsibility of both working and taking classes. In their cultures, neither high school nor college students worked while attending school. They also had little understanding of university graduation requirements prior to enrolling, particularly general education, and were expecting to take classes related only to their major. Other institutional factors affecting student persistence were related to customer service. Those who departed had had negative experiences with bureaucratic and inefficient procedures at the university that had upset them.

All of the students who departed were on work–study scholarships, and each noted that work was a definite factor contributing to their early departure. As work–study students, they must maintain a twenty-hour-per-week job to pay for their tuition, books, and room and board. Unlike the students who persisted, these students did not develop strategies to help them balance work and school. Comments from a Tahitian student are revealing in this regard: "Trying to work and go to school at the same time nearly drove me crazy." When one realizes that Tahitian children do not have jobs while going to high school (it is against the law) it is understandable why work would be difficult to manage. One student from the Cook Islands reported that the hardest part of her first year of school was working. "I had no choice. No job, no school." Students frequently reported that work became a top priority, and their studies suffered as a result.

In addition to the demands of working twenty hours per week, students were quite disoriented by the educational system. Most of these students had never set foot on a university campus, much less one in the United States. They found the systems markedly different from what they were used to. A student from Samoa, for example, who had decided to major in accounting, was disillusioned by "all the GE [general education] I had to take. I thought I could go straight into accounting, but I was stuck in GE classes. Classes I really hated in high school like biology but had to take because they were GE just killed me." She reported that she never really got a grasp of the need for and the structure of general education classes.

A final point regarding institutional factors that caused students difficultly was the institutional bureaucracy and the general lack of what might be considered customer service. A number of students shared frustrations in trying to get consistent information. For example, an admissions officer told one student that she could major in languages and study to be a translator. Once she arrived on campus she discovered that information was incorrect. Of this experience she said, "My whole purpose for going to the university was gone. I really felt like quitting and coming home." Another student reported that she had been admitted without having completed Form Six (high school equivalent). At the end of her first semester, the error was detected and, "They sent me home. I was devastated, but there was nothing I could do. I talked to everyone I thought could help, but no one seemed willing to help, so I left."

The combination of required student employment, an unfamiliar educational system, and the seemingly unyielding organizational structure of the university was more than these students could abide. The need for meaningful orientations based on a clear understanding of students' backgrounds is nowhere more apparent than in their need to understand institutional factors.

Spirituality

A college education decreases students' spirituality and religiousness. According to national survey data, students who rated themselves as "above average" on these two measures compared to their peers entered college with stronger feelings of spirituality and religiousness than they had when they completed college (Saenz & Barrera, 2007). The researchers suggest that while institutions may be preparing students academically, they do not address spiritual development. Indeed, a focus on "'inner' development— the sphere of values and beliefs, emotional maturity, moral development, spirituality, and self-understanding" (Astin, 2004, p. 34) is largely ignored in higher education.

Over the past forty years, according to a national survey accompanied by focus group interviews, incoming college students are increasingly more focused on being well-off financially than on developing a meaningful life philosophy (Lindholm, 2006). In the same time period, the number of students claiming no religious preference has nearly tripled. In spite of this, the majority are actively struggling with religious issues such as questioning their beliefs and trying to understand evil, suffering, and death. Nearly 80 percent report discussing religion and spirituality with friends and praying.

Students reporting religious involvement (attending religious services, workshops, and retreats; and reading religious texts) experience less psychological distress and have better emotional health than those who do not. This includes feeling less overwhelmed by responsibilities; experiencing less stress, anxiety, and depression; and having higher levels of self-esteem. Few of these students report discussing spiritual matters in class or with professors, however.

These data demonstrate that college students struggle with spiritual questions. One would expect students who attend religious institutions to have fewer spiritual struggles. This is not the case. Findings of the national College Students' Beliefs and Values survey indicate that students at religious institutions struggle more spiritually than those at nonsectarian institutions, perhaps because they are faced with investigating their religious beliefs or even debating and critiquing those beliefs (Bryant & Astin, 2007). Disagreeing with accepted doctrines at religiously affiliated institutions may result in further spiritual struggles. On the positive side, spiritual integration at faith-based institutions has been found to positively affect persistence. Generally, students who attend because they desire an education that integrates faith and academic learning are more likely to persist than those who may be attending for other reasons (i.e., parental wishes) (e.g., see Morris, Smith, & Cejda, 2003; Schreiner, 2000; Walter, 2000).

All of the international students interviewed belonged to the sponsoring religious organization of the institution. On one level, this provided them with an immediate sense of belonging in that they shared the same values and religious beliefs as their peers. One would expect this to somewhat compensate for differences in language, culture, and educational background. Students who persisted were strengthened by their involvement in religious activities and the atmosphere of the campus. Their personal religious beliefs and commitments supported them in times of difficulty as did their associations with others with similar faith. The experience of a religious proselytizing mission frequently instilled and strengthened a commitment to education and established patterns of discipline necessary for academic success.

In contrast, those who departed had sometimes violated some of the religious tenets of the institution as defined in the honor code, which caused them to feel guilty. In some cases, this led to students' voluntary departure so that they would not be formally dismissed. We now discuss how spirituality and the religious nature of the institution had either positive or negative effects on students.

Students who persisted. Membership in the sponsoring religious organization had an immensely positive effect on the international students who were successful. For many, the church, through the influence of its teachings and leaders, was responsible for their resolve to pursue an education. A student from the Pacific Islands expressed her determination to get an education due to the influence of church teachings. "The church has taught me the importance of education."

As students arrived on campus and experienced challenges related to their social, academic, and cultural adjustment, engaging in the religious activities of the institution, such as church and devotional attendance, and in personal religious practices, especially prayer and scripture study, strengthened them and helped them overcome challenges. A Pacific Island student illustrates: "There is a scripture, if you put God first everything will be fine . . . I study the scriptures . . . Prayer is a must, in the prayer you might ask for something, so that helps."

Voluntary full-time missionary service in the church either before their admission to the university or during a leave of absence was key to the students' success. Through this experience they were exposed to other walks of life, gained discipline and confidence, improved their English skills, and formed higher expectations of themselves and what they could accomplish in life than prior to this experience. A student from Asia commented: "After my mission, I know the main reason why I want to get education because I want to have that knowledge to be able to apply in my future life. And that motivate [sic] me." A Pacific Island student observed: "I dealt with the people, finding out what their concerns are, and really be able to feel worthwhile and helping on my mission. . . . You never realize that doing something for someone else is different, helps you learn to learn a lot."

In addition to the influence of church teachings regarding education, prayer and religious study, and mission experiences, students commonly expressed gratitude for the religious atmosphere of the school. They attributed their ability to be successful to their faith and religious practices. Through their campus experiences, their knowledge of the church increased, and they felt they had grown not only intellectually, but also spiritually. From a Pacific Island student: "I would say what really helped me is the church, really helped me." For international students who persisted, the influence of the church was critical. It resulted in greater focus and commitment, helped them develop confidence, and eased their anxieties and stress. The religious environment and the students' individual religious beliefs and experiences were key to academic success.

Students who departed. As with the students who persisted, all the students who did not complete their education were members of the sponsoring church. The impact this religious affiliation had on these students is quite apparent by the things they said after they had returned home. Their inability to abide by the tenets and honor code of the institution clearly had a negative impact on their academic accomplishments.

A requirement for all students admitted to the university is to sign and abide by a code of conduct outlined by the sponsoring church. In several cases students violated this code and found themselves feeling guilty and unable to focus on school matters. One student described her dilemma in these terms: "I had made some bad choices early on. Everything in my life was all mixed up, not just my self-esteem, but my spiritual life went very low too. It got my spiritual life as well as my education." She further reported that after three months of struggling over her situation, she "packed up and left for home before they kicked me out which would have been even more shameful for me." Another student who had violated the honor code remarked how much she wanted to stay in school but realized that she needed to get her life straightened out. "I had to come home and get things straightened out especially my spirituality."

A high school teacher suggested a possible reason why spirituality may be a factor contributing to these students' ability to succeed or lack of ability to succeed in terms of independence. This insightful teacher suggested that independence might be best understood from a religious perspective:

> We talk about how important it is to be independent yet these students are raised in a highly communal culture where young people are tightly fit into a role they are supposed to maintain. . . . Christianity teaches individualism, yet that runs counter to these cultures. It may well be that those students who do well here are those that are able to practice the individualism preached by their church.

The comparisons between those students who maintain that their spiritual moorings were influential in their academic success and those students who had broken away from their spiritual anchor and not persisted are intriguing. Clearly, as current research suggests, this is an area of student life that warrants further investigation (Astin, 2004; Lindholm, 2006).

The Importance of Structure

The way students structure their environment, so that they can adapt, be successful, and form meaningful relationships, potentially impacts persistence. Students enter institutions of higher education with a variety of psychological attributes (Bean & Eaton, 2002). As they interact with the academic and social systems within the university, students form general feelings about their experiences and make adjustments to feel comfortable and integrated (Bean & Eaton, 2002). The adaptive strategies students engage in can be described by a number of psychological theories, such as attribution and self-regulated learning.

Attribution theory examines the process of attributing causes for life's experiences and events, and the impact of this process on individuals (Weiner, 1979, 1986). The explanations (causal attributions) that people make for outcomes and events in their lives affect their subsequent thoughts, emotions, and behaviors. These causal attributions also affect academic achievement, specifically how students view their successes and failures and the responsibility they take for their own learning.

Students who attribute their failures to external causes beyond their control, such as the teacher, their own ability, or the environment, are likely to believe they cannot change their performance and will be unmotivated to change. This may cause them to study less, miss class, or pay less attention in class, resulting in poor performance and possibly withdrawal. In contrast, those who view their failure as a lack of effort or ineffective study strategies believe that they are responsible for their own performance and that it is within their control to do better. They are likely to adjust the behavior causing the poor performance, try harder, and feel that future success is possible.

In addition to causal attributions, self-regulated learning strategies have been demonstrated to affect achievement. A number of researchers (Zimmerman, 1994; Zimmerman, Greenberg, & Weinstein, 1994; Zimmerman & Risemberg, 1997) argue that research on learning and motivation should focus on teaching students to manage their achievement through self-regulated learning strategies rather than on the learner's ability and the social environment. Students who are able to motivate themselves, possess a large number of learning strategies and know when and how to use them, manage their time effectively, seek assistance from others, restructure their physical environment to make it conducive to study, and monitor and evaluate their own learning are more successful academically than students who do not possess these qualities (Dembo & Eaton, 2000).

Both theories provide explanations for why students may fail to be academically successful and suggest how they can appropriately respond to challenges. Academically successful students are more likely to be integrated into the university and committed to graduating. In addition to structuring their academic success through positive causal attributions and effective learning strategies, students need to structure their environment through appropriate navigation of barriers.

Viewing persistence through these lenses may increase our understanding of why students either persist or depart from institutions of higher education. International students could be expected to have greater adjustment difficulties and different approaches to structuring based on their cultural and educational backgrounds. For them, navigating the institutional environment requires cultural and educational adjustment strategies as well as institution-specific adjustment skills. The ability to structure their environment was a critical factor in the experiences of the students who persisted and departed.

Students who persisted. The international students who were successful had learned how to structure their lives prior to their arrival at the university, or as the result of missionary service. These students had formed successful study habits, took responsibility for their actions, and made effective use of their time. This does not mean they were perfect or that they did not have adjustment difficulties, but they had found ways to balance their responsibilities, get appropriate help when needed, and form some type of study system that worked for them. They met barriers but were able to overcome them. A Pacific Island student shares his approach when having academic difficulties: "I go talk to the teacher. I get to know more what the teacher expects." This student demonstrates a strategy that likely was not appropriate in his own culture, indicating that he had learned to negotiate the American educational system and implement appropriate social skills to increase academic success.

Study habits and approaches among the students varied, with no particular method appearing to have a greater influence on persistence than another. Some of the study habits mentioned were reading the assignments (or at least skimming them if time was an issue), taking reading notes, making outlines of the readings, rereading materials before an exam, summarizing, studying in groups, and self-testing. Most students mentioned that they attended class regularly and tried to understand the concepts being taught rather than just memorizing material. In general, the students planned, set goals, reviewed their goals, organized their time well, started early, and avoided distractions and procrastination. Many students expressed that they had learned to be goal-oriented and use time effectively on their missions.

They were not perfect, however. Some reported still struggling with study skills or felt that they were not very proficient in this area. An Asian student reported: "I like to study very last second. I don't like to study too long, but I have to study very hard in order to get a good grade. . . . When the teacher gives us the study guides or syllabus, I usually break it in certain parts and on certain days finish certain part." Others, as indicated in the following quote, attributed their ability to overcome barriers to prayer and scripture study and to relationships: "It's the religion background, I pray about it. . . . Religion set the standard for all the students, and also people have that religion background, and they're more accepting and they're more patient and charitable to help you."

These students exhibited many of the characteristics related to attribution and self-regulated learning theories such as taking responsibility for their own performance, managing their time effectively, seeking assistance from others, restructuring their physical environment, and evaluating their own learning. They overcame barriers by relying on personal support, seeking appropriate help, and exercising spiritual strength.

Students who departed. The most important factor for students who did not persist was freedom. Students came from cultures and home backgrounds in which parents largely controlled their lives. Coming to university in the United States was seen as a way out and an opportunity to experience life on their own. However, they were not prepared for the amount of freedom they experienced and were unable to discipline themselves in ways that would contribute to their educational success.

To understand how some students can be so overwhelmed by freedom that they lose sight and control of their objectives, it is helpful to hear how a student in that situation perceives it. An insightful student from Fiji describes the issue this way:

Polynesian culture is a family oriented culture. Parents keep a close eye on the family. We don't leave our homes until we are quite old. And you know coming here we are faced with so much freedom that we have never had before that we just cannot control it. It's a disease; you know when we have this freedom and a little bit of money in our pocket, we just can't control. . . . With a dollar we can get on a bus and go movie hopping at [the mall]. We have never had such freedom. Some students take several years to get over it. And it cost them so much. Some lose their student status and never return.

This new-found freedom was the most frequently discussed factor contributing to a student's failure to persist. Students, parents, faculty, and administrators who were interviewed concurred with this student's insightful comments. Freedom is a "disease" that some Pacific Island students have not learned how to handle.

Several factors seem to contribute to this challenge: family upbringing, as noted by the student from Fiji, and the educational system. One teacher saw the independence problem this way: "The nail that stands out gets hammered down in this culture. And once the students get to the university in the United States, they are supposed to think just the opposite." A high school principal described the problem as an artifact of the school system: "Here we follow the British system in school, and we are very exam oriented. We train our students to be exam takers but not independent thinkers. So nearly every aspect of these young peoples' lives here in the Pacific works against them knowing how to be independent." A counselor in the same high school added to this principal's comments by suggesting that "A 19-year-old coming from the Pacific is generally 5 or 6 years behind his American counterpart when it comes to standing on his own and making decisions."

While students who persisted to graduation demonstrated characteristics related to attribution and self-regulated learning theories, just the opposite seemed to be true for students who did not persist. They were generally ineffective in finding strategies to overcome their barriers, particularly when it came to relying on themselves to find solutions for new challenges.

SYNTHESIZING THE STUDENTS' EXPERIENCES

The acknowledged limitations of not having the voices of nonpersisting Asian students, and having students from only one university necessitate that conclusions be limited. Similarly, findings from qualitative studies may not be generalizable. They represent only the experiences of the specific students interviewed. Nevertheless, these students' insights are compelling. What follows are a few preliminary thoughts on these factors. The reasons students in these studies experienced success and failure are intriguing. In many ways these studies have revealed opposite sides of the same coin: families can be influential to academic attainment or failure; peers are likely to make a difference in a student's achievement or defeat; and having a vision, a clear goal, or lack thereof can be a powerful influence toward academic success or failure. Furthermore, spiritual moorings that stabilize, and knowledge of how to structure responsibility seem to be factors promoting persistence.

It is also significant to note that certain of these factors, family, relationships, institutional factors, and vision, have been shown to impact domestic students in similar ways. Family has consistently been identified as a contributor to persistence or nonpersistence (Astin, 1993; Atinasi, 1989; Bean, 2005; Tinto, 1993). This is particularly true if students are first-generation college students (Roueche & Roueche, 1994). The power of relationships on student success is not only at the core of Tinto's integration model and Astin's notion of involvement, but it is also consistently a factor noted in retention research (Astin, 1993; Bean, 2002; Braxton, 2002; Pascarella & Terenzini, 2005; Seidman, 2005; Tinto, 2005). Institutional factors are also very much a part of retention research. The current focus is not to determine if institutional factors affect persistence but to determine which factors are most influential (Pascarella & Terenzini, 2005). Finally, vision, or having a clear reason for attending higher education, has long been identified as a contributing factor to student retention. Commitment to institution and graduation are fundamental aspects of Tinto's retention model (Tinto, 1993).

While domestic and international student retention may be similar in some regards, they are quite different in others. For example, the impact that a lack of structure had on the Pacific Island students who departed is significant. As noted, freedom was by far the most often cited reason given by students, parents, teachers, and administrators for Pacific Island students' early departure from the university. However, those who had learned to structure their university experience (e.g., balance work and study, manage their time, be responsible, and stay focused on their goal) were successful. This points to the need for intervention to help students develop these skills and habits as needed.

Even so, one of the keys to success was having a strong vision. Without this, attempts to provide more structure for students would likely be ineffective. It appears that students have to know why an education is important and strongly desire it. Beyond that, having supportive family, friends, faculty, and staff, and reliance on spiritual faith can serve to strengthen this vision.

For students to have identified spirituality as a contributing factor to their persistence or early departure is noteworthy. To date little research has been conducted on the influence of spirituality on student retention and general success in the university. Astin has taken particular interest in this topic, and maintains that it may indeed be one of the key elements that we have overlooked in our study of student life in the university (Astin, 2004). It may well be that further research will identify spirituality as one of many factors that affect both domestic and international student retention.

In summary, a point that is clear from these studies and retention research in general is that each group of international students, indeed each individual, comes with unique needs that must be understood for meaningful retention programming to be implemented. Understanding group similarities and differences is perhaps the best first step leading to our understanding of individual differences.

SUMMARY

As noted in chapter 2, retention continues to be a priority on the research agenda of higher education. This sustained interest is indicative of the many unresolved retention issues. Student retention in higher education is a "complicated, confusing, and context dependent" issue that may never be completely understood (Hagedorn, 2005, p. 89). In many ways, retention is an ill-defined problem, and as such resolution and understanding will have to come from multiple sources, and be based on the context under consideration (Braxton, 2002; Braxton & Hirschy, 2005). The studies in this chapter focus on a group of students who have received little attention in persistence research; yet their experiences provide important insights to persistence. These studies also support the notion that the retention question is as complex as the varied student populations entering higher education.

The narratives related here emphasize several key issues. For instance, the fact that students reported spirituality as a positive factor in their decision to stay the course even through hard times suggests the need for much more investigation on a topic that as yet has a limited research foundation in general retention research and no research to date for international students. Also, the detrimental effect freedom had on Polynesian students is a topic of considerable interest. Other international students from similar upbringings may be impacted in comparable ways when they leave the highly structured confines of their families and traditional communities to enter the wide-open options of U.S. higher education. Each of these themes calls for more research as we strive to understand the different contexts from which international students come.

Far too often, the label *international or foreign student* is as specific as we get when referring to the students who cross international borders to study on our campuses, yet such a categorization is a gross misrepresentation and oversimplification of these students and the issues they face. This chapter examined two key groups of international students—Asians and Pacific Islanders. Insights from their experiences suggest the necessity to consider international students not as one large group of students with similar needs, but as many groups with unique requirements. The fact that international students come to our campuses with a variety of needs makes Seidman's (2005) retention formula (see chapter 2), which calls for early, intensive, and continuous intervention based on a clear understanding of students' needs, a potentially useful tool in an international student context.

The remaining chapters in this book present programming based on the principles of knowing students' needs and offering support that extends beyond cursory attempts to help. The institutions are as diverse as community colleges, liberal arts, and major research universities. The students they are aiming to support come from all corners of the globe. Some are seeking graduate degrees while others are visiting scholars, and many are undergraduate students. The one thing all of these students have in common is that their needs are unique.

REFERENCES

Allen, D. (1999). Desire to finish college: An empirical link between motivation and persistence. *Research in Higher Education, 40*(4), 461–485.

Astin, A. W. (1984). Student involvement: A developmental theory for higher education. *Journal of College Student Personnel, 25,* 297–308.

———. (1993). *What matters in college? Four critical years revisited.* San Francisco: Jossey-Bass.

———. (2004). Why spirituality deserves a central place in higher education. *Liberal Education, 90*(2), 34–41.

Attinasi, L. C. J. (1989). Getting in: Mexican Americans' perceptions of university attendance and the implications for freshman year persistence. *Journal of Higher Education, 60*(3), 247–277.

———. (1992). Rethinking the study of the outcomes of college attendance. *Journal of College Student Development, 33*(1), 61–70.

Bean, J. P. (2005). Nine themes of college student retention. In A. Seidman (Ed.), *College student retention: Formula for student success.* Westport, CT: American Council on Education/Praeger.

Bean, J. P., & Eaton, S. B. (2002). The psychology underlying successful retention practices. *Journal of College Student Development, 3*(1), 73–89.

Bourdieu, P. (1986). The forms of capital. In J. G. Richardson (Ed.), *Handbook of theory and research for the sociology of education* (pp. 241–258). New York: Greenwood.

Braxton, J. M. (2002). *Reworking the student departure puzzle.* Nashville, TN: Vanderbilt University Press.

Braxton, J. M., & Hirschy, A. S. (2005). Theoretical developments in the study of college student departure. In A. Seidman (Ed.), *College student retention: Formula for student success*. Westport, CT: American Council on Education/Praeger.

Brown, L. L., & Robinson Kurpius, S. E. (1997). Psychosocial factors influencing academic persistence of American Indian college students. *Journal of College Student Development, 38*(1), 3–12.

Bryant, A. N., & Astin, H. A. (2007). The spiritual struggles of college students. *Journal of Higher Education* (forthcoming). Retrieved July 19, 2007, from http://spirituality .ucla.edu/Publication percent20& percent20Reports/Spiritual percent20Struggle percent20Submit percent20to percent20JHE_Revised_9_22_06.pdf

Cabrera, A. F., Nora, A., Terenzini, P. T., Pascarella, E., & Hagedorn, L. S. (1999). Campus racial climate and the adjustment of students to college: A comparison between White students and African-American students. *Journal of Higher Education, 70*(2), 134–160.

Chapdelaine, R. F., & Alexitch, L. R. (2004). Social skills difficulty: Model of culture shock for international graduate students. *Journal of College Student Development, 45*(2), 167–184.

Coleman, J. S. (1988). Social capital in the creation of human capital. *American Journal of Sociology, 94*, 95–120.

Dembo, M. H., & Eaton, M. J. (2000). Self-regulation of academic learning in middle-level schools. *The Elementary School Journal, 100*(5), 473–490.

Eimers, M. T., & Pike, G. R. (1997). Minority and nonminority adjustment to college: Differences or similarities? *Research in Higher Education, 38*(1), 77–97.

Elkins, S., Braxton, J. M., & James, G. W. (2000). Tinto's separation and its influence on first-semester college student persistence. *Research in Higher Education, 41*(2), 251–268.

Furnham, A., & Bochner, S. (1982). Social difficulty in a foreign culture: An empirical analysis of culture shock. In S. Bochner (Ed.), *Cultures in contact: Studies in cross-cultural interaction* (pp. 161–198). Oxford: Pergamon.

Hagedorn, L. S. (2005). How to define retention: A new look at an old problem. In A. Seidman (Ed.), *College student retention: Formula for student success*. Westport, CT: American Council on Education/Praeger.

Hechanova-Alampay, R., Beehr, T. A., Christiansen, N. D., & Van Horn, R. K. (2002). Adjustment and strain among domestic and international student sojourners: A longitudinal study. *School Psychology International, 23*(4): 458–474.

Hendricks, A. D. (1996). A grounded theory approach to determining the factors related to the persistence of minority students in professional programs. *Innovative Higher Education, 21*(2), 113–126.

Hernandez, J. C. (2000). Understanding the retention of Latino college students. *Journal of College Student Development, 41*(6), 575–588.

Hurtado, S., Sax, L. J., Saenz, V., Harper, C. E., Oseguera, L., Curley, J., Lopez, L., Wolf, D., & Arellano, L. (2007). Findings from the 2005 Administration of Your College First Year (YCFY): National aggregates. Retrieved July 19, 2007, from http://www .gseis.ucla.edu/heri/PDFs/2005_YFCY_REPORT_FINAL.pdf

Jacob, E. J., & Greggo, J. W. (2001). Using counselor training and collaborative programming strategies in working with international students. *Journal of Multicultural Counseling and Development, 29*(1), 73–88.

Lindholm, J. A. (2006). The "interior" lives of American college students: Preliminary findings from a national study. In J. L. Heft (Ed.), *Passing on the faith: Transforming traditions for the next generation of Jews, Christians, and Muslims* (pp. 75–102). New York: Fordham University Press.

Mendelsohn, D. (2002). The lecture buddy project: An experiment in EAP listening comprehension. *TESL Canada Journal, 20*(1), 64–73.

Morris, J. M., Smith, A. B., & Cejda, B. D. (2003). Spiritual integration as a predictor of persistence at a Christian institution of higher education. *Christian Higher Education, 2*(4), 341–351.

Nora, A. (2002). The depiction of significant others in Tinto's "rites of passage": A reconceptualization of the influence of family and community in the persistence process. *Journal of College Student Retention, 3*(1), 41–56.

Nora, A., & Cabrera, A. F. (1996). The role of perceptions of prejudice and discrimination on the adjustment of minority students to college. *Journal of Higher Education, 37*(4), 427–452.

Pascarella, E. T., & Terenzini, P. T. (1991). *How college affects students.* San Francisco: Jossey-Bass.

———. (2005). *How college affects students: A third decade of research, volume 2.* San Francisco: Jossey-Bass.

Rajapaksa, S., & Dundes, L. (2002). It's a long way home: International student adjustment to living in the United States. *College Student Retention, 4*(1), 15–28.

Roueche, J. E., & Roueche, S. D. (1994). Responding to the challenge of the at-risk student. *Community College Journal of Research and Practice, 18*, 1–11.

Saenz, V. B., & Barrera, D. S. (2007). Findings from the 2005 College Student Survey (CSS): National aggregates. Los Angeles: Higher Education Research Institute. Retrieved July 19, 2007, from http://www.gseis.ucla.edu/heri/publications -brp.php

Schreiner, L. (2000, October). Spiritual fit. FIPSE through the eyes of retention. Washington, DC: Council for Christian Colleges and Universities. Retrieved July 20, 2007, from http://www.cccu.org/docLib/20020321_FIPSE percent20- percent20 Through percent20the percent20Eyes percent20of percent20Retention.rtf

Seidman, A. (Ed.). (2005). *College student retention: Formula for student success.* Westport, CT: American Council on Education/Praeger.

Taylor, E. W. (1994). Intercultural competency: A transformative learning process. *Adult Education Quarterly, 44*, 154–174.

Tierney, W. G. (1992). An anthropological analysis of student participation in college. *Journal of Higher Education, 63*(6), 603–618.

Tinto, V. (1987, 1993). *Leaving college: Rethinking the causes and cures of student attrition.* Chicago: University of Chicago Press.

———. (2005). College student retention: Formula for success. In A. Seidman (Ed.), *College student retention: Formula for student success.* Westport, CT: American Council on Education/Praeger.

Tompson, H. B., & Tompson, G. H. (1996). Confronting diversity issues in the classroom with strategies to improve satisfaction and retention of international students. *Journal of Education for Business, 72*(1), 53–57.

Trice, A. (2003). Faculty perceptions of graduate international students: The benefits and challenges. *Journal of Studies in International Education, 7*(4), 379–403.

Walter, K. L. (2000). *Staying or leaving: A multilevel approach to explaining variations in persistence rates among Christian college undergraduates.* Unpublished doctoral dissertation, University of Arizona, Tucson.

Weiner, B. (1979). A theory of motivation for some classroom experiences. *Journal of Educational Psychology, 71*(2), 3–25.

———. (1986). *An attributional theory of motivation and emotion.* New York: Springer-Verlag.

Zimmerman, B. J. (1994). Dimensions of academic self-regulation: A conceptual framework for education. In D. H. Schunk & B. J. Zimmerman (Eds.), *Self-regulation of learning and performance: Issues and educational applications* (pp. 3–21). Hillsdale, NJ: Erlbaum.

Zimmerman, B. J., Greenberg, D., & Weinstein, C. E. (1994). Self-regulated academic study time: A strategy approach. In D. H. Schunk & B. J. Zimmerman (Eds.), *Self-regulation of learning and performance: Issues and educational applications* (pp. 181–199). Hillsdale, NJ: Erlbaum.

Zimmerman, B. J., & Risemberg, R. (1997). Self-regulatory dimensions of academic learning and motivation. In G. D. Phye (Ed.), *Handbook of academic learning: Construction of knowledge* (pp. 105–125). San Diego: Academic Press.

4

Recruitment

Schools recruit international students for the same reason they recruit domestic students: the students and the institution have something to offer each other. International students may be seen as a way to strengthen or build new programs in language or cultural studies; to reinforce enrollments in declining academic units, such as the sciences or accounting; to help internationalize the campus and curriculum; or to augment enrollments and revenues. Regardless of the reasons, properly recruiting international students can be a complex task that is compounded by linguistic, educational, and cultural differences, not to mention geographic distances. For these reasons and more, international student recruiting practices need to be both ethically and procedurally sound (Thachaberry & Liston, 1986; NAFSA, 2006). This becomes particularly important as more and more universities and nations compete for international students (Forrest, 2008).

Some institutions have been hosting international students for years and have refined their recruitment practices to the point that they are able to keep international enrollments at an optimum level with minimal costs. Recruiting fairs, international travel, professional agencies, word of mouth, and technology are all means that they can readily employ. Other schools may be just beginning to internationalize their campuses; consequently, they have limited experience and resources. Additionally, some institutions may be facing budget constraints and must recruit the same number of students they have recruited in the past with considerably fewer resources. Regardless of a school's circumstance, effective, efficient recruiting is a must (Allen, 2008).

The contributors to this chapter offer a variety of insights and suggestions for recruiting that are based on years of experience. A common component each contributor brings to the discussion is how an institution can both efficiently and effectively recruit.

Negar Davis of Penn State discusses recruiting from the standpoint of a large, multicampus university. The blended approach to recruiting that Penn State has developed depends on internal cohesion and external collaboration to achieve enrollment and internationalization goals. Similarly, Ted McKown presents ways that Kent State University has built synergy among three separate offices on campus that work with international students. In so doing, they have brought the international advisor and the student to the center of their recruiting model.

Writing from years of experience in international education, Ravi Kallur begins by advocating that schools need a clear recruiting plan that includes a variety of strategies that other institutions might adapt or adopt for their specific needs. Bridget Canty follows with specific examples of how the University of Houston uses armchair recruiting strategies that require limited travel and minimal expenses.

This chapter concludes with Cheryl Darrup-Boychuck's compelling presentation on how and why institutions can predict and measure the return on their investment in international students. While each institution will approach this accounting question in a unique way, there are common elements among the programs that will allow for a straightforward way to measure the rate at which recruiting costs are recouped.

The recruiting suggestions in this chapter are in no way intended to be comprehensive. They do, however, offer important principles that can help an institution, large or small, make the most of its recruiting budget while working toward a variety of enrollment goals.

International Student Recruiting: A Blended Approach

Negar Davis

RATIONALE

International student recruiting, when done correctly, is a complex task with many individuals involved and much at stake. Consequently, institutions that develop a strategic recruitment plan will see a much higher success rate than those that take a less organized approach. Such a plan can be developed in a number of ways, depending on an institution's mission and philosophy regarding internationalization of the campus. A factor that cannot be overlooked—but often is—is the need for the recruitment plan to be inclusive. This inclusion needs to embrace colleagues on the same campus as well as those at other institutions.

Too often the administrative offices and academic departments on campuses that have an interest in international student recruiting do not communicate with each other on important issues that impact enrollments and students (see McKown in this chapter). For example, faculty members are seldom consulted on recruiting decisions, yet their expertise, interests, and input are integral to the process. Including the knowledge, insights, and resources of faculty, staff, and students in a school's recruiting efforts can help achieve internationalization objectives.

Furthermore, external partnerships with institutions, governments, and corporations can help a university's recruiting efforts. According to the Institute of International Education, the number of international students in the United States will increase as the number of college-age students increases worldwide (Bhandari & Chow, 2007). However, underestimating the power and will of other countries that are interested in the same market would be a mistake. This is becoming particularly apparent in Europe as the Bologna Process makes the European educational system more attractive to international students (Foley, 2007).

As a result, the best guarantee of mutually beneficial recruiting is to develop strategic partnerships with organizations outside of the university. Joint ventures with corporate, government, and educational institutions will enable each organization to benefit from the others' unique expertise. The recruiting model described here illustrates how Penn State blends strategic international partnerships with the expertise of professionals on campus to achieve institutional curricular and enrollment goals in relation to recruiting international students.

DESCRIPTION OF INSTITUTION AND STUDENTS

The Pennsylvania State University is a land-grant, comprehensive, multicampus research university with a long tradition of including international students as part of the student body. Currently over four thousand international students from more than 135 countries are enrolled at Penn State's twenty-four campuses. International students, therefore, represent approximately 4.3 percent of Penn State's total student body of ninety-two thousand.

As with many other institutions throughout the United States, the largest sending countries are China, India, and Korea. However, to maintain balance, a key recruiting goal has been to diversify international enrollments by focusing on regions that are underrepresented, such as Africa, South and Central America, the Middle East, and Eastern Europe. In addition, Penn State is working to significantly increase its total international student enrollment. These ambitious goals require a recruiting program that is both efficient and effective.

PROGRAM DESCRIPTION

The University Office of Global Programs (UOGP), in partnership with the Undergraduate Admissions Office, the Graduate School, and the Intensive English Communication program, began conversations about expanding recruitment efforts to increase international student enrollments from underrepresented countries.

In addition to increasing enrollments, the aim was also to reduce recruitment costs by working together and improving the admissions process and the programs and services offered to international students, scholars, researchers, and their dependents. In addition, developing external partnerships with community, state, government, corporate, and educational institutions was seen as a way to achieve recruiting goals in a more systematic and sustainable manner. Blending internal cohesion with external collaboration is Penn State's way of being responsive to all stakeholders—students, faculty, the university, and external organizations.

Internal Cohesion

At Penn State, as with many other institutions in the United States, domestic and international student recruiting has typically been handled by one office—the Undergraduate Admissions Office. However, other units, including UOIP, the Intensive English Communication program, the MBA admissions office, and academic departments, were also recruiting students on their own. Unfortunately, coordination among these entities was nonexistent. This fragmented effort resulted in only slight undergraduate enrollment growth. Over a span of ten years, international undergraduate student enrollments increased by less than five hundred students.

The need to develop internal partnerships became essential to increase enrollments, improve customer centeredness, and reflect a welcoming and inclusive campus environment. To overcome the challenges caused by these disjointed recruiting efforts, UOIP joined forces with the Undergraduate Admissions Office. This partnership involved meeting regularly and, for UOIP, playing a larger role in the recruitment process. UOIP developed a recruitment plan to complement the efforts of the Undergraduate Admissions Office, and the two offices shared their annual recruitment plans to create transparency and coordinate travel plans.

At the same time, UOIP also targeted interested offices, such as the Intensive English Communication program, the Graduate School, the MBA admissions office, and academic departments, and invited staff to joint meetings where they could discuss admissions and enrollment issues. This approach was clearly welcomed by all of the above participants as well as the chancellors at other Penn State campuses who were also eager to internationalize their student bodies and curricula.

This internal partnership effort has resulted in several obvious advantages. It has facilitated joint meetings with international visitors, such as academic advisors at overseas educational advising centers, and university representatives interested in various partnerships with the university. In the past, many campus officials working on international student recruiting were unaware such meetings were even taking place.

In addition, internal partnerships have also resulted in cost savings, since plans are shared and discussed, and redundant activities are either canceled or changed. Internal cohesion also allows for cross-training with regard to the admissions process and requirements and enables faculty and nonadmissions staff to market Penn State more broadly and accurately. Working jointly and strategically toward the goal of increasing student enrollment and diversifying the overall student body has been a positive change at Penn State.

External Collaboration

While internal cohesion is vital to recruiting efforts, campus internationalization cannot be fully achieved without collaboration with partner institutions and corporations outside the university. For the past several years, the Office of International Programs has engaged in international outreach events that include several internationalization goals such as teaching, research, and service for the university. These events also include activities and meetings with international alumni, scholars, prospective students, parents, academic advisors, government officials, partner institutions, and corporate partners. A specific example is perhaps the best way to illustrate the nature of these partnerships and to explain how they are formed and how they contribute to Penn State's objectives.

On a recent four-day visit to Doha, Qatar, the Penn State recruiting officer's agenda consisted of participation in a two-day international higher-education fair to market Penn State to prospective students; a visit and tour of the Qatar University to consider partnerships with the university; meetings with officials from the gas and petroleum companies to investigate the possibilities of joint ventures; meetings with the Qatar Foundation to learn about future educational needs; a tour of the Education City for a firsthand observation of the educational system from which international students transfer; interviews with local newspapers as part of the higher education fair; visits to high schools to inform counselors about the Penn State admissions process; and meetings with prospective students, parents of currently enrolled students, and alumni to enhance relationships.

Blending on-campus expertise with international outreach helps accomplish many objectives with positive results. With one short trip abroad, representatives of the university recruit students at all levels; consider possible exchange programs; build partnerships; network with colleagues; and meet with alumni, parents, sponsored student program officers, embassy and foreign government officials, and university officials. This approach contributes significantly to the university's overall internationalization efforts.

EVALUATION

As with any initiative, assessment is critical to success. Assessment of Penn State's recruiting efforts follows a similar principle to the one used for recruiting itself, namely, drawing on the expertise of many for one cause. Staff from UOIP meet frequently with others on campus to measure the success of all recruiting efforts. To justify recruitment efforts, it is important that administrators see data and trends. Therefore, data are compiled and analyzed by UOIP on an ongoing basis to determine if efforts have been productive. Each country that is visited is monitored for increased enrollments. Recent efforts in Malaysia, for example, have resulted in eighty additional sponsored students enrolling from that country.

Issues of value are also frequently discussed: is time better spent staffing a booth for five hours at a recruiting fair or meeting with a minister of education? Issues such as these are now openly discussed in joint meetings attended by campus representatives. The number of applications received and the number of actual enrollments for each of the target countries are compiled and analyzed to measure change. If changes are not apparent within a period of three years, recruiting approaches are reviewed and modified accordingly. It is essential to note that results from recruiting efforts are not likely to be immediate for any institution.

APPLICABILITY TO OTHER INSTITUTIONS

The blending of international outreach and partnerships can be of benefit to other institutions. A blended model can be modified for use at any campus, regardless of its organizational structure or size. The main objective of this model is to provide internal partnership opportunities between the academic departments and administrative units while building partnerships with external organizations that have an interest in sending students to the United States for educational purposes.

This integrated approach allows for better communication, transparency, and cross-training to market the institution locally and internationally. It also provides an opportunity for internationally minded faculty to interact with administrative units to assist with recruiting and alumni outreach efforts. Faculty, staff, and students can collectively contribute to internationalization by blending their expertise and world views. Much can be gained both internally and externally.

Synergizing Admissions and Advising to Improve International Recruitment

Ted R. McKown II

RATIONALE

Higher education is truly in a new and challenging age of recruitment for at least three reasons. First, the demographics of college-bound students are shifting. The United States is experiencing the end of inflated enrollments. Echo boomers (children of the baby boomers) are now in high school, signifying the end of an influx of college-aged students in the United States. (Burmeister, 2008). Second, to deal with a weak economy, the education sector is restructuring units and departments, eliminating programs, and reducing staff. The challenge of doing more with less is a common charge at many institutions. Third, students today will go where they are offered the best deal, and they change institutions multiple times to reach their desired level of attention.

International student enrollment can provide a partial solution to these issues. Open Doors estimates that every fifty international students who attend a particular institution generate $1,000,000 for that institution (Bhandari & Chow, 2007). This being the case, there is a large return on investment when recruiting international students (see Darrup-Boychuck in this chapter).

If universities expect an increase in international enrollment to be a meaningful response to the changing higher education environment, then they will need to change the way they respond to international students. At a university in the United States, it is common to find three distinct and separate groups working within international education: international admissions, international student and scholar services, and education abroad. The potential for disconnect among these various departments is significant. Furthermore, such separation can distract from the common goals of assisting international students and building momentum to increase future enrollments.

While the possibility of problems is great, an equally strong potential for good exists. By synergizing international education, particularly in the areas of international admissions and student advising, the university mission will be promoted and both the international students and the university will benefit. At Kent State University, we realized the potential for good that would come from uniting efforts; it made sense to come together and use knowledge of specialized areas to work toward the common mission of serving international students from recruitment to graduation.

DESCRIPTION OF THE INSTITUTION AND STUDENTS

Kent State is a large public doctoral/research university in the Great Lakes region of the Midwest. Kent currently enrolls thirty-five thousand students annually, of which eight hundred to one thousand are international students. Founded in 1910 as a land grant normal school by the state of Ohio, Kent State relies on traditional undergraduate freshmen each year for tuition dollars. Since it is a public institution, it has always relied on tuition dollars for a large percentage of its operating budget.

The student body historically had been drawn from a fifty-mile radius within northeast Ohio. However, as enrollment dynamics changed, attempts were made to enroll students from other areas and surrounding states. These efforts proved to be generally ineffectual. Consequently, the university has had to turn to new sources of revenue. The administration recently stated that meeting enrollment needs would be accomplished by placing a high priority on recruiting higher quality students and drawing those students from more diverse areas. In addition, the administration made it clear that recruiting international students and providing international experiences for all students would be high priorities.

PROGRAM DESCRIPTION

By definition, synergy is designed to get people to work together to accomplish a common goal. Building synergy between international admissions and student advising at Kent State University is seen as an opportunity to diversify the classroom while increasing enrollments and generating revenue. The international student advisor, as a part of the Office of International

Affairs, is the centerpiece of activity, interacting with applicants, processing immigration documents, and providing advising and programming to current international students. This unifying effort improves communication not only within international units on campus but with the international applicant as well. In short, this process allows employees in international education to work together to significantly increase international enrollment and further the mission of international and intercultural exchange at the university.

Many institutions do not have strong connections between international marketing, recruitment, and admissions efforts. Most recruitment is performed by marketing or admissions personnel who have little to no intercultural training and probably have limited personal contact with international students. In addition, once the recruitment cycle is complete, the admission professional moves to the next recruitment cycle and may not have any further contact with the recently admitted students.

As Kent State moves into the future, the international student advisor is becoming the key component in making international recruitment and retention efforts more efficient by being more meaningfully involved in the relationship-building process with international applicants and students. Relationships that an international student advisor develops with students are at the core of a synergized marketing concept.

The principle behind this approach is that one individual, in this case the international advisor, possesses all the information a student needs to make a decision about selecting a college/university within the United States. An advisor works closely with those offices on campus that would service an international student, thereby making it possible to assist the prospective and current students with concerns and problems. In addition, an advisor has the ability to demonstrate concern for the international student by responding to emotional needs. The aim is to provide students with a positive experience with the university, which can have lasting effects for both the student and the institution. This nurturing environment begins when a prospective student is first contacted, and it continues through graduation.

Kent State's efforts to build synergy in the international student recruiting process have had success—but not without opposition. In synergizing admissions with international student services, international student advisors were projected to become the lead people in the international application process by developing relationships with students. Communication between advisors and applicants would ensure smooth processing of application materials and initiate a long-term connection between the student and the advisor. The relationship would continue to build until the student graduated from Kent State. An immediate challenge to this concept was the resistance raised by the advising staff. They wanted to manage current international students and their immigration issues, but they had little desire to recruit new students.

One recent step in this gradual transition of responsibilities was engaging the advisors in the admissions process. Advisors were given the tasks of responding to prospective applicant questions, tracking the application progress, and staying in close contact with the applicants throughout the process. The goal was to reduce the application process time to two weeks. The advisors exceeded this goal, reducing the average process time of an international application to five business days. Prior to this change it had taken four to six weeks to process an application. However, it took the Office of International Affairs two admissions cycles to get to the higher level of productivity.

International student advisors and application processors became a team, communicating several times per day to proactively eliminate the issues that arose regarding applications. The advisor would then communicate these issues to the applicant. Having the advisors participate in the admissions process was a huge success as it allowed the application processor to produce a quick turnaround of applications.

As Kent State University gradually moves the international student advisor into a pivotal position in the application process, the future student is the focal point. The advisor is able to work with and help a student from first contact to graduation. In this process, the advisor builds personal connections with current students who, when they graduate and return home, are likely to positively promote the university to future students.

EVALUATION

While this is a work in progress, combining international admissions and advising is beginning to demonstrate positive results. The most recent recruitment cycle was productive. New international student enrollment has increased by 7.4 percent. Applicants received more prompt responses to their applications than ever before because the international advisor was in the center of the process.

While increased enrollments and the revenue they generate are often used as metrics of success, these are not the only signs that the new model of admissions and advising is working. Success can also be seen as advisors quickly recognize problems and international students are better served. International students already feel more connected to the university because of the synergy taking place. This is demonstrated by increased enrollment numbers and higher student participation at programming events. In addition, the international advisors are building relationships with the international students at first contact, which allows for a more proactive early understanding of the students and their academic needs. Relationship building has become a centerpiece of activity for the advisor and is accomplished through programming, advising, and meeting with students.

APPLICABILITY TO OTHER INSTITUTIONS

This approach applies to any institution within the United States regardless of size or type. This model can be adapted according to institutional goals, core values, and missions. With the right training and skills, the international student advisor can become the ideal person at an institution to synergize admissions and advisement and to combine recruitment efforts and follow-up activities with relationship building. This powerful combination allows the university to increase enrollment, elevate retention, and create a perpetual marketing tool as international students graduate and return home to promote their positive experiences at the university. In this regard, the advisor–student relationship could have tremendous future benefits to any university.

Helpful Strategies for International Student Recruitment

Ravi Kallur

RATIONALE

International students' success on American college and university campuses begins with recruitment. Effective recruitment allows the institution to establish appropriate linguistic and cultural diversity as well as enhance intercultural learning opportunities. Since recruitment plays such a pivotal role in the international experience, it is critical to understand how students are recruited, what information they are given, and how American institutions can remain competitive in attracting international students. The strategies presented here are intended to aid institutions and, by extension, their students in the vital recruiting process.

Before proceeding with a discussion of recruiting strategies, two key principles must be established. First, the institution's mission and philosophy, which often drive resource allocations, must support international student recruitment. Failure to provide resources will jeopardize the students' success, derail the efforts of the institution, and hamper future international student recruitment.

Many professional associations agree that an institution should have a clear statement defining its rationale for enrolling international students and clearly stating its goals regarding enrollment. This statement should be directly related to the institution's mission statement and goals. Second, ethical recruitment and admissions practices should be an integral part of international recruitment. Principal recruiting goals ought to increase international student enrollments with the aim of promoting global awareness and international understanding.

DESCRIPTION OF THE INSTITUTION

There is no one-size-fits-all strategy for recruiting students. As such, it is important to identify the most efficient ways to recruit international students based on the size and type of institution. For example, English-as-second-language schools and undergraduate programs will benefit by traveling to recruit and by meeting with school and advisement center counselors. Parents of students who are applying to these types of institutions are actively involved in decision making, and it is comforting for them to meet a school representative in person. Graduate schools, on the other hand, typically recruit more mature students who rely a great deal on technology and are hungry for immediate, current information available through the Internet. Personal contact with a recruiter for these students is not a critical factor. For such institutions, armchair recruitment, chat rooms, and websites can be effective ways to reach students.

PROGRAM DESCRIPTION

Recruitment is a complex process in any context, but it becomes especially intricate when the international aspect is factored in. Any institution, regardless of its type or mission, that ventures into the international recruiting arena needs to understand that certain preparatory steps must be taken before deciding on which type of recruitment method to use.

Preparation

Before international student recruitment can begin, an institution needs to develop a plan based on sound data. This process can vary among institutions, but three basic components should be considered. First, a self-study of the institution and its existing resources is needed. This includes a survey of currently enrolled and recently graduated international students. To facilitate this, the Council for Advancement of Standards in Higher Education (www.cas.edu/) has published self-assessment guides (SAGs) with standards and guidelines. Next, an outside consultant or colleague from a different successful program can provide invaluable insights on current practices and resources and can make recommendations. Finally, no plan is complete until the self-study and corresponding data and consultant reports are reviewed with administrators and decision makers.

The next logical step is to develop a three- or five-year recruitment plan based on the data collected. This plan should include budget for support services, travel, an ESL program, and other needs identified in the self-study. Such a plan should include establishing an advisory committee consisting of representatives from financial aid, admissions, the registrar, housing, food service, campus security, and the faculty. The same committee should help in implementing the plan and conduct a thorough annual review. Such a review will offer insight into the progress made and the issues faced in the previous year.

Types of Recruitment

Armchair recruitment. For institutions with a limited budget and a small offering of programs, armchair recruitment is a good starting strategy. Armchair recruitment is not exempt from the planning described above. However, it will require a relatively small budget and only moderate support services. Key factors in preparing for armchair recruitment include developing a three-year plan, establishing a budget, and hiring any additional staff the plan calls for to respond to inquiries from prospective students and organizations.

Institutions should focus on a few countries that send large numbers of students to the United States. Information collected in the self-study report may be helpful in identifying countries to target in the recruitment process. Once target countries are identified, potential students can be contacted through inexpensive strategies such as mail campaigns, which can be done through Army post office (APO) mailboxes to reduce international mailing costs. Advertising in publications that are widely viewed by international students is another inexpensive method. Publications like *Study USA* and *Petersons* are good places to start.

Another important aspect of armchair recruiting is developing an alumni network. Alumni are a valuable resource. They can give presentations at schools and colleges during college career days. They can also attend educational fairs sponsored by the Institute for International Education (IIE). Savings can be significant, and who represents a school better than a successful graduate? Similarly, faculty and current international students planning business or personal trips abroad can be superb ambassadors. They know the schools and people in their hometowns. They can visit their former schools and talk to advisors or speak to a group of students who might be interested in studying abroad.

Regardless of the recruiting method used, two cautionary notes are in order. First, careful tracking of inquiries, applications, admissions, and enrollments is a must. The need for accurate record keeping and tracking systems cannot be overstated. This will provide solid information on which to measure growth trends and base financial decisions.

The second caution is to be careful of agents. Many countries have entrepreneurial individuals who help students with the admission process and placement at an American institution. These agents work for fees, which they collect from the prospective student as well as the school where the student enrolls. Because agents generally do not work for a single institution, they may not have any knowledge about an institution, the services provided, or whether the particular student they are helping is a good fit. As such, it is important that, if agents are involved, expectations and guidelines be in writing. Recruiters should visit the agents' offices while traveling abroad, and agents should be invited to campus at least once every two years. Review contracts and agreements annually.

Travel recruitment. More and more school representatives are venturing into the world, traveling by themselves or with groups to meet prospective students, parents, and educational advisors abroad. This method of recruitment is more effective than armchair recruiting for many reasons. Meeting prospective students in their home countries provides the recruiter with new perspectives and an appreciation of the students' countries and cultures. The recruiter will have an opportunity to understand the country's economy and educational system as well as the students' ability to afford the school. A preliminary review of credentials helps the recruiter inform students of the programs most likely to meet their educational needs. Parents, who are usually included in these meetings, generally feel more comfortable sending their child to a school where they can identify an individual by name and face.

Travel recruitment requires careful planning and execution. When an institution plans recruitment travel, a well-defined plan should be in place that includes timelines, number of trips per year, budgets, and support personnel. A good follow-up with candidates and schools should also be part of the recruitment plan.

One of the first realities an international recruiter learns is that international recruitment travel is cumbersome and complicated. Accordingly, institutions may want to send their recruiters with U.S. recruitment groups in the initial year of travel recruiting. Recruitment groups or agencies typically plan the itinerary, identify schools to visit, arrange visits and briefings at the U.S. consulate or embassy, and set up educational fairs for students and parents to meet with the school representatives. Generally, tours will have fifteen to forty representatives from different institutions traveling in the group. These schools will vary in size, academic offerings, and locations.

A benefit of group travel recruitment is the opportunity to interact with colleagues from other schools and learn from their experiences as well as exchange ideas for publications and advertisements. In addition, traveling with a group is less strenuous than traveling alone, and it gives the representative more time to meet students, alumni, and school officials while the tour organizer takes care of hotel arrangements, transportation, and other logistical matters.

The Institute of International Education is a good source for information regarding recruiting tours. They regularly publish information about different groups and their itineraries. Finding out which schools have participated in the past is also helpful. This information is generally available on group tour websites. If an institution chooses to not join a tour group and sends their recruiter out alone, the individual should be a veteran traveler with a thorough knowledge of the institution and should be able (i.e., both knowledgeable and empowered) to make decisions while on the road.

Recruitment within the United States. If an institution is targeting the undergraduate international student population, one of the most economical ways to recruit students is through community colleges and ESL programs in the United States. There are more than eighty-six thousand international students in community colleges (Bhandari & Chow, 2007). Participating in community college and ESL recruitment fairs will reduce the international travel related costs including airfare, lodging, and shipping expenses. It will also alleviate any problems and costs associated with cancellation of trips and revision to the travel itinerary that may arise due to changes in political situations in the host country. In addition to being less expensive for travel reasons, domestic educational fairs are useful, inexpensive training grounds for the new staff members.

Network recruitment. Attending national conferences hosted by organizations like NAFSA: Association of International Educators, American Association of Collegiate Registrars and Admissions Officers (AACRAO), and the Association of International Education Administrators (AIEA) is an indirect but effective avenue for recruitment. These conferences provide opportunities to meet representatives from educational advising centers, international schools, ESL programs, and community colleges. This type of recruitment also enables school representatives to connect with individuals in similar positions at other schools and establish initial contacts in person.

Visibility of an institution is a critical aspect of recruitment. In this regard, visits to the education department offices in the embassies in Washington, DC, will help. Several foreign governments financially support students who wish to study in the United States. These embassies can provide information regarding the number of students they send, the areas of specialization, and the requirements for admission. Furthermore, visiting embassies helps an institution establish direct links with the governments that send students.

EVALUATION

While serving as the director of International Student Affairs at the University of Missouri, Kansas City, I developed various international recruitment plans. The plans were of three-year durations and were part of an overall strategy to increase international enrollment. The plans included timelines, budgets, staffing needs, international travel destinations, and community college and ESL program recruitment. Success of our efforts can be measured in various ways, but enrollment is an accurate metric. International student enrollment over a five-year period increased from approximately six hundred to nine hundred students. We also expanded our exchange program agreements with other schools, provided community college transfer, and awarded out-of-state tuition scholarships.

APPLICABILITY TO OTHER INSTITUTIONS

Several institutions seeking advice on how they could increase their international recruiting efforts have followed guidelines similar to those outlined above. At the request of the vice chancellor for Student Affairs at Southern Illinois University, Carbondale, a colleague and I reviewed the international programs at SIU, Carbondale and submitted an advisory report suggesting many of the recommendations outlined here. Nearly all of the recommendations have been implemented with better coordination of recruitment, admissions, advising, and retention.

In addition, Park University in Parkville, Missouri, requested a review and assessment of its program in an effort to increase international enrollments. Park University also implemented a recruitment plan following many of these guidelines. Its success can also be measured by enrollment numbers. In a three-year period, the university's international enrollments increased by 43 percent and the number of countries represented on their campus increased by nearly 20 percent.

The ideas suggested are applicable and adaptable to most institutions interested in recruiting international students. The extent to which the ideas can be implemented depends on the type of institution as well as the extent of support and resources available. It is also absolutely essential that institutions have a clear vision of their mission related to international students to respond to the special needs of this population.

International Armchair Recruitment: Enhancing Your Assets with a Limited Budget

Bridget E. Canty

RATIONALE

Most would agree that the international education arena has changed dramatically in the past decade. Aside from changes in immigration laws after 9/11, other factors are forcing U.S. institutions to rethink their current recruitment practices. One factor is the Bologna Process, an international educational agreement that allows students in Europe to have a seamless experience when transferring from one European university to another. Such an agreement makes higher education in Europe an attractive option to international students who are searching for educational opportunities.

Another factor is the rapidly increasing capacity of the Internet. With the readily available information that the Internet provides international students, it should come as no surprise that students are becoming more selective and increasingly more demanding about which institution they attend. To address these global changes and the competitive markets that they have spawned, the University of Houston has been forced to reevaluate and revise its international recruitment.

DESCRIPTION OF THE INSTITUTION AND STUDENTS

The University of Houston (UH) is located in the fourth largest city in the United States. *U.S. News & World Report* (America's Best, 2008) stated that UH is the second most ethnically diverse research university in the United

States. In fact, UH's three thousand international students and scholars represent over 130 different nations and compose an average of 9 percent (well above the 4 percent national average) of the total thirty-five thousand undergraduate and graduate student body. UH receives in excess of six thousand international applications a year. The majority of the international applicants come from the following five countries in descending order: India, Republic of China, Republic of Korea, Nigeria, and Taiwan.

PROGRAM DESCRIPTION

The Office of International Admissions (OIA) at UH has addressed the challenges of a new competitive global market and a limited budget by improving its armchair recruitment strategies and understanding that quality customer service is a must. Armchair recruiting is essentially what the name suggests: cost-effective recruiting that is conducted by means of print publications and electronic and web-based communications, which is done without leaving one's desk. At UH, armchair recruiting includes three central elements: (a) marketing, (b) e-communications, and (c) collaborative agreements.

Marketing

The American Marketing Association (Zinkhan & Williams, 2007) recently released a new definition of marketing: "Marketing is an organizational function and a set of processes for creating, communicating and delivering value to customers and for managing customer relationships in ways that benefit the organization and its stakeholders" (p. 285). To adequately market the institution, UH defines and clearly articulates the uniqueness of the university on its websites and in brochures. In this process, UH focuses on its strengths. An emphasis on strong academic programs, a generally warm climate, and a student population that is as diverse as the city are all marketed as reasons UH should be the institution of choice for international students.

One of the most beneficial international marketing strategies used at UH has been collaboration with the university's marketing team. This has proven beneficial in two ways. First, it has minimized the cost of promotional brochures and handbooks because in-house services are less expensive than outside providers. Second, working with the university's marketing team has allowed OIA to learn what other departments on campus are doing to promote their areas.

The university confidently markets who it is and what it has to offer by finding creative ways to make a limited budget count. The OIA website, which offers free marketing, was designed by the OIA and the UH marketing team. Market research is obtained by working with a technical marketing team to gain information on the type of applicants who visit the website. Data are collected on students' areas of interest, country location, gender, and age. The website is also analyzed to determine what links get the most hits. This information is used to design web pages and marketing materials for twelve feeder countries. The main page provides general information while the web pages for the feeder countries list country-specific information. They include specific requirements for each educational level, information on student organizations at UH, and pictures of current and alumnus students from various countries.

E-Communication

In addition to marketing, e-communication is essential for recruiting in a competitive market, especially for those students whose world revolves around the latest technology. UH has begun to use e-communication as its principal form of communication with prospective students. Although the new generation of college students uses technology a great deal for communication purposes, they also want and expect quality customer service. In this context, customer service means an easy-to-navigate website with quick and concise responses from the university. It also means that the information provided electronically to students is efficient, correct, personal, generationally appropriate, and up-to-date. This takes effort from the marketing team, the technical support staff, and the admissions office, which all work together to assist international students in making UH their choice.

Another form of e-communication implemented across campus is the Apply Texas Application (ATA). This allows applicants to apply online at anytime and submit their application fee with a credit card payment. Within forty-eight hours of the application submission, the information is downloaded electronically into the UH system. The electronic application process has reduced human error and has made the process less flawed. Once the university moved to the ATA application, the number of applications UH received increased by 20 percent annually. E-communication has been one of UH's biggest recruitment assets and in many ways has allowed the university to become paperless.

Collaborative On-Campus and Two-Year College Agreements

In addition to marketing and e-communication strategies, UH recruits using armchair strategies by collaborating with other on-campus and off-campus programs. One of the biggest on-campus partners is the Language and Culture Center (LCC) Intensive English program. To recruit international students, OIA has collaborated with LCC to implement two ways to enable international students to qualify for enrollment. First, undergraduate students studying in the LCC who wish to attend UH may complete Level 6, the final level in the program, in place of the TOEFL. Second, UH has agreements with some sponsor programs that allow students to apply to the Intensive English program while their applications and credentials are reviewed by International Admissions to determine admissibility. These agreements have been beneficial to both departments by increasing the number of applications from international students.

OIA has also begun working with domestic recruiters, articulation coordinators, and support staff to include international recruitment with domestic local recruitment. For OIA, this means learning domestic admissions requirements for UH and networking with those outside the international arena to increase our population of international students transferring from two-year colleges. OIA has also had to articulate to new colleagues at two-year colleges how working together would be advantageous for all parties. Prospective students are now able to take advantage of the two-plus-two agreement, which allows community college students to complete the first two years at a community college and their junior and senior years at UH.

The main objective of these recruiting efforts is to have students choose UH; however, the fundamental principle that underlies all recruitment efforts is customer service. In these efforts, OIA left the comfort of working in isolation and strategically thought of new ways to proactively address the vastly changing international arena. OIA has continued to change and evolve to maintain an edge in what has become a global competitive market.

EVALUATION

Each phase of the OIA marketing strategies is assessed using different measuring tools. For instance, the website and written materials are evaluated by student focus groups; the students provided invaluable feedback about the look of the website regarding what worked and what did not. Feedback from these focus groups was instrumental in updating the website. The e-communications system is assessed by performing statistical tests to determine how frequently students receive communication, how smooth the process is for them, and how accurately data are processed in the system. Finally, the success of the collaborative on-campus agreements with community colleges is also measurable. Each on-campus agreement is assigned a special code that identifies the students and the program. Students are tracked by their special code, which allows data to be collected on the number of applications received from a particular program.

With unprecedented global competition, a limited recruitment budget, and no international travel, we have found multiple ways to continue to attract international students by focusing on our strengths, improving our processes, working collaboratively with others on campus, and working with community colleges to help students further their education by matriculating to UH.

APPLICABILITY TO OTHER INSTITUTIONS

This brief guide to international armchair recruitment should be beneficial to any university with the all-too-common challenge of a limited recruitment budget. Although each university is different, the principles of developing a marketing plan, using e-communication, and obtaining collaborative on-campus and two-year college agreements all have potential for improving recruiting. They may have to be adapted to local circumstances, but the costs are minimal.

For instance, something as simple and inexpensive as forming student focus groups through student organizations can assist with marketing plans. Getting students' input on websites and brochures is easily done and can make a positive impact on an institution's international marketing plan. E-communication is used in conjunction with marketing endeavors. Because technology is such a pervasive element in the lives of many students today, the use of e-communication is not only imperative for any institution seeking to recruit students, but it is also inexpensive.

Finally, developing internal and external collaborative agreements entails reaching out to those on and off campus who have the same goal—to recruit international students. Having a limited budget makes international recruitment challenging, but not impossible. Recruiting goals can be met, even exceeded, from an armchair and on a shoestring.

A Simple Approach to Measuring Return on Investment in International Student Recruitment

Cheryl Darrup-Boychuck

RATIONALE

Educational administrators responsible for enrollment management across the United States, and indeed around the world, increasingly demand solid justification for every penny in their staff's budgets. In an effort to make financial accountability possible and transparent, domestic admissions departments over the years have established formulas that attempt to calculate an equivalent to what the corporate world calls "customer acquisition costs." In the case of the business world, every attempt is made to determine how much it costs to acquire a customer. Having such figures allows companies to make informed decisions and maintain reasonable profit margins.

The same can be said for higher education as well. Knowing how much it costs to recruit a student helps administrators make informed decisions and maintain healthy budgets. Despite the apparent advantage of knowing what it costs to acquire a domestic student, most institutions do not know with any degree of specificity the cost to recruit an international student.

The 2006 National Association of College Admissions Counselors (NACAC) Admissions Trends Survey provides invaluable data on the cost of recruiting domestic students. It indicates that the cost to enroll one domestic student (based on all categories in the total admissions budget) averaged $2,350 overall. The mean cost for private institutions was about $2,802, while public institutions' average came in at $1,083 (Hawkins & Clinedinst, 2007). However, the corporatization of U.S. higher education, coupled with

96

intense global competition for talent, has shed new light on the importance of universities being able to measure their return on investment (ROI) in international student recruitment.

One reason for the lack of data on international student recruiting costs is that the potential number of quantifiably elusive variables seems limited only by the imagination. For instance, how do we account for such factors as foreign currency fluctuations, research in external markets, or word-of-mouth referrals? Another less obvious reason for the lack of data has to do with the mindset of today's senior international educators. According to the 2006 NAFSA: Association of International Educators membership survey, 54 percent of NAFSA members are between the ages of forty-one and fifty-nine. These colleagues helped breathe life into the idealistic hopes and dreams of the post–World War II generation before them, believing that education across borders was the solution for many of the world's shortcomings.

Several of today's prominent fifty- and sixty-year-old international educators contributed to designing the structure of the current global student mobility machine (Gardner, 2007). For today's mature international educators, there was always a "greater purpose" to their work—one that was impossible to define by numbers with dollar signs in front of them. Whatever past reasons were for not quantifying the costs of recruiting international students, current economic and market demands mandate that educational institutions find reliable ways to measure gains from their investments.

PROGRAM DESCRIPTION

The formula for measuring ROI for international student recruitment is illustrated by three examples. The purpose of the examples is to demonstrate how ROI for international student recruitment can be measured despite the fact that many colleagues and scholars have deemed it impossible to accurately measure on an industry-wide basis because of the substantial complexities of international student recruitment.

The logical place to begin to establish an ROI model for international admissions is to consider the formula used to calculate domestic student ROI. The NACAC formula is simply a matter of comparing the initial investment to subsequent profits produced by that investment. In other words, recruitment costs (such as website development, travel to recruitment events, and direct mail) and financial aid packages were subtracted from student tuition. Since variability from one campus to another is significant, the most reasonable approach for calculating ROI for international students is to focus on individual campuses and apply the mathematical model used by domestic admissions when analyzing international admissions on that same campus.

Once the ROI model for domestic admissions is established, then the international admissions office can begin plugging in its own figures to arrive at an accurate comparison on that particular campus. At bare minimum, the basic equation for measuring ROI in international student recruitment is a matter of subtracting recruitment costs—such as travel, commissions, scholarships, advertising, and overseas fairs—from the tuition and fees that international students pay.

This deliberately simplistic approach is most helpful when considering the comparative benefits of different recruitment initiatives. The elementary equation isolates the recruitment expenses, inherently recognizing that the ROI could be zero or even a negative figure if, in fact, no students enroll as a result of that particular effort. Consider the following three scenarios involving domestic travel, overseas agent engagement, and online promotions.

Domestic Travel

One colleague spent $1,200 for a flight, hotel, and meals in Washington, DC, for a visit to the Saudi Cultural Mission. Later that year, twenty Saudi scholarship students arrived on his campus as a direct result of that visit. The financial gains from his visit were about $143,000 in tuition and fees and an impressive ROI (Darrup-Boychuck, 2008). Most recruitment initiatives do not realize returns of such magnitude so quickly. The Saudi example is instructive, however, in emphasizing the importance of staying alert to current events and projected trends in this dynamic industry.

Overseas Agent Engagement

This particular case transpired over the course of four years and illuminates the industry's trend toward quality over quantity. A U.S.-based colleague worked with an education agent in Busan, South Korea, to coordinate an exclusive information session for his community college. Of the ten students in attendance, four ended up enrolling in English as a Second Language courses and degree programs, generating $47,840. Expenses included an agent workshop, three flights, hotels and meals, event and equipment fees, plus commissions, totaling $13,800. ROI equals $34,040 over four years (Elliott, 2007).

Online Promotions

Technology-based promotions feature inherent filtering, targeting, and tracking mechanisms. The Internet, and indeed all electronic media, provide a powerful platform to correspond with the world's most affluent students and parents. Another differentiating factor between online promotions and other recruitment initiatives involves time. Colleagues expect a quicker ROI from Internet advertisements when compared to recruitment travel outside of the United States, for example. The cost of online promotions varies widely, but in this specific case, the annual advertising fee was $1,195. A university-based extension program enrolled ten students in their ten-week sessions, generating $33,150 for an ROI of $31,955, which was directly due to their online promotion (Darrup-Boychuck, 2008).

These few illustrations provide a simple foundation for further research. Ultimately, the industry will need to collect and share hundreds of such examples to establish baseline data on which the United States as a whole can benefit in the extremely competitive marketplace of global student mobility.

To secure appropriate funding for effective international student recruitment in the United States, colleagues need to articulate compelling arguments in the language used by their vice presidents responsible for enrollment management—language that most certainly includes numbers with dollar signs in front of them. Unfortunately, the complexity of international recruitment grossly inhibits the establishment of one broad, national formula that fits all contexts for measuring ROI for international student admissions. Fortunately, a comparative analysis with domestic admission costs on each individual campus may very well provide the hard data needed to boost the budget for international admissions.

Hard data are what the industry needs now to proceed with measuring ROI in international student recruitment. Analyzing individual campuses is a logical place to begin the research. Within a single campus environment, dozens of quantifiably elusive factors must be purposely omitted from a broad ROI formula for the sake of accuracy. These factors include those listed in table 4.1.

How important are any of these factors in analyzing the success or failure of specific international student recruitment initiatives? A few of these factors may weigh heavily in a solid ROI equation for any given institution; other factors may not matter at all for another campus' particular intents and purposes. For example, some campuses pride themselves on the vast diversity of their international student population. They may be willing to spend more (in scholarships perhaps) to recruit a student from a country that is not currently represented in their mix, as opposed to recruiting another student from a country that is already well represented on campus. The point to remember is that individual campuses select the factors that most accurately represent their specific context.

Table 4.1.   Individual Campus Factors Affecting ROI

Factor	Outcome
Prestige factors	The university can claim that internationalization is part of the campus mission.
Diversity factors	The university can boast a certain number of countries represented on campus.
Word-of-mouth referrals	Referrals can produce more enrollees for very little cost.
Research into external markets	Recruiters will understand which academic programs sell well in which countries.
Follow-up mechanisms	The university can respond promptly to initial inquiries.
Staff time and salaries	Time and money can be devoted to recruitment and/or alumni networks.
Foreign-born faculty members	These faculty members may be able travel back to their home country to recruit informally.
Monetary gains	International student fees can fund scholarships for other international students.
Currency fluctuations	Fluctuations can make the cost of a U.S. education more or less affordable.

EVALUATION AND APPLICABILITY

How do you measure such factors as those listed in table 4.1? The corporate world has proposed a few mathematical models designed to estimate how much of each customer's value stems from purchases or tuition and fees, in the case of higher education, and how much from referrals, to arrive at a customer's lifetime value (Kumar, Petersen, & Leone, 2007). These types of equations could predict a dependent variable, such as the likelihood of enrolling an international student based on the different costs of recruitment (e.g., overseas travel, alumni connections, or print publications).

There certainly is some value in collecting data and crunching numbers to accurately calculate the ROI in international student recruitment for any segment of the population. That value can increase exponentially for the United States as a global education destination if the ROI results (from both domestic and international admissions) are shared widely. For example, a colleague may be struggling to justify resource allocation for a full-time international student recruiter. Or perhaps another colleague wants to prove that his community college has a high probability of success in a particular emerging student market. The most solid arguments may be based on dollars-and-cents case studies from peer institutions that faced similar circumstances in recent years.

At this point, the challenge is to build a library of case studies that address the various scenarios in measuring ROI in international student recruitment. Because very little hard data currently exists, and given the complex dynamics of the industry, younger colleagues would do well to invest time speaking to seasoned international admissions professionals on campus now to more effectively frame future planning. After all, the colleagues with the most overseas recruiting experience are starting to retire.

Armed with appropriate "tools of the trade" in a field that increasingly resembles corporate America, international educators can work more effectively with their administrators when they speak their language. Quantifiable case studies, coupled with concise anecdotes, will serve the industry well during campus-wide discussions about budget allocations and internationalization strategies.

REFERENCES

Allen, C. E. (2008, Spring). Initiating an international recruitment program at a large research university. *IIE Networker Magazine.* Retrieved October 7, 2008, from http://www.iienetwork.org/page/124191/

America's Best Colleges 2008. (2008). *U.S. News & World Report.* Retrieved November 28, 2007, from http://colleges.usnews.rankingsandreviews.com/usnews/edu/college/

Bhandari, R., & Chow, P. (2007). *Open doors: Report on international educational exchange.* New York: Institute of International Education.

Burmeister, M. (2008). *From boomers to bloggers: Success strategies across generations.* Fairfax, VA: Synergy Press.

Darrup-Boychuck, C. (2008, Spring). Measuring return on investment in international student recruitment. *IIE Networker Magazine.* Retrieved June 24, 2008, from http://www.iienetwork.org/page/124187/

Elliott, W. (2007). Request for input: Working with agents. *The Marketing and Recruiting Idea Factory Forum.* NAFSA: Association of International Educators' Recruitment, Admissions and Preparation Knowledge Community: Marketing and Recruiting Network Discussion Forum. Retrieved October 28, 2008, from http://www.nafsa.org/cms_login?came_from=http://www.nafsa.org/knowledge_community_network.sec/recruitment_admissions/recruiting_and_marketing/connect_with_your_colleagues_13/mridea_request_for/index_html&retry=&

Foley, C. (2007). Introduction to the Bologna Process. *International Educator, 16*(3), 3.

Forrest, S. (2008). Staying competitive with Europe. *International Educator, 17*(3), 88–91.

Gardner, D. (2007). *Open doors: Report on international educational exchange.* New York: Institute of International Education.

Hawkins, D., & Clinedinst, M. (2007). *State of college admission 2007* (NACAC Annual Report 2007). Alexandria, VA: National Association of College Admissions Counselors.

Kumar, V., Petersen, J. A., & Leone, R. P. (2007). How valuable is word of mouth? *Harvard Business Review, 85*(10), 139–146.

NAFSA: Association of International Educators. (2006, January). *Guidelines for ethical practices in international student recruitment.* Retrieved October 7, 2008, from http://www.nafsa.org/publication.sec/documentlibrary.dlib/students_coming_to _the/guidelines_for_ethical

Thachaberry, M. D., & Liston, A. (1986). Recruitment and admissions: Special issues and ethical considerations. In K. Pyle (Ed.), *Guiding the development of foreign students.* San Francisco: Jossey-Bass.

Zinkhan, G. M., & Williams, B. C. (2007). The new American Marketing Association definition of marketing: An alternative assessment. *Journal of Public Policy & Marketing, 26*(2), 284–288.

5

Orientation

For domestic students, the transition to university can be exciting, unfamiliar, and certainly challenging. For the international student, it is all of that and more; "for them, the experience is like falling from the nest and hitting the ground forty feet below" (Shumway, 1994, p. 2). Much is unfamiliar to a new international student: the culture, the environment, the climate, and usually the language. The challenges for international students are numerous and the learning curve is often steep. Most universities recognize this and offer a variety of support services, the most common of which is new student orientation.

Nearly every institution offers its new students an orientation to welcome and inform, yet their methods vary widely. The focus of this chapter is to provide alternatives and insights from professionals who have a wide range of expertise and experience in orienting international students on small campuses, community colleges, and major universities.

At the beginning of this chapter, Francine Wilson presents the orientation Cornell University has developed for Hubert H. Humphrey scholars over the past twenty-eight years. While this discussion focuses on orienting visiting scholars at Cornell, the principles are applicable in a variety of settings.

The next three contributors demonstrate how peers, faculty, and the curriculum can be key components to an effective orientation. Heather Housley at Georgia State University discusses how a program utilizing volunteer students can strengthen the orientation process, and how students helping students is an effective, low-cost approach to adjustment. The cost factor involved in orienting students is also discussed by Laura Kimoto, who suggests ways in which the University of Hawaii at Hilo makes use both of the English as a Second Language (ESL) faculty and of the ESL course curriculum to familiarize international students with the many support services on campus. This model is particularly efficient and effective since it extends orientation over the course of a full semester and absorbs orientation costs into classes that are already being taught. Similarly, the Community College of Southern Nevada incorporates its orientation into a full-semester course designed specifically for international students. As Tammy Silver points out, this model allows for in-depth discussion and considerable feedback at a time when students are likely to be encountering issues related to adjusting to a new country, culture, and language.

The final contributions focus on the possible uses of technology in the orientation process—specifically, offering online orientation courses and familiarizing foreign students with current technology. Gary Rhodes, Laurie Cox, and Jodi Ebner present an orientation currently being developed by the Center for Global Education at Loyola Marymount University. This approach is a compelling alternative to the standard two- or three-day orientation format, for reasons relating both to cost and pedagogy. Their model allows students to gain valuable information at a time and pace conducive to their level of adjustment.

While Rhodes, Cox, and Ebner suggest ways that technology can be the mode of orienting new students, Greg Kessler suggests that technology ought to be a topic for orientations to present. As campus services become more dependent on technology (see Calvert and Szasz, chapter 6) it becomes increasingly necessary to ensure that students know how to use that technology. Everything from using the library to registering for classes requires a practical knowledge of technology, but not all international students come from countries where technology is so central to their lives.

As long as international students are part of the U.S. university system, orienting them to expectations and opportunities remains essential to their success. The format of orientations will certainly change with changing needs and expectations, but the fundamental principles illustrated in this chapter will likely remain the same. The objective should be to make students' transition from homeland to U.S. higher education as smooth and welcoming as possible.

Humphrey Fellowship Program Orientation: A Pattern for Success

Francine M. Wilson

RATIONALE

A new visiting scholar traveling to Cornell University arrives at Kennedy International Airport in New York City. He calls Cornell University's Humphrey Fellowship program in Ithaca, New York, to announce his arrival and asks to be picked up. Although the staff member who answers his call tells him that New York City is approximately 225 miles from Ithaca and that he can take a bus for less than $50, this new visitor still has no clear point of reference for his location in relation to his final destination, so he decides to take a taxi, and the driver gladly agrees to drive him upstate—for $500. This true story is an old one (circa 1993, taken from the archives of lessons learned in orienting new visiting scholars), but the principles it teaches about the importance of properly orienting international students to their new environment are timeless.

International educators' research (Kinsella & Smith-Simonet, 2002; Rhodes & Hong, 2005) provides evidence that "effective orientation is critical for student success" (Rhodes & Hong, 2005, p. 39). Although the content, purpose, and duration of orientation programs vary depending on the participants (undergraduates, graduates, or short-term trainees), the necessity for integrating this activity into the overall experience for students and scholars cannot be overstated. An effective orientation must go beyond focusing primarily on cultural adjustment (Lin & Yi, 1997). Participants must learn about resources to help them succeed academically, professionally, and culturally. Furthermore, issues and students' needs are constantly changing. Consequently, a successful orientation must be dynamic—responsive to the needs of students and the mission of the institution. It is just such a dynamic model that Cornell University has adopted for its Hubert H. Humphrey Fellowship program orientation.

DESCRIPTION OF THE INSTITUTION AND STUDENTS

Cornell University was one of the first universities to participate in the Humphrey Fellowship program and has continued to serve as a host for twenty-eight years. Cornell University's College of Agriculture has maintained this honor through its reputation as a leader in international development and international relations as well as its strong land-grant tradition of seeking to increase and apply knowledge to meet human needs.

The purpose of the Humphrey Fellowship program, sponsored by the U.S. Department of State, Fulbright Education and Exchanges, is to bring accomplished professionals from selected countries in Africa, Asia, Latin America, Europe, the Caribbean, and the Middle East to the United States for ten months of nondegree study and practical professional experiences. Each year, thousands of applicants apply to the fellowship program, but the final number of awards ranges from 160 to 175 per year. Humphrey fellow alumni number 3,755 from 156 countries. Of the approximately 160 Humphrey fellows nationwide, seven to fifteen fellows participate in the Cornell University program each year.

PROGRAM DESCRIPTION

Since 1979, the International Programs Office in the College of Agriculture and Life Sciences (IPO/CALS) at Cornell University has hosted Humphrey fellows with the aim of helping them expand their knowledge and expertise in public service leadership through interactions with their professional counterparts in the United States as well as with people from other countries. A key factor contributing to the fellowship program's success has been the Humphrey fellows orientation. The structure and content of the orientation come from two sources: student needs and insights from international student professionals.

Almost from its inception, the Humphrey fellows orientation has been shaped according to student needs. The story of the new fellow who paid nearly a third of his monthly stipend for a taxi ride from the airport to his new home in Ithaca serves as a good example. The new fellow learned from this experience that his relationship with coordinating staff is key to successful navigation in a new and different environment. More importantly, the coordinators also learned from his experience that more detailed information about travel for future visitors is critical, and this has been incorporated into the orientation process. This story is just one of many examples of how the orientation program is modified in response to students' needs.

International educators across the country have much to offer when designing student orientation. Cornell's orientation process has been positively influenced by scholarship focused on international students' needs. Research suggests that international students and scholars experience several adjustment stages during their transition (D'Agostino, Senders, & Reilly, 2007; Lin & Yi, 1997). These stages, pre-arrival, initial adjustment, ongoing, and return home, serve as guiding principles for the content and structure of Cornell University's program and define the university's dynamic orientation.

Pre-Arrival

Before the Humphrey fellows ever step foot on campus, Cornell has begun addressing the necessities of shelter, food, health, safety, and cultural competency. This is accomplished by mailing a welcome package to each fellow three months before arrival. The package contains information about the campus; program expectations; contact information for coordinators; a list of Humphrey fellow alumni in their country; and information about arrival, housing, and stipend amounts. Recently, technology has aided in the pre-arrival phase by making information available more quickly and at a reduced cost. Relevant information is now available on the Humphrey fellows website. Fellows are also encouraged to interact with each other on a blog that has been created especially for them.

On-Campus Orientation

Shortly after their arrival, the Humphrey fellows participate in a three-week, on-campus orientation that forms the foundation of the fellowship program by providing guidelines on practical day-to-day matters as well as direction for fulfilling key objectives including interaction with U.S. counterparts, leadership development, and mutual understanding among cultures.

Practical matters. During the orientation, fellows receive information about leases and financial matters from budgeting to paying bills, understanding taxes, and tipping etiquette. A graduate student helps fellows locate suitable accommodations for those who prefer housing other than that prearranged by the program staff. Key resource people, such as academic advisors, friendship partners, and administrative partners, are introduced. Effective techniques for using e-mail and websites and for avoiding fraud and scams are covered to prevent Humphrey fellows from experiencing major misunderstandings and legal incidents.

During the three-week orientation, university staff introduce fellows to academic support resources on campus, including libraries, computer facilities, and English and writing courses. In addition, they are introduced to community and professional resources available for their program.

Interactions with U.S. counterparts. Interaction with Americans begins at the airport, where Ithaca residents interested in cultural exchange participate in what is known as Friendship Partners. They welcome the fellows at the airport and assist with settling in. A picnic to help fellows and friendship partners become acquainted is held shortly after the fellows' arrival. Going on field trips to cultural sites, such as the New York State Fair, museums, and musical events; visiting local residents' homes; and participating in sporting events, clubs, and volunteering yield positive results in aiding Humphrey fellows' familiarity and ease in interacting with Americans.

Leadership development. Honing leadership skills begins during orientation by arranging for fellows to meet with local leaders such as the mayor of Ithaca and the director of a local food distribution network for the working poor, Loaves and Fishes. Fellows participate in a team-building outdoor activity at a nature center, which involves a ropes course. They learn how global citizens with different backgrounds can come together to make decisions, organize themselves as a group, respect each others' opinions in meetings, and acknowledge different leadership styles. The university provides fellows with business cards and a brochure containing profiles on each fellow to help them network with each other. Before classes begin, a college-wide event, Crops and Cultures of the World, is scheduled at Cornell Plantations to introduce Humphrey fellows to resources in the fields of agriculture and natural resource management. They also go to Agricultural Progress Days in Pennsylvania to meet nonacademic leaders and professionals.

Mutual understanding. Building mutual understanding among cultures within a ten-month period is achieved in a variety of ways. Humphrey fellows are housed together, allowing them to share information, identify professional goals, and discuss their country's development challenges. They must agree to be part of a group and discuss what it means to be a Humphrey fellow. They develop a group social contract to which everyone must contribute principles such as how decisions and majority consensus will be reached. This is done in an atmosphere of openness and trust. Everyone receives and signs a copy of this contract, which is posted in the Humphrey fellows' room.

Ongoing Orientation

Work toward achieving the program's key objectives does not end the last week prior to the start of school, but continues throughout the ten-month program. Program staff, academic advisors, and friendship partners in the community help with the Cornell Humphrey fellows' adjustment during the academic year. The advisor meets with each fellow to ascertain the best way to assist. They may introduce the fellow to colleagues in his or her professional network or even travel with the fellow to a conference. The advisor may seek the fellow's advice on a project a professor is working on and suggest possible interesting courses. Fellows work toward meeting the program goals by developing an action plan shortly after their initial orientation. This plan is based on the program objective outlined in the fellow's application. For example, one fellow's plan was to design educational materials for farming families in transition by learning from rural programs in the United States. Fellows make presentations of their work, using resources such as the library and audio-visual materials—all of which they learn about during the three-week orientation.

Return Home/Follow-Up

As noted earlier, Cornell's orientation reaches out to fellows before their arrival on campus, throughout their time on campus, and after their return home. The latter is accomplished by keeping the fellows informed and involved. Cornell's Humphrey Fellowship program uses a newsletter to communicate with alumni. Alumni frequently communicate with the Cornell Humphrey program staff as well, so that the coordinators are aware of the progress of alumni and problems with readjustment. Fellows also often join a professional organization during their time in the United States, so they receive the organization's newsletter, which helps them stay abreast of current events in their fields. Fellows stay involved in the program by serving on candidate review committees to select new candidates and providing an informal pre-departure orientation for new fellows. Furthermore, Cornell faculty and friendship partners who travel to a country of former Humphrey fellows make efforts to meet with alumni. These receptions are warm and welcoming.

EVALUATION

To ensure that an orientation program is dynamic (Griffiths, 2007), evaluation is key. Evaluations given during orientation, in the middle of the school year, and at the end of the program provide valuable feedback that helps coordinators continually refine the program.

Cornell University's program evaluations begin with individual interviews shortly after Humphrey fellows arrive on campus. These interviews have two purposes: (1) to determine whether the fellows received the pre-arrival materials mailed to them, participated in the online blog to learn more about each other and the program, or talked with alumni, and (2) to find out what questions the fellows have about the program guidelines. These evaluative interviews are an ongoing aspect of the program. The coordination team seeks formative insights during scheduled meetings, in social settings, and from talking to third parties, such as the fellow's advisor or friendship partner.

The second format used for evaluations is summative questionnaires, which the fellows complete anonymously. They answer questions about their process of settling in, how useful they found program assistance, how much time they spent in orientations for various field trips, what they thought of the academic environment, and how much they learned about each other and resources on and off campus. The anonymous summative evaluations have provided insightful criticism as well as praise and commendations. All input is considered and contributes to a dynamic, responsive orientation program.

APPLICABILITY TO OTHER INSTITUTIONS

While the orientation program described is designed for the Humphrey Fellows program, its principles can be adapted and applied in other settings. Short-term study abroad, experiential learning, service learning, professional development, and training programs will reap benefits from using the model presented here. When an orientation begins before students depart from their homelands, continues through their initial days on campus, and extends to their return home, both the institution and the individuals benefit. Specifically, such programs help students reach academic goals, adjust to new cultures, and build professional skills.

Creating Connections

Heather Housley

RATIONALE

International students arriving in the United States face many challenges. Rather than leave them all alone to navigate the complex processes of immigration, campus administration, and integration into the local community, most universities offer an orientation program to assist with these issues. Program lengths vary from a few hours to several days, and the content differs according to the needs of the individual campus and its available support.

On many campuses, current international students are recruited to assist with orientation, working alongside full-time staff or faculty. The use of peer leaders in facilitating international orientation leads to many benefits. It provides additional staff during a busy time for most international offices, thus increasing the amount of support that can be provided to new students. For the students, peer leaders provide a trustworthy information source for key orientation content—for example, learning about the U.S. classroom; navigating the university administration; and finding out where to eat, live, and play in the local community (Beasley, 1997). Students tend to be more comfortable asking questions of peers than of authority figures (Mynard & Almarzouqi, 2006). This leadership development opportunity helps peer leaders share knowledge, hone communication and teamwork skills, and develop skills outside the classroom. Additionally, it allows for small-group interaction, which enables better connection with fellow students and the campus community.

To assist with the more than three hundred new international students arriving on campus each fall semester, Georgia State University's International Student and Scholar Services (ISSS) has created a team of fifteen to twenty student leaders who help coordinate its four-day orientation program. These students are called Volunteer International Student Assistant (VISA) Leaders and are an invaluable part of the orientation program. With the help of a well-trained, well-informed, and cohesive group of student assistants, orientation at Georgia State flows smoothly and connects incoming students to their new environment.

DESCRIPTION OF THE INSTITUTION AND THE STUDENTS

Georgia State University, founded in 1913, is a research university located in the heart of downtown Atlanta. The largest university in the Atlanta metropolitan area, Georgia State is known for its top-ranked business programs and has a total enrollment of more than twenty-seven thousand undergraduate and graduate students. International students make up 1,500 of the total student body and represent over 140 countries. On-campus housing is limited to 2,500 beds, so most international students live off campus and must find apartments and roommates when they arrive.

PROGRAM DESCRIPTION

All incoming international students at Georgia State attend international orientation, a mandatory program held the week before classes start each semester. The program length varies from four days in the fall semester to two days for the spring and summer terms. The following are the goals of new international student orientation at Georgia State.

- Provide information about immigration regulations, cultural adjustment, the U.S. classroom, university procedures, housing, food, transportation, and finances.
- Carry out various administrative processes for the university, such as testing, academic advising, registering for courses, and copying immigration documents.
- Create connections with the students' academic departments; with peers to form initial friendships and receive advice and support; and with relevant campus services, programs, and facilities.
- Welcome the students in a positive, friendly, and helpful way.

VISA leaders help tremendously in achieving these goals and present a welcome, friendly face during the extensive orientation program. International Student and Scholar Services carefully select and train continuing students for the leadership roles. Both domestic and international students are encouraged to apply and are selected based on a written application and a personal interview. VISA leaders are chosen not only based on their enthusiasm, personalities, and communication and leadership skills but also based on geographic and academic program diversity.

Once selected, the VISA leaders attend a three-day training program. One and a half days are devoted to learning about the content and structure of orientation, campus, and community adjustment information and to planning the sessions and social events. The other half of the training focuses on team-building activities—group games aimed at improving communication and trust and a challenge activity, such as a high ropes course or a white-water rafting trip to North Carolina. Needless to say, this half is the leaders' favorite part. Seeing this diverse group of individuals emerge from the three days of training as a cohesive, well-functioning group of friends and teammates is extremely rewarding. The leadership lessons they continue to learn during orientation only strengthen this initial bonding.

During orientation, VISA leaders do the following:

- Greet new international students with a smile and a warm welcome.
- Individually lead a four-hour small group session of ten to twenty new international students; this session includes an icebreaker, a campus tour, and an information component.
- Provide information about course registration, housing options, banking, and campus life as well as general information about adjusting to life in the United States, in Atlanta, and at the university.
- Help international students submit immigration documents for copying.
- Provide help and advice during course registration.
- Take lost or late students to the proper locations on campus.
- Help staff with the general administration of the orientation.
- Organize and present four general orientation sessions (Life in Atlanta, How to Succeed in the Georgia State Classroom, Finding an On-Campus Job, and Technology 101).
- Plan the social event that ends orientation (Global Grillout).
- Provide daily feedback to staff about the orientation program and areas for improvement.
- Answer students' questions and be as helpful as possible.

VISA leaders are paid $300 for their work during fall orientation and are each given a polo shirt and T-shirt to wear as uniforms. They also are given a 10 percent discount on books at the University Bookstore. VISA leaders are paid less during spring and summer orientations ($250 and $200, respectively) due to the smaller amount of time involved for orientation and training. Funding for orientation and the VISA leader program at Georgia State comes from a $5 international education fee per student for each term. Half of the funds generated from the fee go to International Services for SEVIS-related expenses and orientation, and the other half go to Study Abroad programs for staffing and student scholarships. In the past, VISA leaders were unpaid volunteers; however, the current stipend attracts a larger and more diverse group of applicants and ensures timely attendance during training and orientation.

EVALUATION

Assessment tools clearly indicate that students who participate in orientation have a smoother transition to the start of their academic program. Three types of assessment are used. First, VISA leaders fill out a qualitative evaluation form at the end of orientation to provide feedback about their experience. Second, VISA leaders finish each day of orientation by sitting down as a group with International Services' staff to discuss the program—what went well and what can be improved. Recommendations are typed up and examined during the planning of the next semester's orientation. Third, new students participating in the orientation are asked to complete a quantitative evaluation of the orientation program, which includes questions regarding the effectiveness and friendliness of their VISA leader.

Results from the VISA leaders' evaluations show that they gain valuable leadership skills during the program, increase in self-confidence, enjoy providing assistance to new international students, and build strong friendships within their VISA leader group. This experience is often a platform for students' further leadership roles on campus (Tenney & Houck, 2004).

New international students repeatedly state on their evaluations that the best part of orientation was their friendly and helpful VISA leaders. Comments such as the following are very common: "All VISA leaders were very helpful, friendly and knowledgeable. They made all the difference!" Another frequent response highlights the importance of peer interaction: "It was helpful to have an international VISA leader who had been through the same troubles as we did." Both the small-group sessions and the large general sessions led by the VISA leaders invariably get high scores from the students. Perhaps the best indicator of the success of the program is the frequent queries by new students during and after orientation about how to apply for the program.

As a further measure of success, VISA leaders' friendships both with each other and with the new students continue well beyond the time of orientation. VISA leaders have invited members of their orientation groups to birthday parties and other social events on campus and continued assisting new students well after the end of the orientation. The VISA leaders seem proud of their new United Nations–like circle of friends and enjoy reuniting and reconnecting with them throughout their studies. The experience is frequently brought up by former participants in job interviews—they specifically mention the aspects of teamwork, communication, and problem-solving skills.

APPLICABILITY TO OTHER INSTITUTIONS

Any institution can benefit from the use of a student peer program to assist with international student orientation. Continuing international students are often eager to assist new students in their transition to campus; thus, student peer leaders should not be hard to come by.

Creating a similar program requires a small investment of staff time and funding resources. The coordinator of the orientation program needs time away from other duties to plan and lead the training program, though other campus offices can share the time burden and expertise required. For example, a campus visitors' center can train students how to lead a campus tour, and recreation or student affairs staff can help with the team-building or challenge program component. Additional funding is needed for student stipends and training costs unless students are recruited as unpaid volunteers and training costs are minimized. The white-water rafting or challenge activity does add to the cost ($25 per person at Georgia State), so if funding is limited, perhaps a simple hiking trip, picnic, or other off-campus adventure can achieve the same team-building goal. Free perks from around campus (e.g., discounts, T-shirts, food, recognition, tickets) can be used as an alternative incentive for the student peer leaders if funds are not available to provide a stipend.

The benefits of a peer leader program similar to the VISA leader program at Georgia State greatly outweigh the associated time and costs. The perspective and experience of a fellow student is invaluable in creating the all-important early connections between new international students and their campus and community. The additional connections made among the VISA leaders themselves and between them and the new students are a rewarding outcome of a program ultimately meant to provide hospitality and friendship to those far away from home.

The English Language Instructor: A Bridge to Support Services on Campus

Laura Kimoto

RATIONALE

Most universities and colleges in the United States offer comprehensive orientation programs at the beginning of each semester to help newly arrived international students adjust to their surroundings. Such factors as the erratic arrivals of new students, inconsistent motivation, diverse preoccupations, and varying levels of English proficiency all detract from the effectiveness of orientation (Barsoum & Durham, 2006). Furthermore, overloading new students with information at the beginning of the semester does not guarantee retention or utilization of that information, especially given the linguistic barriers. Experience has shown that even after the initial introduction to the campus and community, international students still have an enormous learning curve to overcome before they feel comfortable in their new surroundings. While an extended orientation may ameliorate some of these challenges, not all institutions have the means to prolong orientation, regardless of how helpful that may be.

One way of extending orientation without adding extra costs to the institution is through the ESL curriculum. Often, international students enroll in ESL classes during their first few semesters of school. By passing the orientation baton from student services staff to the ESL faculty, universities can provide an excellent semester-long student orientation. This program description outlines general guidelines for involving ESL instructors in the orientation process and helping international students build a bridge to key support services in the university.

DESCRIPTION OF THE INSTITUTION AND STUDENTS

Situated in the middle of the Pacific Basin, the University of Hawaii at Hilo (UHH), located on the island of Hawaii, is a four-year undergraduate institution that emphasizes internationalizing its campus. Ranked sixth by *U.S. News and World Report* (*"U.S. News* Ranks U. H. Hilo,"* 2007) for student ethnic and racial diversity among liberal arts colleges in the United States, UHH serves approximately 3,600 students. Of these, four hundred are from international origins, mostly Asian (e.g., Japan, Korea, Taiwan, China) and Pacific Island nations (e.g., Marshall Islands, the Federated States of Micronesia).

The strengths of UHH are its small classes, low student-to-faculty ratio; diverse student body; active faculty who encourage student participation in research and community service; and perhaps most importantly, a friendly, collegial attitude sometimes referred to as the "aloha spirit" that epitomizes UHH's student-centered approach.

The university has an office of international student services, which provides immigration advising for its international students. It also has a Center for Global Education and Exchange to support the approximately eighty inbound and outbound international exchange students per semester. UHH also recently began an English Language Institute (ELI) to support the English language skill development of the increasing number of international students who attend the school independently or through institutional exchange agreements. The ELI typically offers academic English language instruction to one hundred or more students during the fall semester and sixty or more students during the spring semester. Courses are offered at three levels and focus on listening/speaking, reading, writing, and grammar skills.

DESCRIPTION OF THE PROGRAM

For a variety of reasons, many international students do not take advantage of campus support services. Volunteer programs, counseling and career centers, and student employment offices are some of the least-utilized resources (Abe, Talbot, & Geelhoed, 1998). To overcome this problem and help international students succeed, instructors in the ELI at UHH implemented projects in their classes to accomplish several key functions. First, students are given an authentic context and task to accomplish, and second, students develop their language skills as they practice help- and information-seeking behaviors needed for smooth access to student services. All the projects are flexible—they can be a simple homework assignment or lead to a formal presentation with PowerPoint slides.

The instructors are free to adapt the projects to fit their curriculum, objectives, and assessment needs. The following are examples of projects that have been implemented at UHH:

- An instructor invited a staff member from the university's Women's Center to talk about domestic violence and sexual harassment. The speaker presented information and statistics and instructed students on how to say no. This project raised awareness of the challenges that women (or any underrepresented group) may face in getting an education and of the need to support all segments of the student population and provide equal access to higher education. Students were empowered with tools to deal with sexual harassment, something usually not addressed in universities in their home countries.
- Students investigated offices and programs listed in the school's general catalog under Learning Resources or Student Affairs. They read about an office, scheduled an interview, and visited the office. They then reported back to classmates on their experience and on what they learned. This assignment helped students recognize that UHH has staff specializing in assisting students in various areas and that students are expected to seek out services from the appropriate source. The aim of this project was to make students more comfortable visiting offices and create personal contacts with staff members for possible needs in the future.
- Students researched a degree program that they were interested in. They read about the degree requirements in the general catalog and scheduled an interview with a professor from the department. Interviews focused on the faculty member's professional interests and career or on the degree program and career opportunities. (Students could also interview a U.S. student majoring in that subject or observe a class.) Students were surprised by how approachable professors are in the United States—something that may be rare in universities in their home countries. They also learned that students are responsible for seeking help from their professors during office hours and that they should not expect the professor to invite them in for consultations as teachers do in some Asian countries.
- Students read university regulations and procedures, such as information about the foreign credentials evaluation or how to apply for graduation. They interviewed the appropriate staff members and compared the procedures with those of universities in their home countries. Many students were surprised to learn that *they* were responsible for applying for graduation. Normally universities in their home countries notify students about graduation or students graduate in a predetermined time span.

- Students learned how to write a resume and cover letter. They discovered that in the United States, personal achievement is valued and therefore included in a resume. They could compare this to resume writing in their own countries.

To fully utilize ESL instructors in familiarizing international students with campus support services, several criteria should be met. First, teachers must be made aware of the communication skills their students need to access student services. This awareness logically leads to the need to build a bridge between instructors and key student services staff members who work with international students. Once these connections and common goals are established, the instructor and staff members can create meaningful learning situations, projects, and opportunities for students. In addition, instructors should be allowed to make adjustments to their curriculum. If they have this creative freedom, they will be more open to using real-life situations for their international students while meeting the learning outcomes of their course or program. Finally, instructors' potential role in the transition, retention, and success of international students at their institution should be acknowledged.

EVALUATION

These projects were implemented at UHH for students in the ELI at all levels of instruction to help them discover resources for their success. Based on informal feedback gathered via in-class discussion and e-mail from students, staff, and instructors, the overall reaction to the projects was positive.

International students reported that they learned more about their university. For instance, they were surprised to learn that there was a special office just for women (the Women's Center), support services for gay and lesbian students, and a domestic student exchange program office. They learned how to calculate their GPA—something that many people assume international students know. Students gained confidence in their language skills as they experienced success in communicating with others. They also appreciated the opportunity to make personal acquaintances with staff and faculty members. Students reported that they were less hesitant to approach staff members for assistance since they already knew them and were familiar with the services they offered. Students said they would not have had the confidence to make initial contact on their own, and that they were willing to share their newly gained knowledge with friends from their own countries.

The student services staff members were glad to have individual contact with the international students. They were willing to share their resources and offer their services. The projects were further enhanced by the professional on-campus connections ESL instructors and staff members established when the instructor contacted the staff or faculty members to briefly explain the objectives of the projects.

The benefits for the ESL instructor were also clear. Instructors felt more like part of a team in their institution. It was refreshing for them to establish professional contacts with other staff members who truly care for international students.

APPLICABILITY TO OTHER INSTITUTIONS

These projects are highly applicable to other institutions as they meet critical needs of international students: learning about campus resources; developing English skills; making connections with support staff, instructors, and other students on campus; and transitioning successfully into the host culture. Students in intensive English programs (IEP) can particularly benefit as they are often marginalized and intentionally shut out from services offered to matriculated students.

The projects presented are part of a skills-based curriculum, but they can be adapted to fit many curriculum designs if the instructor has the freedom and time to make adjustments. In fact, most ESL professionals would welcome the use of real-life contexts. These projects could also be part of a University 101, Freshman Experience, or even a Study Skills/Life Skills course for both international and domestic students.

Foundations of Success for International Students: An Extended Orientation Class

Tammy J. Silver

RATIONALE

International students coming to the United States for the first time often experience difficulties adjusting to their new environment. These adjustment issues are related to cultural incongruence, a lack of understanding of academic expectations, and complex visa status regulations. In addition, students must face all of these challenges using a new language (Andrade, 2006). Cultural challenges include differences in diet, problems with accommodations, discrimination as a result of cultural differences, and misunderstandings due to misinterpretation of the language or the accepted norms of the host nation.

Additionally, international students must adjust to a new academic structure and are further challenged by issues such as difficulty understanding lectures, instructors' accents, test constructions, and teaching styles (Lin & Yi, 1997). Because of linguistic challenges such as difficulty with reading comprehension and limited vocabulary, international students often need more time to read their textbooks and have a difficult time expressing their topical knowledge in essays (Lin & Yi, 1997). Furthermore, international students attending two-year colleges have a higher risk of dropping out than those attending universities, because two-year colleges tend to accept students with a lower level of English ability.

Zhai (2002) found that the top challenges international students face include differences between the educational systems in the United States and in their home countries, cultural and language differences, food, living practicalities, time management, and social integration. The majority of the students Zhai interviewed suggested that academic and cultural orientation programs would be helpful. Lin and Yi (1997) consider such programs essential. They suggest that "orientation programs . . . need to emphasize the U.S. culture, language and university adjustment" (Lin & Yi, 1997). They propose that workshops within the first six months include topics such as U.S. culture and traditions, stress management, sexual and racial harassment, financial planning resources, banking and health care systems, counseling services, and university rules and regulations, and that support mentor programs be provided to help students develop English language skills.

Tinto (1988) shows that the first semester "is critical to the student's eventual persistence until degree completion" (p. 451). He further recommends that "rather than [concentrating] their attention on the few days just prior to the beginning of the academic year, orientation programs should span the first six weeks of the first year, if not the first semester" (p. 451). Programs designed to assist international students with academic and sociocultural transitions contribute to retention.

To facilitate a successful college experience that leads to academic goal attainment, the International Center at the College of Southern Nevada (CSN) requires all first-semester international students to enroll in an internally developed course entitled Foundations of Success for International Students. The goal of the Foundations course is to facilitate a connection to the campus by teaching international students to successfully navigate complex higher education systems, cope with cultural ambiguity, and follow specific immigration regulations.

DESCRIPTION OF THE INSTITUTION AND THE STUDENTS

Founded in 1971, CSN is Nevada's largest institution of higher education and the fourth largest community college of its kind in the nation. CSN operates in over fifty locations, including three main campuses and eleven learning centers in four counties covering forty-two thousand square miles. With student success as the number one priority, CSN educates over seventy thousand students annually in over two hundred career fields and offers more than eighty associate degree and certificate programs.

The importance of international students and international education to the state of Nevada is reflected in the May 12, 2005, passage of Senate Concurrent Resolution 38, the International Education Policy Resolution. The resolution supports international education and foreign exchange programs as a critical component of higher education. This resolution led to the revision of the state's higher education master plan, encouraging campuses to increase opportunities for students to engage in international education activities.

The International Center at CSN works closely with Student Affairs, Human Resources, and the Executive Director of International Development to achieve this goal, which is in accordance with the college's strategic plan to enhance internationalization of student life and campus culture. For the past decade, the center has provided comprehensive services to F-1 students and the college community by overseeing recruitment, admissions, orientation, assessment, registration, institutional reporting and compliance, and ongoing advisement for approximately 750 international students from over sixty countries. The center also oversees the Foundations course. CSN's international students come primarily from Asia, with the highest percentage coming from South Korea, followed by Japan, the Philippines, Thailand, and Taiwan. The minimum criterion of English proficiency for admission is 450 PBT/45 IBT (paper-based TOEFL/Internet-based TOEFL) or its equivalent on other English proficiency measures. Most students' English ability falls between 450 and 470 on the PBT (45 and 52 IBT).

PROGRAM DESCRIPTION

The foundations course is based on the belief that international students experience a higher level of academic success and cultural competence as a result of planned interventions rather than a sink-or-swim approach. The content of the foundations course focuses on three areas: honing academic skills, addressing cultural adjustment issues, and applying regulatory compliance knowledge. As such, the course gives international students tools to become academically successful and socially integrated within an unfamiliar environment while maintaining immigration status. Course topics include expectations of students in the U.S. higher education system, strategies for success, institutional policies and procedures, and campus resources and support services. The course also teaches students how to differentiate between the norms of their culture and the norms of U.S. culture. Subsequently, international students learn to recognize and contextualize situations that may impact them negatively if they lack this knowledge.

Communicating the importance of complying with institutional policies and federal regulations and the impact of noncompliance on immigration status is also important. For example, first-time international students do not intuitively make a connection between paying tuition on time each semester and being administratively withdrawn from all classes, which potentially harms their visa status. Therefore, demonstrating how regulatory compliance applies to academic goal achievement is incorporated into the curriculum. The course reveals how academic adjustment, cultural adjustment, and immigration issues are inherently intertwined and how disruption in one area can cause a domino effect on the others.

The foundations course serves as a catalyst to the social integration process by providing a forum for newcomers to feel welcome, develop a support network among classmates experiencing similar difficulties, and cultivate a trusting relationship with the International Center advisors who teach the course. Figure 5.1 illustrates the model for student success that forms the basis of the course, which contains academic, cultural, and regulatory issues. Examples of academic issues include the U.S. educational system, graduation requirements, plagiarism, and registration. Cultural adjustment focuses on such topics as stages of cultural adjustment, community involvement, and cultural norms in and out of the classroom. Regulatory issues include an overview of SEVIS, immigration documents, termination and reinstatement, reduced course loads, transferring, and work authorization. These categories are not taught as isolated units. Topics are introduced so that students' most critical needs are served first; then the topics are integrated and recycled throughout the course to demonstrate interdependence among categories. Learning outcomes include creating a successful college experience, making informed decisions, navigating unfamiliar organizations, strengthening critical thinking and problem-solving abilities, identifying and utilizing academic and student support systems, and developing cultural awareness of self and others.

Figure 5.1. Model for foundations curriculum.

In alignment with student persistence research, Foundations was deliberately created as a five-week course, offering one elective credit transferable to all Nevada System of Higher Education institutions. Moreover, the course material becomes meaningful because the duration of the course coincides with the international students' initial adjustment period.

EVALUATION

Online class surveys using a pre- and post-test design are used to assess student learning outcomes of the foundations course. Program outcomes measured on the pre-test are different from those on the post-test, but the learning outcomes measured are the same on both surveys. Programmatic aspects of the pre-test focus on student experiences prior to the beginning of the semester, such as the accuracy of pre-arrival information and the benefits of the orientation. The post-test focuses on student experiences once the semester has begun, such as satisfaction with various aspects of the International Center and staff assistance. Questions related to learning outcomes measure differences in students' self-perceived abilities to explain concepts and make appropriate decisions in the three content areas as a result of the course intervention.

On the first day of class, students are instructed to access the survey online and submit it as part of their homework assignment before the next class period. The same procedure is followed during the last week of class. The first semester the instrument was implemented, a total of forty-one students took the pre-test and thirty-nine completed the post-test. The results demonstrate a notable increase in overall learning in the three content areas. Further analysis of discrete items allows for closing the assessment loop by implementing course improvements. For example, 22 percent of the students surveyed indicated after the pre-test that they understood the concept of reduced course loads, whereas this number increased to 79 percent after the post-test. Even though this increase demonstrates significant learning related to the concept of reduced course loads, we can use this information to implement curricular revisions so that the post-test learning outcome is closer to 100 percent.

One test item revealed what was initially interpreted as a decrease in learning. The question asked whether students have decided on a major. The results suggested that more students had a major upon entering the college than at the end of the semester. This suggests that students initially have an idea of what they want to study but may change their minds—often as a result of the course—after gaining a better understanding of the variety of academic programs available and the ease of changing majors. However, this may also be influenced simply by exposure to the curriculum outside of the foundations course through sources such as faculty members and other students.

APPLICABILITY TO OTHER INSTITUTIONS

The foundations course can be adapted to fit the needs of both two- and four-year institutions. While the concepts of academic success, cultural adjustment, and immigration transcend institutional types, the application of knowledge may differ depending on the programs and services available. For example, two-year colleges typically do not have health centers on campus. Therefore, learning how to access medical care is a more critical topic for two-year college students. Colleges and universities that have residence halls may add this dimension to the cultural adjustment aspect of the course, which would not necessarily be included in the two-year college curriculum. Course adaptation is institution specific and depends on institutional policies and procedures, academic expectations, and programs and services that provide opportunities for international students to learn how to navigate complex systems and engage in sociocultural interaction.

While the need for an extended orientation course is clear, the practicalities of implementation include human and other campus resources. Institutions may require approval through their curriculum committees as well as through the state's higher education system if the course is to be credit-bearing and transferable. Additionally, staff must be able to create, update, and teach the curriculum, and physical space issues for teaching must be addressed. However, the economic and cultural benefits that international students bring to the campus and community support are more than a fair exchange for the challenges of program implementation.

Orientation and Reentry Programming for International Students: The PLUS Project

Gary Rhodes, Laurie Cox, and Jodi Ebner

RATIONALE

Many higher education institutions are concerned about the academic and social development of students and see the value of orienting them to the United States as well as to a particular college campus (Hanson & Zambito, 2003). Unfortunately, recognizing a need does not always translate into a best practice. Too often, orientation programs for international students are less than ideal. For instance, some institutions compress their programs into an unrealistic time frame. Many last less than a day, most last from only one to three days, and they generally take place before the beginning of the student's first semester (Cox, 2007). Properly orienting students takes time and "requires considerably more than a one-day program" (O'Connell, 1994, p.75).

International students often arrive late due to visa and flight challenges and miss orientation entirely. They may also experience significant transitional issues such as jet lag, homesickness, and culture shock at the time of orientation. All of these make it difficult for students to fully comprehend vital information. In addition, orientation topics often address basic survival skills for the first semester but fail to address subsequent adjustment issues. The latter include helping students recognize that they have adapted and changed while living in the United States and preparing them for the adjustments and re-acculturation involved in moving back to their home countries.

Although a prolonged, comprehensive orientation would be ideal, the practicalities of limited resources often make such programming impossible.

For this reason, the Center for Global Education at Loyola Marymount University (LMU) has designed the Project for Learning in the United States (PLUS), a program that uses technology to address many of the limitations of current orientation programming. Although the PLUS program is in developmental stages, it is based on principles that offer international students the opportunity to address transitional issues over a full semester or longer, which results in a comprehensive learning experience at a time and pace suitable for student learning.

DESCRIPTION OF THE INSTITUTION AND STUDENTS

The Center for Global Education was developed at the University of Southern California and later moved to LMU, a comprehensive university located in Los Angeles, California, with 5,500 undergraduate and three thousand graduate students. The center collaborates with organizations around the world to promote international education and to foster cross-cultural awareness, cooperation, and understanding.

The center has developed many online resources to support U.S. colleges and universities that maintain study abroad programs. One such resource is PLUS. Supported by the Fund for the Improvement of Postsecondary Education (FIPSE), the purpose of PLUS is to enable colleges and universities to have a positive impact on international students by better orienting and integrating them onto their campuses as well as providing support for their return home.

PROGRAM DESCRIPTION

One of the center's key resources is an online curriculum, which addresses three critical periods in an international student's experience: prior to arrival, during the first semester, and following degree completion. The online delivery of the courses enables them to be easily accessible to international students before, during, and after their study in the United States. The more ownership a university takes the more impact the courses can have, particularly if universities choose to offer these courses for credit. The center has also developed an administrator/teacher capability for institutions to create groups, enroll students, and monitor course completion.

Course 1: Pre–U.S. Study

The pre–U.S. study course provides resources and information to help international students through the application process and prepare them for the many facets of campus life. Course content includes essential pre-departure topics such as securing admission and financial support, learning about the United States, and preparing to share information about one's home country while in the United States. The course also focuses on such topics as obtaining a visa, finding appropriate housing, and dealing with health and safety issues. In addition, the course prepares students for future transitions in their higher education experience. The content and focus of this course closely validates and promotes the perspective that the ideal orientation begins prior to arrival in the United States (Pang & Barlas, 1996).

Course 2: First Semester in the United States

The second course in the series aims to assist international students with practical, academic, and intercultural support during their first semester. It provides resources through ten modules, which address such common topics as health, safety, culture shock, and academic and social success. While the principal focus of this educational program is on the students' first semester in the United States, additional information is provided that supports students throughout their study. It provides them with transition tips and important information on opportunities to help them make the most of their time in the United States. Furthermore, since the course is not institution specific, colleges and universities may customize it with information about their campus, local community, and mentoring and outreach opportunities to provide a more personalized and comprehensive course for international students on their campus.

Course 3: Transitions: Study/Employment/Reentry

Course 3 integrates the experience international students have had studying in the United States into their academic and extracurricular lives as they continue their education, training, and professional lives either in the United States or in their home countries. Students are provided with guidance about education and internship and work opportunities to expand upon previous learning in the United States and enhance their future studies and careers. The ten modules for course 3 contain information about continuing studies in the United States at the next academic level and about participating in an internship or Optional Practical Training (OPT). The modules also help students understand and cope with the reentry/reverse culture shock process. The online workshop these modules offer may be the best way to provide international students with key information after they return to their home countries because they are able to secure "immediate support when they are most ready to receive it" (Cox, 2006, p. 150).

Global Scholar Certificate

To support and encourage students in their extracurricular international learning, the center is developing a "Global Scholar Certificate" that international students may earn in recognition of their participation in the PLUS online courses. The certificate will be offered to encourage international students to complete each course and to reward them for their time, energy, attention, and persistence. The formal Global Scholar Certificate can also enhance international student resumes as they transition to higher degree programs and work opportunities.

EVALUATION

Students who enroll in the three courses will be asked to participate in an online survey following the completion of each module. The information gathered from the surveys will be used by the center to determine the usefulness, relevance, and comprehensiveness of the courses. Faculty and staff nationwide who utilize the PLUS materials to prepare courses for their international students will be invited to complete a survey to assess the intervention efficacy and to determine whether the content helped them meet their intended goals for students on their campuses. This information will be used by the center staff to modify the courses to better orient students to their campuses and support their learning in the United States.

APPLICABILITY TO OTHER INSTITUTIONS

One of the fundamental aspects of the PLUS program is that it can be adapted by the institutions that use it. In this way, PLUS is applicable to any institution that admits international students. Through PLUS, the center intends to help make study in the United States more inclusive, inviting, and accessible. It also seeks to provide resources and an online curriculum to both students and faculty/staff to support comprehensive orientation and transition assistance at any U.S. college or university. PLUS provides support for international students and recognizes their participation with a Global Scholar Certificate. These resources can assist institutions in aiding international students in making the transition to campus and, later, to life back home.

Instructional Technology for International Students

Greg Kessler

RATIONALE

While students around the world are familiar with computers, the Internet, and other forms of technology used for communication and entertainment, students outside the United States may not have extensive experience with the types of technology used in U.S. universities. Universities across the United States have made impressive progress in the area of instructional technology to make information and resources more accessible. This best practice description provides an overview of the infrastructure uniquely common to U.S. universities as well as the expectations of students participating in today's learning environments. Extensive personal experience teaching international students suggests that they lack familiarity and comfort with technological resources. In many cases, students are expected to understand the systems and requirements without any formal preparation. Considering that these environments are typically designed for U.S. students, it is clearly necessary to assist international students as they navigate the digital realm of contemporary education.

Utilizing computer-assisted language learning technology to assist international students with their development in English is common at U.S. universities (Kessler, 2006). However, it is widely recognized that students may not benefit from these resources and practices without the requisite orientation and training in the use of the technology (Hubbard, 2004; Kolaitis, Mahoney, Pomann, & Hubbard, 2006). While there is no extant research into the need for such preparation beyond the language-learning environment, it is prudent to consider extending these principles to the broader technology needs of international students. The following description offers some of the practices and details of a program for familiarizing international students with the technology-oriented resources, expectations, and realities of a typical U.S. university environment.

DESCRIPTION OF THE INSTITUTION AND THE STUDENTS

Ohio University is a research institution with slightly over twenty thousand students. The international student population is composed almost entirely of graduate students with very few international undergraduate students. This composition results in an intensified focus on teaching and research skills as part of international student orientation. In particular, the university's orientation program familiarizes international students and scholars with the technology-related resources available and emphasizes the importance of students' use of these systems. Some resources are necessary for orientation to the campus itself while others benefit students interested in joining social communities. Others are needed for registering for classes, managing financial obligations, and monitoring grades. Regardless of the potential impact, students must be familiar with these resources to make the most of their university experience.

PROGRAM DESCRIPTION

This instructional technology orientation program consists of a series of four two-hour workshops. In each workshop, instructors introduce students to the technology and allow them time for hands-on practice. These workshops focus on four components:

- Course Management Systems
- Libraries
- Wireless Internet and Portable Technologies
- Communication and Social Networking

Course Management Systems

The most obvious distinction for an international student may be the ubiquitous nature of the course management system (CMS). Systems such as Blackboard, WebCT, and Moodle are used by nearly every university in the United States. These systems may serve as the core of a class or simply as a place to store documents. At Ohio University, the use of Blackboard has become a standardized and expected part of all classes. Since adopting Blackboard, a number of local studies have shown that use is typically limited to the dissemination of syllabi and other common course documents. However, there is a small cadre of faculty and teaching assistants who use the other features extensively. This extended use typically involves discussion boards, grade books, whiteboards, and links to digital materials available through the library or other external sources. In the courses where the instructor employs Blackboard's extended features, it is critical that students stay connected through Blackboard.

Students may be required to participate in online discussions within the CMS on a regular basis. They may be required to submit their homework through the CMS interface. The CMS may be where students check their course grades, previous grades, or even their overall status as a student. Some systems integrate all of the students' information within the CMS interface. Such integration certainly simplifies things for students as long as they are prepared to visit frequently and understand what information is available. Students must establish a sense of the role of the CMS in their particular university, department, and individual classes. Some faculty members may be so used to using the local CMS that they neglect to inform students about how they use it in their class. It is in the students' best interest to check in with the system on a regular basis and seek clarification from instructors.

To assist international students in their adjustment to these applications of technology, one orientation workshop introduces them to the CMS at Ohio University. Students obtain their university e-mail address and log in to the university's CMS. Once logged in, they are guided through a virtual tour of the CMS system, including browsing through potential course offerings, communication tools, and other CMS-based materials. Students participate in a mock discussion forum about the use of this technology for instruction to provide them with a feel for how they may participate in the classroom in the near future.

Libraries

University libraries have undergone major changes in recent years. Many campuses have more digital holdings than traditional print holdings, particularly for the most recent publications (Marcum, 2003). These digital holdings are not limited to text-based materials. They may include video, interactive media, and visual and audio collections. The digital library may be available to students from anywhere on campus, in the country, or possibly around the world, and allows students unprecedented access to information.

At Ohio University, the library has made digital holdings available in various ways. Most current academic journals are available digitally. Many books are available through digital checkout, allowing users to access the book for two-hour blocks of time. Entire databases of artistic collections, cultural artifacts, documentaries, feature films, and other forms of multimedia are made available through the extensive OhioLink Network (OhioLink, 2008). This network of Ohio institutions allows collaboration across a spectrum of users, interests, and academic institutions.

In the library orientation workshop, students visit the library's website with their research area in mind and locate four distinct resources: books, journal articles, media, and dissertations or theses. They are able to save full text or citations to their university-hosted network storage space. At the end of the session, they share what they were able to find, including the quality of the materials and the number of sources that require a physical visit to the library.

Wireless Internet and Portable Devices

The expansion of wireless networks across campuses has introduced a number of interesting expectations and complications. Students are able, and encouraged, to be connected to the Internet whenever they like. This means that a student may be sitting in a class while taking notes on a laptop and responding to surveys or other automated online questions with information related to the class. It may also mean that students are engaged in a distracting activity.

Students can get hands-on experience with wireless laptops and networks in the workshop. They are encouraged to imagine situations in which these portable technologies might be useful. They are also encouraged to consider the challenges they may present. As many of the international students at our university are also teaching assistants, it is important for them to consider their own positions on student use of laptops rather than traditional paper notebooks in the classroom. They discuss implications for use in and out of the classroom of the portable and increasingly ubiquitous devices. With many campuses having 100 percent wireless network coverage, members of the university community are able to access web-based information from any location on campus at any time. Information can be shared through the use of laptop computers, portable digital assistants, or other networked devices. In some cases, sharing information can be an expected part of the curriculum.

Communication and Social Networking

Universities in the United States communicate with students through electronic means. The amount and nature of such communication may vary from school to school, but it is a reality international students need to be made aware of early in their university experience. From the first contact, a university may rely solely upon e-mail for disseminating information about registration, advising, housing, grades, or anything else it needs to share with students. Students who do not check for this information on a regular basis may find themselves facing unnecessary difficulties.

At Ohio University, all regular interaction between the registrar's and bursar's offices and students is conducted through e-mail. Special requests for information can be conducted either in person or through a web interface. All registration is conducted online as well, unless special permission requires that a student register in person. Students schedule meetings with advisors, purchase textbooks, and identify dining hall menus through a web browser.

Recently, students at Ohio University and other institutions have begun using the Internet to communicate on a new level. Increasingly, universities are relying on social networking and virtual environments to aid communication and outreach to students. University social groups, clubs, and even departments and research groups are utilizing these systems to stay in touch with students. These attempts are driven by the popularity of such sites as MySpace and Facebook among U.S. undergraduate students. While these systems may be unfamiliar to international students, they will be expected to become familiar with the extant and emerging systems at their given institution to engage in a successful academic experience.

The fourth orientation workshop walks students through each of the communication and social networking systems that are used locally: Blackboard Discussion Forum, Facebook, and Second Life. Students are presented with information regarding the benefits and drawbacks of each of these systems. Finally, they are allowed to experiment with each of them on their own at the end of the session, interacting with other students in the room as well as with other members of the university community.

EVALUATION

To gather the assessment information necessary for keeping Ohio University's program relevant in the future, each attendee is required to complete an orientation evaluation. Over the past four years, the instructional technology portion of the overall orientation has consistently ranked among the most positively received. Typically, previous participants are invited to share their experiences, and they are always eager to do so. These international students share their frustrations, successes, and surprises with new students as they highlight the importance of an instructional technology orientation. Each year numerous orientation attendees respond. Some of them have shared the following statements:

"I never would have anticipated this kind of use of technology."
"We didn't use computers for anything other than word processing at my previous university."
"This orientation certainly made my transition easier."

APPLICABILITY TO OTHER INSTITUTIONS

The descriptions of the orientation technology workshops demonstrate how familiarity with different forms of instructional technology and organizational communication is critical to international students. While each institution has its own technological culture, resources, and tools, the technology is likely to be quite similar to the programs and applications mentioned. These workshops could easily be adapted for other institutions by allowing the local needs and available resources to shape the specifics of the information.

REFERENCES

Abe, J., Talbot, D. M., & Geelhoed, R. J. (1998). Effects of a peer program in international student adjustment. *Journal of College Student Development, 39*(6), 539–547.

Andrade, M. (2006). International students in English-speaking universities: Adjustment factors. *Journal of Research in International Education, 5*(2), 131–154.

Barsoum, S., & Durham, D. (Eds.). (2006). *International student advising: Academy spring training handbook 2006.* Washington, DC: NAFSA Academy for International Education.

Beasley, C. (1997, February). Students as teachers: The benefits of peer tutoring. In R. Pospisil, & L. Willcoxson (Eds.), *Learning through teaching. Proceedings of the 6th Annual Teaching Learning Forum, Murdoch University.* Perth: Murdoch University. Retrieved February 19, 2008, from http://lsn.curtin.edu.au/tlf/tlf1997/beasley.html

Cox, L. (2006). Going home: Perceptions of international students on the efficacy of a reentry workshop (Doctoral dissertation, University of Southern California, 2006). *ProQuest Digital Dissertations Database* (Publication No. AAT 3237190).

———. (2007). [Orientation and Re-Entry Study for International Students in the U.S.]. Unpublished raw data.

D'Agostino, T. J., Senders, S., & Reilly, D. (2007, spring). The promise of integrated program design, Hobart and William Smith College. *IIE Networker.* Fulbright Fellows Handbook 2006–07.

Griffiths, L. G. (2007, March 30). Comprehensive internationalization strategies for provosts, deans, and faculty. Paper presented at the 2nd Annual IIE Best Prac-

tices Conference. Retrieved July 29, 2007, from http://www.iienetwork.org/
?p=IIEConference_2007

Hanson, L., & Zambito, J. (2003). The troubling issues facing international students today. *The Journal of Student Affairs at Colorado State University, 12,* 7. Retrieved November 14, 2008, from http://www.colostate.edu/Depts/SAHE/JOURNAL2/2003/HansonZambito.htm

Hubbard, P. (2004). Learner training for effective use of CALL. In S. Fotos & C. Browne (Eds.), *New perspectives on CALL for second language classrooms* (pp. 3–14). Mahwah, NJ: Erlbaum.

Kessler, G. (2006). Assessing CALL teacher training: What are we doing and what could we do better? In P. Hubbard & M. Levy (Eds.), *Teacher education in CALL* (pp. 23–42). Amsterdam: John Benjamins.

Kinsella, J., & Smith-Simonet, M. (2002). Orientation and reentry. In K. Tuma (Ed.), *The guide to successful short-term programs abroad* (pp. 203–237). Washington, DC: NAFSA.

Kolaitis, M., Mahoney, M. A., Pomann, H., & Hubbard, P. (2006). Training ourselves to train our students for CALL. In P. Hubbard & M. Levy (Eds.), *Teacher education in CALL* (pp. 317–332). Amsterdam: John Benjamins.

Lin, J .G., & Yi, K. Y. (1997). Asian international students' adjustment: Issues and program suggestions. *College Student Journal, 31*(4), 473–479. Retrieved July 29, 2007, from http://vnweb.hwwilsonweb.com.ezproxy.library.unlv.edu/hww/shared/shared_main.jhtml?_requestid=14909

Marcum, D. (2003). Requirements for the future digital library. *The Journal of Academic Librarianship, 29*(5), 276–279.

Mynard, J., & Almarzouqi, I. (2006). Investigating peer tutoring. *ELT Journal, 60*(1), 13–22.

O'Connell, W. (1994). Foreign student education at two-year colleges. Washington, DC: NAFSA.

OhioLink. (2008). The Ohio Library and Information Network. Retrieved October 16, 2008, from http://www.ohiolink.edu/

Pang, G., & Barlas, R. (1996). *Culture shock! All you need to know about studying overseas.* Portland, OR: Graphic Arts Center Publishing Company.

Rhodes, G., & Hong, H. (2005). The Project for Learning Abroad, Training and Outreach (PLATO): An integrated study abroad, training, certification, and diversity outreach program. *IIE Networker, Fall,* 39–41.

Shumway, E. B. (1994). Welcome to Laie. Opening remarks presented at the NAFSA Spring Conference. Brigham Young University Hawaii, Laie, HI.

Tenney, A., & Houck, B. (2004). Learning about leadership. *Journal of College Science Teaching, 33*(6), 25–29.

Tinto, V. (1988, July–August). Stages of student departure: Reflections on the longitudinal character of student leaving. *Journal of Higher Education, 59*(4), 438–455.

U.S. News Ranks UH Hilo among Leaders in Diversity. Retrieved October 14, 2007, from http://www.uhh.hawaii.edu/news/press/view/588/

Zhai, L. (2002). *Studying international students: Adjustment issues and social support.* (ERIC Document Reproduction Service No. ED474481). Retrieved July 29, 2007, from http://www.eric.ed.gov/ERICDocs/data/ericdocs2sql/content_storage_01/0000019b/80/1a/e2/95.pdf

6

English Language Programs and Academic Support

International students come to the United States to earn a degree in their chosen field. Central to their success in achieving this goal are strong English language skills. Although most higher education institutions require evidence that students have the requisite English skills for success, this judgment is often made on the basis of standardized English language proficiency tests, which indicate what students know about the language rather than their ability to use it. International students who are nonnative speakers of English attest to the challenges they face with regard to their course work, as do their professors. Even those with strong English skills often have to spend more time on readings and assignments than native speakers do and may not fully comprehend course materials. International students also face cultural and educational differences that impact success in the classroom. These include unfamiliar written and spoken discourse styles, classroom interaction patterns, expectations, and learning styles.

Recognizing these challenges, institutions across the nation have developed innovative ways to support international students' English language development and academic adjustment. The first three program descriptions in this chapter present creative variations of English language programming. To begin, Kelley Calvert and Patricia Szasz describe how students enrolled in the English for Academic and Professional Purposes (EAPP) program at the Monterey Institute of International Studies benefit from the use of an online course management system that supports cooperative learning, social interaction, and authentic language practice. Students build technology skills while learning academic English and becoming comfortable with expectations for active learning. Next, Enid Rosenstiel, Julianne Taaffe, and Laura Thomas share the benefits of a summer bridge program for matriculated international graduate students at The Ohio State University. The Graduate Preparation program provides linguistic, academic, and cultural support to prepare students for their disciplines and help them integrate socially. Finally, Marcia Babbitt and Tara Weiss present a learning community model at Kingsborough Community College in which students are enrolled in English language courses that are linked with content courses such as psychology and sociology. Students who participate in this model have greater language gains than students in traditional stand-alone English language courses.

Strong writing skills are necessary for academic success, particularly for graduate work, which often requires a thesis or dissertation. English language learners not only have to develop sufficient fluency in the language to be able to analyze and express complex ideas but they must be able to do so clearly and accurately. Christine Jensen Sundstrom explains how international graduate students at the University of Kansas receive this support through formal classes, tutorials, workshops, and writing support groups. Courses focus on professional writing, thesis and dissertation writing, and professional presentations, all of which address specific problems encountered by nonnative speakers.

The final two contributions in the chapter present distinct pieces related to English language and academic support. Joan Friedenberg makes a compelling case for a complete departure from the intensive English language program model common in U.S. higher education. She argues for the use of bilingual and sheltered language teaching techniques, citing the higher education context in Europe to illustrate the benefits of supporting multiple languages of instruction. Last, Mary Ellen Duncan of Howard Community College advocates the use of a comprehensive array of support practices involving the community, the faculty, and campus services. This approach enables the internationalization of an entire campus.

From community college to graduate-level studies, these examples of best practices demonstrate how institutions are supporting the English language development and academic adjustment of international students who are nonnative English speakers. They indicate a rich variety of thinking on the issues and innovative solutions.

Using Moodle to Create Community in the Classroom and Beyond

Kelley Calvert and Patricia Szasz

RATIONALE

Current research indicates that students expect teachers to use technology in the classroom. One study reports that 72 percent of the students surveyed agreed that professors should use technology (Imus, Ployhart, Ritzer, & Sleigh, 2004). This high percentage may reflect students' desire to use the kinds of resources at school that they use in daily activities (Imus et al., 2004). Increasingly, both educational institutions and the workplace rely on computer technology. International students who come from developing countries may or may not arrive with the tools necessary to be successful in these environments. If we consider our position as educators, we see that encouraging technological literacy is as important as teaching informational literacy for our international students.

In the area of language learning, the use of computers gives students access to an array of resources unavailable in traditional language classrooms. These include authentic materials, communication capabilities through networking, multimedia capabilities, and nonlinear (hypermedia) structure of information (Chun & Plass, 2000). With these tools, nonnative speakers of English can further develop their English skills.

Moodle (Modular Object-Oriented Dynamic Learning Environment) is an online course-management system that makes utilizing these benefits much easier. Based on socioconstructivist pedagogy, the goal of Moodle is to promote a discovery-based approach to learning (Brandl, 2005). Used alone or as a supplement to classroom learning, Moodle, which students access on the World Wide Web, enables teachers to present a course in week-by-week segments, giving previews, objectives, and assignments in clearly demarcated sections. Moodle also allows teachers to easily include resources like Word documents (e.g., syllabi and assignments), links to other websites (e.g., readings, additional information on grammar points), PowerPoint presentations, and audio/visual materials (e.g., MP3 files).

Teachers may also use wikis (i.e., Web pages that all users can access and edit) and forums (i.e., interactive, teacher-moderated discussions) to facilitate cooperation and interaction among students (Brandl, 2005). The benefit of a wiki is that the class can generate dictionary entries for unfamiliar vocabulary and concepts in an interactive and memorable way. Using forums allows students more time to think about and respond to topics (Gonglewski & DuBravac, 2006). As a result, some students who may not be comfortable stating opinions in class are able to be more direct and open in discussion forums. Additionally, the use of forums allows students to keep in contact with other students and the teacher outside of the classroom. Students can ask questions, express concerns, and communicate at any time, thus keeping them connected to their language learning even when not physically present in class.

DESCRIPTION OF THE INSTITUTION AND STUDENTS

The Monterey Institute of International Studies is primarily a professional graduate school, offering master's degrees in international business, translation and interpretation, language teaching, and international policy. The international focus of the campus is reflected in a student body of approximately 750 students representing over fifty countries. Approximately 90 percent of the American students have lived abroad, and approximately one-third of both faculty and students come from countries other than the United States (Monterey Institute of International Studies, 2007). To prepare students for careers in international fields, the Institute expects all students to come to campus proficient in a second language.

The campus is also home to a nondegree intensive English program. The Institute's Intensive English program, which enrolls about 120 students annually, provides language instruction to nondegree students of all proficiency levels. Participants are twenty-five years old on average and represent Africa, Latin America, the Caribbean, Europe, and Asia. Beginning- to intermediate-level students attend the Intensive English as a Second Language (ESL) Program. This program provides a combination of skills-focused and content-based courses that emphasize building communication skills.

The Intensive English program also operates an English for Academic and Professional Purposes (EAPP) program for high-intermediate to advanced students. The minimum TOEFL requirement for this program is 500 on the paper-based test or 61 on the Internet-based test. Although the program is designed to prepare students to enter degree programs in English-medium universities, many students also attend the program to build their professional communication skills.

Each module in the EAPP program is eight weeks long, with a total of five sessions offered per year. Per session, students typically take three or four courses that focus on the English language skills and strategies necessary to succeed academically and professionally. Offerings range from courses such as Reading Strategies and Vocabulary Development to Academic Discussion and Presentation. The majority of students in this program go on to pursue graduate degrees at the Monterey Institute or other American universities.

PROGRAM DESCRIPTION

In the spring of 2007, the Monterey Institute of International Studies began to use Moodle as a tool for course management and as a support system for student activity outside the classroom. The decision to do so was largely based on evidence of the enormous potential of the Internet for assisting language learning. Teachers used Moodle to organize classroom materials into a comprehensive week-by-week course syllabus. From this template, students could access readings, post questions and comments, submit assignments, and provide peer feedback. Students could also use forums to discuss current readings and ask questions outside of class.

Student blogs were linked to the Moodle site. A *blog* (Weblog) is often used as an online journal, but its applications to educational writing are numerous. Students in the EAPP program wrote reading response journals about the book *The Clash of Civilizations* (Huntington, 1993). Because blogs are usually accompanied by a comment button, readers can write a reaction, which is then logged and linked with other comments below the original text (Godwin-Jones, 2003). The comment function allows students to interact with one another outside the classroom and continue classroom discussions indefinitely.

As Gonzalez-Lloret (2003) points out, cooperative learning occurs when small groups of students interact, and cooperative language learning has a predominantly social function. Doughty (2000) adds that the target language fills an essential void when classroom activities relate to a learner's immediate communicative needs. Using Moodle and blogs to create a small, interactive, and cooperative environment online takes learning outside the classroom and allows students to interact socially to fulfill specific communicative needs.

Additionally, blogs make heavy use of hypertext, or links to other sites. Therefore, the information available to students through blogs is limitless. One can literally research and connect to site after site. As Furstenberg (1997) put it, student tasks should "exploit the associative nature of hypertext or hypermedia so that students can collaboratively discover and construct new connections, which they combine in a coherent whole" (p. 24). As students linked to blogs and searched for information related to *The Clash of Civilizations* (Huntington, 1993), they simultaneously linked to literally hundreds of other related readings, which facilitated a broader understanding of the content and encouraged greater autonomy in student learning. Many students simply performed a Web search of the phrase "The Clash of Civilizations" and found a series of related articles, blogs, and anecdotes. These related readings, though unassigned, brought unforeseen richness and depth to classroom discussion. Students came to class with comments such as "Personally, I agree with Queen Noor of Jordan, who suggested that there is not a clash of civilization, but a clash of political interest and greed."

In addition to student-generated blogs, participants also used Moodle's online glossary feature to track and build new vocabulary. Students collaborated in the Academic Discussion and Presentation class to build an interactive dictionary of over one hundred context-embedded words and phrases that they had encountered both inside and outside of class, ranging from *atheist* to *geothermal energy* and *sexually transmitted disease*. This feature provided students the opportunity to review key vocabulary, but unlike traditional vocabulary logs, the online dictionary became a resource shared by the entire class. Like the forums, the glossary feature enabled students to learn cooperatively.

Discussion forums allowed students and teachers to reflect on issues raised in class and then expand on the discussion between classroom sessions. For example, in the Active Listening Strategies course, the teacher provided a link to a *New York Times* article that analyzed key words and phrases used during President Bush's 2007 State of the Union address. Students then chose one of the phrases (for example, "Iraq" or "Social Security") and analyzed its frequency and use. Without the teacher being present, students could listen to the speech and then use the newspaper article and related graphics to analyze the speaker's rhetorical decisions. In addition to focusing on vocabulary, the assignment allowed students to consider speech organization at the discourse level. In this way, the teacher was able to raise language awareness even when students were not physically in class.

The final component of the pilot program included audio files of class discussions and lectures that were recorded using an iPod. The audio files were then imported into Moodle and made available as podcasts. These audio files allowed a student in Costa Rica to follow class even though she was unable to be present. These podcasts also allowed students to access and review lectures and discussions. Finally, having podcasts available online provided instructors with a valuable reflective tool, as they could revisit lectures and notice areas for improvement.

EVALUATION

Student perceptions of Moodle were measured by a survey administered at the end of the semester by an independent research team. Students were given the opportunity to provide feedback on three aspects of their experience with Moodle: (a) opinions about the Moodle environment; (b) Moodle features used and their contribution to language learning; and (c) opinions of specific Moodle features (Kavenoki & Osteen, 2007).

Although the students were not asked directly about Moodle's contribution to their cultural adjustment or classroom community, they expressed favorable attitudes toward Moodle use. Responding to statements on a 5-point Likert scale, in which 5 indicated "Strongly Agree" and 1 indicated "Strongly Disagree," students expressed that they felt comfortable using the Moodle environment (mean response: 4.2), and they indicated that Moodle aided class organization (mean response: 4.4) (Kavenoki & Osteen, 2007). Respondents also strongly agreed that they would like to use Moodle again in future classes (mean response: 4.5) (Kavenoki & Osteen, 2007).

Students were also asked to rate particular Moodle features and how they felt these features contributed to their language learning. In response to the statement "*I believe [x feature] helped my language learning,*" students used the same 5-point Likert scale as above. Students rated Internet article postings highest (mean response: 4.3), followed by the online glossary feature (mean response: 4.2) and the discussion forums (mean response: 4.0) (Kavenoki & Osteen, 2007). While the study did not include a quantitative analysis of student proficiency gains over the session, these results do give teachers and administrators insight into how students viewed the online course-management system as aiding their language learning objectives.

As for the features that students enjoyed using most, respondents indicated that they most appreciated Moodle's forums and glossaries as well as the ability to upload assignments online. In their short answer responses, students indicated that they liked the discussion forums because the forums gave them the chance to communicate outside of class (Kavenoki & Osteen, 2007). As one student commented, "I like the Moodle, though I must confess it took me some time to become familiar. But I think it's a good way to be more in contact with our teachers" (p. 29). Although the study was limited by its qualitative focus on student self-reporting, these responses indicate that the use of Moodle or other course management systems could allow international students a new way to voice opinions in any classroom environment.

APPLICABILITY TO OTHER INSTITUTIONS

The EAPP pilot program illuminated Moodle's potential as a classroom management system and distance-learning tool. For students, Moodle creates a community of interaction and engagement that extends beyond the classroom. This community can be particularly important for students who have recently arrived in the United States and may be struggling with cultural differences and language barriers. Having immediate and continual access to a community of supportive language learners can make a significant difference for a learner. Additionally, for learners who lack experience with computers, Moodle can be a useful introduction to many features of the Internet. For teachers, Moodle organizes the often overwhelming elements of syllabus creation, time management, and assignment distribution. It also creates a coherent whole out of week-to-week fragments and assignments.

Though our pilot program focused on international students in an English language classroom, it is important to note that Moodle can benefit any classroom. Recording audio files for later review may benefit nonnative English speakers in any class. Additionally, having online discussion forums and wikis allows reserved students to engage more fully and comfortably in dialogue about the ideas presented in class. The Moodle course delivery system could thus work at any higher education establishment (undergraduate or graduate), regardless of the university's size or typical classroom numbers. Moodle is a versatile teaching and learning tool that can be applied to any educational environment.

Technology is becoming more and more interwoven into the fabric of life. The challenge for educators today is to keep up with the rapid innovations that the Internet inspires. More importantly, we should endeavor to use these innovations to motivate students to create a community and continue interaction outside the four walls of classroom discourse.

The Graduate Preparation Program at The Ohio State University

Enid D. Rosenstiel, Julianne Taaffe, and Laura J. Thomas

RATIONALE

In light of the growing number of students whose primary objective is to prepare for graduate studies in the United States (Powers, 2007), the American Language program at The Ohio State University instituted the Graduate Preparation program (GPP). The GPP is designed as a nine-week intensive and cohesive preparation course offered in the summer for graduate students who have been admitted to university departments for fall. Now in its third year, the program continues to evolve and is informed by recent research on expectations and needs among new international graduate students and their professors. Both groups express a need for more linguistic, academic, and cultural support. Productive oral and written English skills for completing assignments and participating in classes are vital, as is the language needed for daily interacting, networking, and socializing with classmates and professors. Another perceived need is integration into the wider community beyond the campus (Trice, 2001; Yeh & Yang, 2003).

The program description below specifies how the GPP addresses these needs. The theoretical underpinning of the course was provided by research in the following areas: understanding of and strategies for dealing with idiom (Wray, 2005); awareness of the lexical building blocks of language, including collocation (i.e., words that commonly occur together, such as *dead serious*) (Nattinger & DeCarrico, 1992; O'Keefe, McCarthy, & Carter, 2007); and practice in spontaneous classroom interaction, discussion techniques, group project work, and informal and formal presentations (Ferris, 1998;

Ferris & Tagg, 1996; Pritchard, 2005). Students are exposed to global English (Jenkins, 2001; Kirkpatrick, 2007) and made aware of written style and vocabulary usage within and across disciplines (Cargill, 1996; Hyland & Tse, 2007; Swales & Feak, 2004).

DESCRIPTION OF THE INSTITUTION AND STUDENTS

The Ohio State University is a large Midwestern research institution, located in Columbus, Ohio. Currently, the total number of students is approximately fifty-two thousand, of whom ten thousand are graduate students. Twenty-five percent of the graduate students are international, coming mainly from China, East Asia, and, more recently, India. They typically major in the mathematical, physical, and biological sciences and in engineering. English-language support is provided by a post-admission program in composition, international teaching assistant training, and a preadmission intensive program, the American Language program (ALP).

Attached to the ALP is the voluntary GPP, whose students come from a variety of majors, including business, engineering, education, and economics. Students' TOEFL scores are generally above 550. Native languages include Korean, Japanese, Thai, Chinese, and Arabic among others. Although the students' overall language skills are strong enough for university graduate admission, their actual functional abilities vary widely. Especially upon arrival, some students' listening and speaking skills lag behind their overall proficiency. Their vocabulary base in academic vocabulary is generally strong, but their familiarity with idiomatic English (i.e., common expressions used in daily conversation) is sometimes lacking.

PROGRAM DESCRIPTION

The objectives of the GPP are to support the students' language acquisition and their acculturation to the Columbus community, university campus, and academic departments. The program consists of two main parts: a two-hour listening/speaking block in the morning and a two-hour reading and writing block in the afternoon, four days a week. The primary objectives of the listening/speaking class are building vocabulary, fluency, and accuracy in the contexts of both academic and daily language. The objectives of the reading/writing component also focus on academic discourse in the forms of research and report writing, as well as the idiomatic language necessary for functioning in an American university setting.

Class assignments help the students gather information about and establish social contacts with their academic departments. The students are invited to participate in activities provided for the intensive English program students, including a conversation partners program that matches them with Americans and a number of field trips and social events. For example, during one summer program, students attended a departmental faculty picnic where they mingled with faculty, staff, and graduate students from the College of Dentistry, visited the Ohio State Fair, saw a number of movies, and visited a shopping outlet mall south of Columbus. They also had the opportunity to participate in a white-water rafting trip in West Virginia and go canoeing and horseback riding. Students found that time did not permit them to participate in all these activities, but they appreciated those that they did attend.

CURRICULUM

The curriculum of the GPP is designed to provide students with content-based input and activities to bring their English skills to an appropriate level before they begin their graduate programs. The GPP helps students develop strong skills in an academic or formal register and familiarity with more casual and idiomatic daily English. The listening/speaking and reading/writing courses are integrated in terms of schedule, syllabus, assignments, and activities, with teachers in the program communicating daily and holding weekly planning meetings to adjust and develop the curriculum as needed.

Many ongoing activities related to these goals are carried out throughout the quarter. These include developing formal presentations using visual aids and fielding questions from the audience. Tutorials guide the students in such areas as organization and planning, pronunciation, sensitivity to audience, and self-assessment. Discussion skills are addressed through student-led discussions on current event topics of their own choosing. Academic lecture comprehension and note-taking skills are developed through both in-class lectures and online materials organized around content themes. Pronunciation concepts are introduced and practiced. Current, high-frequency idioms encountered in everyday face-to-face interactions, in the media, and even in classroom settings are systematically introduced and practiced. Students are exposed to American dialects and the international varieties and accents of English they may encounter.

The students work with academic themes and topics and with elements of U.S. culture in many registers and from a variety of sources. Weekly reading and writing assignments in the form of journals alternate between purely cultural topics and those more closely related to the students' disciplines. Students develop a field-specific project and conduct research using primary and secondary sources, and from this they write and present a formal research report at the end of the quarter. Course content includes popular films related to cultural issues and themes, articles from popular magazines, and popular mainstream broadcasts, all of which are intended to increase the students' cultural fluency and to illustrate connections between popular culture and academic discourse. Students present cultural information with follow-up discussions both in the classroom and online.

EVALUATION

Various measures have been employed to evaluate the effectiveness of the program in preparing the participants for the academic demands they face upon entering their graduate programs. Mid-quarter assessments give students a chance to reflect on their progress and express their perceived needs for the remainder of the course. The university requires that all students fill out a standard end-of-quarter form commenting upon their course materials, activities, and instructor. In addition, in the first year of the program, students who had taken the GPP and were in their first year of study completed a survey and participated in a group discussion. This information was very useful in informing the GPP teachers of the assignments the students were encountering in their graduate programs and their transitional concerns. One student's progress was tracked during her first year of graduate study, and insights gained through extensive conversations with her helped inform the program. Feedback from the College of Business about student performance was also critical, since more than half of our international student population consisted of prospective MBA students.

These evaluative tools, among others, have presented a highly positive picture of the program's effectiveness thus far. The students have overwhelmingly expressed their belief that the program helped them establish a firm foundation for beginning their graduate studies. They have stressed such factors as greater confidence in their written and spoken English, a better grasp of American culture in general and university culture in particular, and the opportunity to establish their homes in the United States and attend to their family's adjustment needs before the intense demands of their graduate course work began.

The business school has also reported to us that since the inception of our program, none of the students that have completed it have been placed on their academic watch list of international students who are struggling with class demands. In fact, although GPP is a voluntary program, in 2006, the business school began to require it as a condition of admission for any of their applicants in need of language support. Other colleges are showing an interest in doing so as well. The graduate school has endorsed the program from its inception and actively participates in program activities.

APPLICABILITY TO OTHER INSTITUTIONS

Many institutions of higher education in the United States are experiencing solid international graduate student enrollments and may find a program like OSU's useful. While each program needs to adapt to its own institution and student body, we believe that the fundamental structure and philosophy with regard to preparing graduate students as outlined above is sound. Our own GPP benefits from the existing relationship between a strong ESL program and the larger institution. The institution provides students with the necessary infrastructure while the ESL program provides teachers who have the expertise necessary to meet students' linguistic and cultural needs.

Since most academic programs begin in the autumn, students need to have immigration documents permitting them to arrive on campus the summer preceding the start of their graduate program. They need the facilities that a student status can offer them, such as library/research privileges and university computer network access. They also need housing. In short, they need full graduate student privileges a term before their academic programs begin.

Staffing the program is another major consideration. Teachers should have experience in post-admission ESL courses and familiarity with academic discourse communities. Ideally, teachers should be allowed to devote their full attention to GPP while in session, since the curriculum needs to be created and much of its content needs to be constantly updated. Staffing must also take into account that students must meet the immigration requirement of eighteen contact hours per week.

Finally, a program such as this should enjoy the full support of the graduate school and relevant academic departments. This relationship has been mutually beneficial at OSU: as academic departments have become aware of our program, they have begun recommending it to their incoming graduate students as a means of increasing their students' success. Thus, our program continues to grow.

We have learned through our experiences with the GPP that the issues raised here are important to the success of the program. Institutions wanting to establish similar programs on their campuses should consider the logistics of bringing international students to campus prior to their first semester of enrollment, staffing needs, and coordinating the efforts of various departments to support the students' transition.

Learning Community Programs: In Support of Student Success

Marcia Babbitt and Tara Weiss

RATIONALE

At Kingsborough Community College (KCC), the City University of New York (CUNY), two learning communities for entering students flourish side by side: the Intensive ESL Learning Community and the Opening Doors Learning Community. While these programs both serve the ESL international and immigrant student population, Opening Doors also serves developmental students (those who have not passed the CUNY Assessment Exams in reading, writing, and math) and nondevelopmental students (those who have passed the assessments).

These highly successful collaborative and interdisciplinary programs are designed to accelerate both the academic skills and the language proficiency of first-semester college students. They also help students acculturate to their new environment and become academically and socially integrated into the college community through curricular and cocurricular activities.

DESCRIPTION OF THE INSTITUTION AND STUDENTS

Located at the southern tip of Brooklyn, KCC is a large, two-year urban college that serves approximately fifteen thousand full-time students. KCC offers many programs and areas of concentration that lead to degrees in science, applied science, and the arts. In addition to preparing students to become effective critical readers and writers and to transfer to four-year colleges, KCC promotes global citizenship to develop global and multicultural competencies that are embedded in our general education courses. International and immigrant students are a central part of this goal. According to current enrollment data, our 400–450 international and immigrant students come from as many as seventy-three countries and speak approximately 142 languages and dialects. While international students are less numerous than immigrant students, our distinctive learning communities provide optimal learning and community-building opportunities for them.

PROGRAM DESCRIPTION

While the structures of learning communities vary by institution, all share certain commonalities, such as linking courses together for increased coherence, the treatment of interdisciplinary themes, intellectual exchange among faculty and students, collaboration, and active learning (Gabelnick, MacGregor, Matthews, & Smith, 1990). Our Intensive ESL Learning Community consists of a block of five courses: ESL reading and writing (one of three levels), speech, student development (two courses), and a course such as psychology or sociology. In Opening Doors, students take a course in one of several disciplines (biology, business, or health, for example) together with a developmental or freshman English reading and writing course and a student development class.

Since its inception in 1995, the ESL Learning Community had been optional for ESL students entering KCC. However, beginning in fall 1998, incoming students whose test scores indicated the need for intensive ESL study were required to enroll since success rates of learning community participants had consistently surpassed those of students in our stand-alone ESL courses. Virtually all full-time intensive ESL students now register for one of the ESL Learning Community blocks.

The Opening Doors Learning Community, which began in 2003, was modeled on our successful ESL Learning Community. ESL students who do not need intensive language study but still may face challenges in their new academic setting, including difficulties succeeding in college courses with a new language and a new culture and pressure to pass the required CUNY reading and writing assessment exams, are invited to enroll in this program. All ESL and developmental courses have equated credits, which count toward full-time status and financial aid but not toward graduation. International ESL students participate in both types of learning communities.

Faculty development is ongoing in both programs. Through multifaceted collaboration, faculty create joint themes, assignments, projects, and goals. We focus on the pedagogies and curricula that contribute to student success in linked courses by actively engaging students in reading, writing, and thinking critically and interactively about the concepts they study. We expect students to make personal connections with these concepts and to analyze and respond to them. Writing is a complex activity for native speakers; it is all the more difficult for international and immigrant ESL students. Writing in a new language requires programs that facilitate learning through language development and social–academic interaction. Interaction is essential to building communities that underscore learning as we have described it.

Support services such as tutoring, counseling, academic advisement, and early intervention when difficulties surface are essential to building a strong learning community and helping ensure a high level of student success. Students in the integrated reading/writing ESL and developmental English courses receive tutoring in the Reading and Writing Center with tutors who also attend classes with the students. In-class tutor support is also available for all ESL, developmental, and freshman English courses.

Faculty and counselors work closely with librarians to facilitate an information literacy component. Moreover, faculty confer with student development advisers about individual students, and these advisers provide vital advisement, counseling, and referral services. All of these support systems are critical for international and immigrant ESL students' academic success and social and cultural adjustment.

Our learning communities require strong administrative support to function optimally. Our administration has realized that although the programs may seem expensive due to the ESL and English courses being capped at twenty-five students (the non-learning community courses are capped at forty-four), the results of higher GPAs and higher rates of retention offset the costs. KCC has found that more students tend to register for courses in subsequent semesters when they begin their first semester in a learning community. Clearly, soft money is helpful in the start-up of learning communities, which also includes expenses for ongoing faculty development. With the increase of persistence and retention, soft money can be phased out as the program becomes institutionalized.

EVALUATION

Students are academically more successful in college when they are part of a dynamic learning community, working together on course assignments and gaining new insights and perspectives from each other while forming deep social bonds (e.g., see Bruffee, 1993, 1995; Gabelnick et al., 1990; Tinto, 1987, 1997; Tinto, Goodsell Love, & Russo, 1993). Our findings are similar. Currently, results from both programs indicate that students who participate have a greater success rate in their first semester after exiting the program than do nonparticipants, and that being part of a learning community has a positive impact on future success in college.

Bailin Song (2006), a professor at KCC, completed a study of the ESL Learning Community and concludes that performance of the students in first semester ESL courses, in subsequent ESL and developmental English courses, in credit-bearing courses, and in CUNY reading and writing assessments is significantly higher than that of nonparticipants. The ESL Learning Community students achieved higher pass rates and grades in ESL courses than the nonlearning community students. In addition, students in the ESL Learning Community performed better in subsequent semesters; their performance was measured using overall GPA, English proficiency tests, retention and graduation rates. On ACT reading and writing tests, they had a significantly higher pass rate than did nonparticipating students: 61 percent versus 54 percent for reading and 62 percent versus 44 percent for writing. Significantly more of them graduated from KCC with a degree than nonparticipants did (151 vs. 119), and more of them graduated within a four-year period (139 vs. 91). MDRC, the social research organization that funded the first two years of the Opening Doors Learning Community, has found that participants perform significantly better academically and have higher long-term persistence than nonparticipants (Bloom & Sommo, 2005).

APPLICABILITY TO OTHER INSTITUTIONS

KCC's approach to welcoming and working with international and immigrant students has been successful. Because our learning communities are inherently flexible, we strongly believe that they can be easily adapted to meet the specific cultures of other two- and four-year colleges and universities. We have found this to be so as we have shared the basic tenets of our program with other institutions to help them create or enhance their own programs consonant with their students' needs.

A great strength of our learning community model is that, with some modification, it meets the multiple needs not only of international students, but of all ESL, developmental, and nondevelopmental students at any college. This is an advantage for institutions that may not find it economically feasible to have separate programs for these groups or that find it desirable for students to benefit from intercultural exchanges.

Our learning communities help international students meet challenges in their new academic setting. Our students grow academically, gain confidence and self-efficacy, connect to the institution, and are motivated to achieve their academic and career goals. Students benefit from individualized advisement, counseling, and tutoring. All of these support systems are critical for international and immigrant students' academic success and cultural and social adjustment.

International and immigrant students at community colleges deserve a comprehensive first-semester program to help them become confident scholars, critical thinkers, responsible citizens of the college community, and successful shapers of their college careers. Students form meaningful student-centered academic and social learning communities, through which they engage in integrative, multidisciplinary tasks—the hallmark of our programs. We believe that our adaptable model helps international students in other institutions to achieve their desired goals.

Graduate Writing Support Program: The Least We Owe International Graduate Students

Christine Jensen Sundstrom

RATIONALE

Increased cross-cultural collaboration in virtually all research disciplines has led to large numbers of international graduate students attending U.S. universities. Because of this, and because of the strong competition for research dollars, institutions are challenged to articulate exactly what these second-language researchers and writers need to know and do to be successful in their research endeavors. As a result, the University of Kansas (KU) has developed the Graduate Writing Support program to meet the needs of international graduate students. An additional benefit of the program is the opportunity it affords domestic students to hone their research and presentation skills.

We know some of what needs to be articulated for second-language researchers and writers. They must not only develop linguistic competency, but must also understand U.S. knowledge-making traditions, including how to stake claims and structure arguments using culturally appropriate markers of politeness and collegiality while still advancing their own cases. Jensen (2005) has documented that chemists from different cultural and linguistic backgrounds do not think or write about chemistry in the same way. Similarly, Namsaraev (1997), Vassileva (2001), and Yakhontova (1998) have found rhetorical differences between U.S. and non-U.S. research articles in other disciplines. Swales (1990) noted that native English advisers, journal reviewers, and conference proposal vetters respond less to linguistics bloopers than to violations of genre expectations.

Culp (1999) noted that learning the academic writing of undergraduate studies is like learning a second language even for native speakers. Writing within a specific discipline at the graduate level poses an even greater challenge than general academic writing, and disciplinary expectations are often not articulated, let alone taught. This failure to develop students' rhetorical skills may cause unnecessary frustration, pain, and suffering. Graduate students too often fail comprehensive exams because they do not conform to norms and expectations when presenting information, not because they have not mastered the subject matter. These failures are avoidable for both native and nonnative speakers and writers of English if all graduate students are acculturated to the norms and expectations of their disciplines (Berkenkotter & Huckin, 1995; Gosden, 1992; Jacoby & Gonzales, 1991; Kuhn, 1962; Ronald, 1988). Such instruction shows students how to structure texts in an expected way, make claims using a culturally appropriate level of certainty, and balance evaluation and politeness in reporting the research of others.

Learning to write the genres of a discipline in a second language and within an unfamiliar research tradition presents challenges we have only begun to describe and meet (Bloch & Chi, 1995; Swales, 1990). Often, international graduate students must learn the nature of the prescribed research and methodology as it is practiced in their new cultural and linguistic setting (Berkenkotter & Huckin, 1995; Conrad, 1996; Grace, 1995). A significant number of them may also arrive without having had any formal instruction in scientific writing in the research traditions of their own countries (Braine, 2001; Cmerjokava & Danes, 1997; Salager-Meyer, Angelas, Ariza, & Zambrano, 2003; Yakhontova, 2001; Vassileva, 2001; Ventola, 1997). Salager-Meyer et al. (2003) note that places as disparate as Ukraine, France, Spain, and Latin America have only recently published style manuals for writing scientific papers.

Research that compares the rhetorical structure of research article introductions written in other countries by nonnative speakers of English to the structure of introductions written in the United States by native speakers of English has revealed significant differences (Ahmad, 1997; Lee, 2000; Najjar, 1990). Others have noted that Chinese research articles use fewer citations and place less emphasis on summarizing the existing literature than the U.S. tradition does (Bloch & Chi, 1995; Miao, 2003). Hedges and other moderating devices are employed to different degrees and for different purposes in various cultural-linguistic traditions (Hyland, 1996, 1998; Jensen, 2005). In countries such as Russia and Ukraine, researchers establish the credibility of the methods (Rybak-Akimova, 2005) rather than the expertise of the authors, as might be done in the United States. Writers in the United States also seem to feel freer to boost their own claims and point out what is important than their Chinese counterparts do (Miao, 2005).

To address the complex needs of international graduate student writers, the University of Kansas launched its Graduate Writing Support program with a graduate reading/writing course. This course, one of several now offered, is now identified as *professional writing*.

DESCRIPTION OF THE INSTITUTION AND STUDENTS

The University of Kansas (KU) is a leading research institution located near Kansas City, Missouri. About seven thousand (24 percent) of KU's nearly twenty-nine thousand students are graduate students, and about seven hundred (10 percent) of these graduate students are international. International graduate students at KU come from nearly one hundred countries in Europe, Africa, Asia, and the Americas, with the highest enrollments from India, the People's Republic of China, Taiwan, and Korea, and substantial numbers from Saudi Arabia, Japan, Germany, Canada, Italy, Spain, Sri Lanka, Iran, Costa Rica, France, Mexico, the Philippines, Kenya, and Portugal. These international graduates are enrolled primarily in the liberal arts and sciences, engineering, education, business, pharmacy, and fine arts.

PROGRAM DESCRIPTION

The Graduate Writing Support program includes four major components: formal classes, tutorials, workshops, and a writing support group. All program offerings are now open to domestic as well as international students. The formal courses—professional writing, thesis and dissertation writing, and professional presentations—are each offered one or two times a year for three or four hours of credit. The professional writing class focuses on teaching students to summarize without plagiarizing, critique and evaluate the research of others, design and present a written plan for a research project, use background research to determine project feasibility, and outline an effective argument. Students complete a ten- to twenty-page literature review or proposal using rhetorical structures such as problem-solution, critique, argument, and/or analysis. The objective is to teach students to effectively present information in their fields in acceptable formats and to use accurate linguistic forms.

The thesis and dissertation writing class provides support to students as they work on their research proposals, theses, or dissertations. In the course, students read about what makes specific chapters of theses and dissertations effective. They learn to analyze the rhetorical structure of chapters, analyze sample chapters from their own fields, and apply this information as they write their own texts.

In both of the writing classes described above, classroom instruction is supplemented by individualized conferences and tutorials. In conferences, the instructor reviews the content, organization, and genre conventions of papers, while in tutorials the instructor reviews the grammar, proofreading, and editing of the same papers.

The professional presentation class uses the vehicles of speaker introductions, poster sessions, or short research introductions, and longer research presentations to prepare students to present in department seminars, at conferences, and in proposal or thesis/dissertation defenses. Students meet with the instructor to review the appropriate genre for their presentations and to address relevant linguistic needs.

The second component of the support program is an individualized tutorial class, offered for variable credit, in which students receive individualized assistance on a weekly basis as they (a) write such genres as comprehensive exams or research articles, (b) develop proposals, or (c) work on their theses and dissertations. Students submit their work a day or two before each weekly conference, and feedback from their tutors enables them to improve their skills iteratively over the course of the semester. Great care is taken to ensure that department advisers play the leading role in the process. Students are asked to get feedback from their advisers as often as possible. In cases where it is not clear what the adviser is suggesting about the writing, the tutor, student, and adviser meet to develop a cohesive plan for completing the project.

The third component consists of workshops for KU graduate students with titles such as Designing Researchable Projects, Extreme Dissertation Issues, How to Push on Through to Your Degree, and Models of Mentoring for graduate faculty members. The workshops usually consist of panels composed of KU administrators, faculty, and program staff.

The final component is Dissertation Blues, a writing support group, which meets weekly or semiweekly. It has been a popular problem-solving venue for students, a place where they can overcome writer's block, solve problems they may be having with advisers or other committee members, or decide how to face challenges. In addition, it helps students overcome the isolation of their graduate studies.

The Office of Research and Graduate Studies and the Applied English Center (AEC) (KU's intensive English program) collaborated to start the support program. All of the formal courses are graduate level and staffed by the AEC. Though the program is housed in the AEC, the teaching staff has expertise not only in ESL but also in composition and rhetoric, communication studies, and foreign languages. At some schools, such a program might be housed in an English department, but at KU, the English department was stretched to the limit in covering its service courses, freshman composition, and technical writing.

The support program is housed in the intensive English program at KU, but the courses are graduate school courses. An advantage of the relatively independent status of the program is that it is possible to have staff members with expertise in a variety of areas such as ESL, technical writing and editing, composition and rhetoric, communication studies, and foreign languages. Regardless of where such a program is located on campus, it is critical that staff members have expertise in writing graduate and professional genres and that they are comfortable teaching courses with students from many disciplines.

To facilitate working with students from the full spectrum of disciplines, the tutors and students rely on field-specific models of the type of texts the students are writing. These models may be identified by students or by their adviser, the department graduate adviser, or the graduate secretary. In addition, the program coordinator offers training sessions on the major differences among genres in the humanities, social sciences, and sciences/engineering and teaches the staff how to review the field-specific samples efficiently and effectively.

Enrollment in the courses is generally voluntary, although some departments ask students to enroll in the professional writing course to get their graduate careers off to a strong start. In addition, graduate advisers sometimes recommend to students that they enroll. The students who do enroll range from those in dire need of support (i.e., those unable to meet the writing demands of their courses or programs) to those who are skillful writers and speakers intent on improving their craft. The courses enroll domestic as well as international students. The individualized conferences and grammar and editing tutorials allow the needs of the two populations to be addressed in a one-on-one setting.

Student tuition is the primary source of funding, although a National Institute of Health (NIH) grant supports one course offering of the professional writing class each year. The intensive English program pays the administrative costs of the program. The program has a faculty advisory committee, fostering information exchange and collaboration between departments and the program.

EVALUATION

Both formal and informal performance measures show the Graduate Writing Support Program to be a success. In the four years the program has existed, enrollment has increased from eight students to one hundred students per semester. Although the program was implemented as support for international graduate students, domestic students now constitute half of all enrollments, an increase of perhaps 25 percent from when they were first allowed to enroll. The professional writing course is a requirement for some incoming graduate students and is a support course for an NIH grant for premed minority students.

Of the approximately 373 students we have served in the thesis and dissertation writing class and tutorials, over 90 percent successfully completed a comprehensive exam, proposal, thesis, dissertation, or research article either during or after their enrollment in the program. Of the students who came to us because they had failed comprehensive exams, at least 75 percent were able to successfully complete those exams after participating in the program. Of those who enrolled because they had been stuck somewhere in the process for a lengthy period of time (six months to five years), 70 percent were able to complete their projects. One of the strongest measures of the success of the program is the number of students who return to take other classes and those who enroll because previous students have recommended the courses to them.

APPLICABILITY TO OTHER INSTITUTIONS

Graduate students need support in their studies, as attested to by graduate support programs being instituted or planned at such schools as Yale, Illinois, Michigan State, and Old Dominion. The program at KU reflects one institution's administrative structure. Other institutions may find that other structures serve them better. To structure an effective program, interested faculty and administrators should determine what services are already available in their intensive English programs, writing centers, English departments, and content area departments. In addition, they need to know who has an interest in developing services that are not currently available and who has the necessary expertise in writing and presenting professional genres in a variety of fields.

Other factors to explore include finding administrative support and identifying potential funding sources. Institutions that have such Council of Graduate Schools programs as Preparing Future Faculty, Preparing Future Professionals, or Responsible Conduct of Research may want to exploit the natural linkages between these and a graduate support program such as the one described. Although considerable effort and collaboration are required to establish a graduate support program, the results make it well worth the effort.

Treating International Students' Languages as a Resource Rather Than a Deficit

Joan E. Friedenberg

RATIONALE

Despite attempts by the media, businesses, religious institutions, and the K–12 school system to support multilingualism, U.S. higher education is, ironically, the most monolingual institution in U.S. society. Colleges and universities in the United States still embrace policies and practices that treat languages other than English as a problem rather than as a resource, limiting higher education's ability to deliver an accessible, effective, and efficient education to international students, domestic language–minority students, and, equally important, to English-speaking students. Making U.S. higher education multilingual would help address two critical issues: having to compete with other countries for international students and improving foreign language proficiency among English-speaking Americans.

As to the first of these problems, most international students arriving at U.S. colleges and universities with an unacceptable TOEFL score are not permitted to enroll in credit-bearing courses and are usually placed in intensive ESL programs, sometimes taking twenty-five to thirty hours a week of ESL classes for a year or more. My experiences as a former intensive ESL program director led me to conclude that many international students resent the time and resources spent in these programs; after all, they are not studying their chosen disciplines, have few opportunities to use authentic academic materials from their chosen disciplines, are isolated from English-speaking university students, and make little direct progress toward a degree.

Some researchers have criticized this English-only, language-deficit approach to higher education and prefer to view students' native languages as a *resource* (Auerbach, 1995; Edwards, Wesche, Krashen, Clement, & Kruidenier, 1984; Fishman, 1991; Ortega, 1999; Ricento & Hornberger, 1996; Tikoo, 1996; Wiley & Lukes, 1996). However, current policies and practices endure, and the English-only language policies of higher education continue to be taken for granted.

For example, in *Understanding Your International Students*, Flaitz (2003) offers advice for instructors of international and immigrant students, but the instructors in question are mostly ESL teachers rather than content-area professors, and of the forty-seven problem/solution scenarios presented, none addresses how to help international and immigrant students learn academic content. Instead, the authors focus on problems of international students' plagiarizing, not participating in group discussions, not pronouncing English words perfectly, and not making friends with Americans. In one example, the authors indicate that Brazilian students have trouble making English-speaking friends because their English pronunciation makes them sound rude. In another example, when Haitian students do not make progress learning English, the problem is attributed to their embarrassment over their refugee status. These problems and others described in this book may be the result of nonnative English speakers being isolated in intensive ESL programs.

Ortiz (2004) discusses the increased diversity on U.S. campuses but does not address associated language issues. Johns (2004) presents challenges faced by linguistically diverse students across disciplines at U.S. colleges, but despite indicating that a role for students' native languages is important, she focuses on cultural differences and ways to help students improve their English grammar. While nothing is wrong with these suggestions, they do little to enrich the classroom linguistically for international, immigrant, or native English-speaking students. International and immigrant students are, at best, seen as culturally interesting in college classrooms, although always with the view that their language differences are problems that need to be corrected.

While U.S. higher education largely fails to offer courses in languages other than English, throughout the remainder of the world, universities frequently offer credit-bearing content classes in languages other than their national language (Baker & Jones, 1998; Friedenberg, 2002). Indeed, members of the European Union (EU) concluded that one of the best ways to compete for international students is to offer them courses in languages they already understand. The EU's 1999 Bologna Declaration, an agreement among forty-five European countries aiming to establish a common European higher education system, has resulted in an influx of university students throughout the EU.

At a 2002 meeting of the EU in Barcelona, delegates reached consensus on a language goal of M + 2. That is, all citizens of the EU would strive to become competent in their mother tongue plus two additional languages. As a result of the Bologna and Barcelona agreements, many EU countries not only offer *free* intensive language courses to international students, they also offer discipline-related courses in languages these students already understand. To compete effectively for international students, U.S. higher education needs to consider implementing similar policies and practices.

As to the second problem (i.e., the lack of foreign language proficiency of U.S. college students), while international students make important financial contributions to U.S. higher education, they have more than money to contribute, including their rich cultures, technical knowledge, ability to research and teach in critical areas needed by our country, different world views, and the potential to act as ambassadors for our country. Another potential contribution is their language. By offering coursework in languages other than English, universities can accommodate the linguistic needs of international students eager to take academic course work while at the same time helping U.S. students become more proficient in foreign languages, drawing on international classmates who already speak those languages.

DESCRIPTION OF THE INSTITUTION AND THE STUDENTS

The program proposed here is mostly hypothetical for a U.S. context but could be implemented by any college or university with progressive and entrepreneurial attitudes. To best realize a multilingual program, the institution would need enrollments of international or immigrant students—preferably both—an ESL program, and English-speaking students in foreign language programs or classes. Such a multilingual program would effectively support international students in their studies as they are learning English, while providing a naturalistic setting in which U.S. students could strengthen their foreign language skills.

I propose a multilingual program for U.S. universities that offers select credit-bearing academic courses that are taught in a language other than English and that offers content-based language support through the institutions' foreign language and ESL programs. Although the schools' admissions, advisement, and administrative functions would have to be modified to become more multilingual (Friedenberg, 2002), the academic component of the program is modeled somewhat on two-way and one-way immersion programs successfully employed in many U.S. K–12 school systems and, in part, on bilingual vocational training programs used in some U.S. high schools and adult technical centers (Friedenberg, 1995).

PROGRAM DESCRIPTION

As a way to gradually introduce multilingual programming, the college or university would offer one section of a core general education course (e.g., introduction to sociology, psychology, mathematics, art, or world history) in a language other than English. Ideally, the language chosen would be a language common to many of the university's international and immigrant students and would also be a language offered by its foreign language program. The course chosen would be taught by a professor or teaching assistant who was an immigrant or international visitor, a foreign language professor with sufficient subject matter knowledge, or a U.S.-born professor with bilingual ability.

Such a course would allow international and immigrant students better access to credit-bearing course work while learning English and would allow English speakers studying a foreign language an opportunity for a meaningful partial language immersion experience, complete with native speakers as classmates. Imagine the satisfaction it would give to international students to be the ones in the class providing the help instead of always being the ones receiving it. It is only in such a class that international and immigrant students become a true language resource to both the instructor and the English-speaking students.

The instructor teaching the course would need to use sheltered or immersion techniques (e.g., see Echevarria & Graves, 1998; Edwards et al., 1984; Schneider & Friedenberg, 2001) for the benefit of the native English speakers. Sheltered techniques include focusing on vocabulary development and using slow, simplified speech; cooperative instruction techniques; visual aids; graphic organizers (e.g., lists, diagrams, charts); frequent reiteration; and demonstrations. Additionally, a bilingual teaching assistant might be employed to help the instructor translate handouts, lecture notes, and exams into the non-English language and clarify instruction for English speakers, as needed. Although all instruction for the class would be in the non-English language, students working cooperatively would naturally use some English, to the benefit of international and immigrant students in the class.

Content-based language instruction would also be offered to support the multilingual academic instruction described. The content-based language course would be taught by a foreign language instructor to help the English speakers in the class understand the academic instruction taught in another language. For example, if English-speaking Spanish majors are among the students enrolled in a sociology course taught in Spanish (using sheltered techniques and bilingual teaching assistants and materials to help clarify instruction), they could be concurrently enrolled in a Spanish for Sociology course offered by the Spanish department. Offering the native Spanish speakers in the class a concurrent sociology ESL class would be optional because the sociology class in question is offered in their native language.

EVALUATION

As mentioned earlier, universities throughout the world, especially in the EU, Asia, Canada, and the Middle East (e.g., see Baker & Jones, 1998; Edwards et al., 1984; Friedenberg, 2002), have been offering academic course work in more than one language for decades. Over twenty years ago, Edwards et al. (1984) found that English-speaking Canadian college students could be immersed successfully in a psychology class taught in French when sheltered techniques were used. In 2005, the University of Helsinki hosted a conference devoted entirely to multilingual higher education, in which participants from over sixty countries reported on their universities' bi- and multilingual programs (University of Helsinki, 2005). In 2006, the University of Maastricht (the Netherlands) hosted a conference titled "Integrating Content and Language in Higher Education" in which many participants (from non-English-speaking countries) reported on teaching content in a foreign language, often English (University of Maastricht, 2006). Both meetings included numerous papers that discussed the effectiveness of various efforts at bi- and multilingual higher education, and although challenges were certainly reported (Phillipson, 2005; Tudor, 2005), no scholars suggested the efforts should be abandoned.

Challenges to implementing multilingual programming in U.S. higher education include dealing with potential costs and addressing attitudes and assumptions that course work in the United States simply *must* be in English. Several ways to confront English-only attitudes are available. First, it makes sense to become acquainted with the language accommodations European higher education makes for students visiting from other countries (e.g., offering courses in languages these students already know and not insisting they learn the national language before matriculating), how these accommodations result in increased enrollments of international students for these institutions, how offering course work in other languages does not threaten in any way the status of the national language or the integrity of academic content, and how offering course work in other languages can help native-born students learn a foreign language.

Regarding potential costs, while faculty training would be necessary, it is unlikely that hiring special faculty would be necessary, at least in the beginning. Colleges and universities in the United States usually already have bilingual faculty and teaching assistants who would enjoy the opportunity to teach in a language other than English and who could help translate academic materials into other languages. However, modest funding would be needed to train these faculty members to use sheltered techniques.

Similarly, most universities already have foreign language teachers who, with minimal training, could learn content-based language instruction techniques and teach such courses as the Spanish for Sociology mentioned earlier. Funds to support faculty training, content-based language instruction, and materials translation could come from the extra tuition and fees international students already pay for intensive ESL instruction, international advisement, and tuition. Additionally, offering multilingual programming would likely result in increased enrollments and, therefore, increased revenue for the enterprising institution.

APPLICABILITY TO OTHER INSTITUTIONS

As mentioned earlier, the multilingual programming described here could be implemented at almost any U.S. college or university. As such programming becomes more accepted, universities could consider specializing according to language or discipline. For example, universities could specialize in providing bilingual instruction in a variety of disciplines to one language group (e.g., Michigan State in Arabic, the University of Miami in Spanish, etc.). For multilingual areas, the departments at a university could each specialize in one language group (e.g., civil engineering in Arabic, electrical engineering in Mandarin, education in Spanish, etc.).

Conversely, if offering entire course work in another language proves impractical in the beginning, universities should still make classes taught in English more accessible to international and immigrant students and somewhat linguistically richer for English speakers. For example, professors can teach primarily in English using sheltered techniques, but also provide translated versions of their lecture notes, textbook supplements, PowerPoint presentations, exams, and bilingual teaching assistants as instructional aides for the benefit of international and immigrant students in the class.

In this situation (i.e., an academic course taught using sheltered English techniques with bi- or multilingual materials and support), the content-based language course would be taught by an ESL instructor instead of a foreign language instructor to provide additional support for international and immigrant students in understanding the academic instruction in English. Institutions that serve international students likely already have well-trained ESL teachers who would enjoy the opportunity to teach content-based ESL. For example, if international and immigrant students are enrolled in a biology course taught in English (with sheltered and multilingual support), they would be concurrently enrolled in a biology-related ESL course offered by the institution's ESL program.

Whether an institution opts for major programming in other languages, for only a single course, or simply for multilingual support for sheltered English-medium courses, bringing international students' native languages into higher education classrooms benefits everyone, potentially increases enrollments, and demonstrates a true commitment to viewing such students—and their languages—as a resource.

Community Colleges Open Doors for International Students, Too

Mary Ellen Duncan

RATIONALE

What is the test of an inviting environment for international students, post 9/11? For community colleges, the challenges of creating this environment are different than those for other institutions—sometimes easier, sometimes more difficult. The community college environment tends to be very welcoming, especially for the freshman student. Classes are generally small; the faculty know their students well. On the other hand, community colleges without student housing have to find safe ways to house students and transport them to the college. Members of some communities might feel unsure about hosting foreign students. Urban community colleges generally have a very diverse student population, so people from other countries do not necessarily stand out within the student body. Rural colleges are not likely to have diversity in the student body, but the colleges are smaller, more close-knit, and friendlier.

The test of an environment that is inviting to international students and faculty and that is a win-win situation for the college and the visitors includes several important factors: community involvement and support; faculty leadership, creativity, and fervor for internationalizing the curriculum; an office of international education that serves as a home base for international students; student services personnel who capitalize on the knowledge and motivation of the international student; and board and administrative policy that encourages and supports the exchange of faculty and students from a variety of countries throughout the world.

DESCRIPTION OF THE INSTITUTION AND THE STUDENTS

Howard Community College (HCC), Columbia, Maryland, is located between Baltimore and Washington, DC. Founded in 1971, HCC now serves over 8,000 credit students and fifteen thousand noncredit students. HCC serves over one thousand students from over 150 countries around the world. As a comprehensive community college, HCC has large programs in allied health, business, English, math, science, social sciences, technology, visual and performing arts, and world languages. Most students plan to transfer to one of the more than fifty colleges that have articulation agreements with HCC.

PROGRAM DESCRIPTION

HCC is committed to creating a welcoming environment for international students by developing a culture among faculty, staff, and students. Because of that culture, programs are borne to support various activities: faculty exchange, student exchange, recruiting, specialized English language immersion, and much more. It all begins with community support.

Community Support

Community colleges have the advantage of knowing their communities and leveraging the support of community members to provide an extra measure of excellence. For instance, HCC initiated a Commission on the Future to involve the community in shaping the college's strategic direction. A community leadership group of fifteen persons, headed by one of them, recruited over thirty-five others to serve on task forces the group created around a series of topics of major importance to the college (e.g., technology, academic programs, workforce needs, etc.). The commission also introduced the topic of "preparing students as global citizens."

Most recently, the task force was composed of people representing different cultural groups in the community, including Korean Americans, Muslim Americans (from a number of countries), Latin Americans, and so on. These experts, plus a university professor whose service has been in multicultural education, noted that HCC students need to understand that learning about the world we live in is in everyone's best interest. And the opportunity to do this was created by the diversity in the student body and in the community, by encouraging and supporting student and staff global study and travel, by inviting international students to study English and a wide variety of curricular offerings, and by offering multiple world language instruction and internationalizing the curriculum.

One of the recommendations of the commission was to establish a multicultural center to provide a focal point for the various ethnic groups in the community, who now have their own groups but do not always mingle with other groups. Strengthening these community ties is a very effective recruitment tool for international students. A leader in the Korean American community and head of its county-wide organization was a member of the HCC Foundation Board, the fundraising arm of the college. This relationship built confidence in the college among the Korean American population, contributing to a large number of Korean students coming to HCC to study English at the college's English Language Institute (ELI). The community also runs a Chinese School at HCC on Sundays. This relationship also means important connections that facilitate numerous international visitors and exchanges.

Faculty Leadership and Creativity in the Curriculum

At one of my first meetings with the faculty as a new president, Professor Cheryl Berman asked whether or not HCC should have study abroad programs. That began the college's relationship with Universidad International in Cuernavaca, Mexico. Shortly after that, Professor Beckie Mihelcic, a faculty member in the business department, participated in the winter session in Mexico, learning Spanish along with students and participating in a home stay. When she returned, she made a presentation at a college-wide convocation, using the word *humilidad* (humility) on a big screen to summarize her experience. She told the college faculty and staff that it was difficult learning a new language in a foreign country. She said that the experience was "exhilarating, frustrating, comical, and very humbling." She had a new appreciation for the international students at HCC, making her an ideal director of international education.

Professor Mihelcic began the process of building an awareness of the importance and necessity of preparing students to be global citizens and welcoming visiting global students, and she exploited every possible avenue to give faculty international experiences themselves. The faculty are encouraged to participate in Community Colleges for International Development (CCID) study trips to various countries. Twenty-nine percent of the faculty have traveled outside of the United States, thanks for funds from HCC International Grants. Overall, however, 87 percent of the faculty have traveled outside the United States. But the college's goal is to have 100 percent of the faculty experience another culture. The college is in the process of raising funds to match a recent gift designated for faculty travel.

In addition, many interesting things are being done in the classroom by faculty, including linking the classes of native speakers with classes of non-native speakers, pairing world language learners with native speakers, and integrating credit and noncredit students in certain activities, such as a collaborative effort between the ELI and the culinary students in an International Chef Cook-off. International students regularly present to other classes and various learning communities on campus. They also frequently read their works at poetry readings. The noncredit ESL and credit ELI students participate in a "Dine Around" with native speakers, practicing conversation at inexpensive restaurants.

Service learning presents another opportunity for international students, credit and noncredit, to practice communicating and, at the same time, do volunteer work at a local nonprofit. These experiences also give community members the chance to develop friendships with visiting international students. International students regularly participate in the college's "alternate spring break," organized by the director of service learning, Carol Parreco. Carol has taken students to Louisiana and Mississippi to help restore housing and most recently to Franklin, West Virginia to work with Almost Heaven, a local chapter of Habitat for Humanity.

OFFICE OF INTERNATIONAL EDUCATION

At some point in the college's development, a full-time office becomes necessary to manage a multitude of activities surrounding international education. The Office of International Education at HCC connects with about 150 credit and 150 noncredit F-1 visa students. Communication begins when they receive a welcome message from this office before they arrive. The college's website features a link to international education on its front page, making it easy for incoming students to find the services they need and for HCC students to view opportunities for travel and study abroad. This office also manages the exchange programs with Turkey, Denmark, and Mexico. They have coordinated the activities of visiting faculty from Turkey, Macedonia, Mexico, Indonesia, Ghana, and China, among others. Logistics includes everything from detailed paperwork to such mundane activities as making sure that visitors have groceries on the first day of their arrival.

This office also provides orientation and introductions for international students and faculty so that they feel welcome at HCC. Christele Cain, directing the office of International Education has also traveled to the countries with which HCC has formal exchange agreements, developing strong working relationships. This office plans the International Week activities, held annually in November. Many activities occur, including a "study abroad" fair and opportunities to taste food from various countries, speak to international students, listen to prominent speakers, and enjoy cultural events. Professor Jean Svacina, who is associate division chair in the English and world language department, said that "international students are the curriculum" in so many classes, providing one of the best sources of connecting with the rest of the world. Dr. Svacina thinks that HCC's work with international students is one of the best things the college does.

Student Services

The office of student life at HCC conducts elections for the student government association. Recently, the students elected two international students as the president and vice president of the Student Government Association (SGA). The president, Alex Nowodazkij, a German citizen originally from Russia, became very much involved in college life. He told me once that he was on campus during spring break and found himself picking up papers left on the floor. He said that he knew then that this was his college. Alex was very active on the "augmented leadership team" and became very familiar with the details of strategic plan, performance indicators, and political environment of the college. He was a good representative of student interests and was welcome to bring up student issues with the vice president of student services at monthly meetings or anytime in between—and he did.

Two state-elected officials were prompted to ask more about international students at the college when they were greeted by German and Syrian SGA officers at HCC's annual meeting for elected officials, but it gave the college an opportunity to review all its global activities and why they were important to the community. A Lebanese student, Ritta Zeilah, was also a recent SGA president.

Llatetra Brown, director of student life, also manages a host of student clubs, the number of which varies from year to year but has consistently included an international student club. When the president's team meets with them annually, those students are very complimentary about the college, surprised that they have an audience with the college administrators, feel very fortunate to have an opportunity for an education at HCC, and brag about their relationships with faculty and staff. Other clubs include Russian, Persian, African, Muslim, and Jewish.

A recent African Cultural Festival sponsored by the African student club included a speaker who was president of an African nation and a trivia game to name African countries and languages. Director Brown also makes sure that students are invited to participate in "Open Mike" night where they can perform or read poetry, mingle with other students, and practice speaking English. And she notes that international students never pass up the opportunity to travel to New York City on a student day trip.

The office of student life, in cooperation with the diversity committee, invited international speakers, featured international movies, and developed an international peace pole, which was inscribed in many languages. The

Burrill Galleria at the college features flags from all the countries represented by the student body—over one hundred countries—and these flags are also used as part of the graduation ceremony, which is Webcast to families of grads located around the world. At HCC, students can learn about someone else's culture by talking to the students sitting next to them in class or by joining the international club.

EVALUATION

Welcoming international education and international students has long been a way of life at HCC. In 1999, the college's board of trustees formally endorsed the American Association of Community Colleges (AACC) policy statement on international education and adopted it as board policy in 2000. The college opened a ten-thousand-square-foot building with modern laboratories and classrooms where English and world languages are taught and the international education office resides.

The college has been recognized for its accomplishments in global education. The Commission of the Future has complimented the college for translating its suggestion into actual programs and services. Several donors, including faculty, support scholarships for international travel for students and faculty. The college and donors also support faculty travel. The Association of International Educators (NAFSA) awarded HCC the "Senator Paul Simon Award for Internationalizing the Campus, 2005." The American Council on International/Intercultural Exchange recognized HCC in 2005 with the International Intercultural Achievement Award. Additionally, the state of Maryland recognized HCC's ESL program for outstanding student achievement in 2003. And while the 2008 U.S. Senate State Quality Award in Maryland does not focus on the international student or international education per se, this award does speak to the overall quality of education provided for all students at HCC.

APPLICABILITY TO OTHER INSTITUTIONS

Providing an inviting atmosphere for international students serves as a reminder about how all students want to feel at college. Experience in other countries helps faculty, staff, and board members internalize the importance of a welcoming environment. As in most things, the big picture is important, but attention to detail is also critical to avoid the mishaps that can occur without careful planning, strong relationships with international partners, and limited objectives for each project so that initial success is assured.

When the "stars" are aligned—experienced community leaders set high expectations; the board of trustees supports a responsive, community-oriented college and acknowledges the need for global competencies; the administration and faculty work collaboratively and are enthusiastic about new ways to teach and deliver programs to students—great things happen.

REFERENCES

Ahmad, U. K. (1997). Research article introductions in Malay: Rhetoric in an emerging research community. In A. Duszak (Ed.), *Culture and styles of academic discourse* (pp. 273–303). Berlin: Mouton de Gruyter.

Auerbach, E. (1995). The politics of the ESL classroom: Issues in power and pedagogical choices. In J. W. Tollefson (Ed.), *Power and inequality in language education* (pp. 9–33). Cambridge: Cambridge University Press.

Baker, C., & Jones, S. (1998). *Encyclopedia of bilingualism and bilingual education.* Clevedon, UK: Multilingual Matters.

Berkenkotter, C., & Huckin, T. N. (1995). *Genre knowledge in disciplinary communication.* Philadelphia: Erlbaum.

Bloch, J., & Chi, L. (1995). A comparison of the use of citations in Chinese and English academic discourse. In D. Belcher & G. Braine (Eds.), *Academic writing in a second language: Essays on research and pedagogy.* Norwood, NJ: Ablex.

Bloom, D., & Sommo, C. (2005). *Building learning communities: Early results from the Opening Doors demonstration at Kingsborough Community College.* New York: MDRC Report.

Braine, G. (2001). When professors don't cooperate: A critical perspective on EAP research. *English for Specific Purposes, 20,* 293–303.

Brandl, K. (2005). Are you ready to "MOODLE"? *Language Learning & Technology, 9*(2), 16–23. Retrieved July 6, 2007, from http://llt.msu.edu/vol6num3/brandl/

Bruffee, K. A. (1993). Collaboration, conversation, and reacculturation. In K. A. Bruffee (Ed.), *Collaborative learning: Higher education, interdependence, and the authority of knowledge* (pp. 15–27). Baltimore, MD: Johns Hopkins University Press.

———. (1995). Sharing our toys: Cooperative learning versus collaborative learning. *Change, 27*(1), 12–18.

Cargill, M. (1996). An integrated bridging program for international postgraduate students. *Higher Education Research & Development, 15,* 177–188.

Chun, D. M., & Plass, J. L. (2000). Networked multimedia environments for second language acquisition. In M. Warshauer & R. Kern (Eds.), *Network-based language teaching: Concepts and practice* (pp. 151–170). New York: Cambridge University Press.

Cmerjokava, S., & Danes, F. (1997). Academic writing and cultural identity: The case of Czech academic writing. In A. Duszak (Ed.), *Culture and styles of academic discourses* (pp. 41–63). Berlin: Mouton de Gruyter.

Conrad, S. (1996). Academic discourse in two disciplines: Professional writing and student development in biology and history (Doctoral dissertation, Northern Arizona University, 1996). *Dissertation Abstracts International, 57*(04), 1593 (AAT 9625751).

Culp, L.-A. (1999). Academic English is no one's first language: A multidisciplinary approach to teaching writing (Doctoral dissertation, University of Arizona, 1999). *Dissertation Abstracts International, 60*(04A), 1113 (AAT 9927467).

Doughty, C. (2000). Negotiating the L2 linguistic environment. *University of Hawai'i Working Papers in ESL, 18*, 47–83.

Echevarria, J., & Graves, A. (1998). *Sheltered content instruction: Teaching English language learners with diverse abilities.* Boston: Allyn & Bacon.

Edwards, H., Wesche, M., Krashen, S., Clement, R., & Kruidenier, B. (1984). Second language acquisition through subject matter learning: A study of sheltered psychology classes at University of Ottawa. *The Canadian Modern Language Review, 41*, 261–281.

Ferris, D. (1998). Students' views of academic aural/oral skills: A comparative needs analysis. *TESOL Quarterly, 32*, 289–318.

Ferris, D., & Tagg, T. (1996). Academic listening/speaking tasks for ESL students: Problems, suggestions, and implications. *TESOL Quarterly, 30*, 297–320.

Fishman, J. (1991). *Reversing language shift.* Clevedon, UK: Multilingual Matters.

Flaitz, J. (2003). *Understanding your international students: An educational, cultural, and linguistic guide.* Ann Arbor: University of Michigan Press.

Friedenberg, J. (1995). *The vocational and language development of limited English proficient adults.* Columbus, OH: Center on Education and Training for Employment.

———. (2002). The linguistic inaccessibility of U.S. higher education and the inherent inequity of U.S. IEPs: An argument for multilingual higher education. *Bilingual Research Journal, 26*(2), 309–326.

Furstenberg, G. (1997). Teaching with technology: What is at stake? *ADFL Bulletin, 28*(3), 21–25.

Gabelnick, F., MacGregor, J., Matthews, R., & Smith, B. (Eds.). (1990). Learning communities: Creating connections among students, faculty, and disciplines. *New Directions for Teaching and Learning, 41.*

Godwin-Jones, B. (2003). Tools for distance education: Towards convergence and integration. *Language Learning & Technology, 7*(3), 18–22. Retrieved July 6, 2007, from http://llt.msu.edu/vol7num3/emerging/

Gonglewski, M., & DuBravac, S. (2006). Multiliteracy: Second language literacy in the multimedia environment. In L. Ducate & N. Arnold (Eds.), *Calling on CALL: From theory and research to new directions in foreign language teaching* (pp. 43–68). San Marcos, TX: CALICO.

Gonzalez-Lloret, M. (2003). Designing task-based CALL to promote interaction: En busca de esmeraldas. *Language Learning & Technology, 7*(1), 86–104. Retrieved July 6, 2007, from http://llt.msu.edu/vol7num1/gonzalez/

Gosden, H. (1992). Research writing and NNSs: From the editors. *Journal of Second Language Writing, 1*(2), 123–139.

Grace, S. (1995). *Entering a North American graduate school community: The beginning of the experience for one nonnative speaker of English.* Unpublished manuscript.

Huntington, S. P. (1993). The clash of civilizations. *Foreign Affairs, 72*(3), 22–49.

Hyland, K. (1996). Writing without conviction? Hedging in science research articles. *Applied Linguistics, 17*(4), 433–454.

————. (1998). Boosting, hedging, and the negotiating of academic knowledge. *Text, 18*(3), 349–382.

Hyland, K., & Tse, P. (2007). Is there an "academic vocabulary"? *TESOL Quarterly, 41*, 235–253.

Imus, A., Ployhart, R., Ritzer, D., & Sleigh, M. (2004). Technology: A boom or a bust? An undertaking of students' perceptions of technology use in the classroom. *Inventio: Creative thinking about language and teaching, 6*(1). Retrieved July 6, 2007, from http://www.doit.gmu.edu/inventio/issue_past.html

Jacoby, S., & Gonzales, P. (1991). The constitution of expert-novice in scientific discourse. *Issues in Applied Linguistics, 2*, 150–181.

Jenkins, J. (2001). *The phonology of English as an international language.* Oxford: Oxford University Press.

Jensen, C. (2005). Claim strength and argument structure in international research articles: A case study using Chinese, Ukrainian, and U.S. chemistry texts. (Doctoral dissertation, University of Kansas, 2006). *Dissertation Abstracts International, 66*(12) (AAT 3203256).

Johns, A. (2004). Linguistic diversity and instructional practices. In A. Johns & M. Sipp (Eds.), *Diversity in college classrooms: Practices for today's campuses* (pp. 133–151). Ann Arbor: University of Michigan Press.

Kavenoki, G., & Osteen, J. (2007). *Moodle satisfaction.* Unpublished manuscript.

Kirkpatrick, A. (2007). *World Englishes: Implications for international communication and English language teaching.* Cambridge: Cambridge University Press.

Kuhn, T. S. (1962). *The structure of scientific revolutions.* Chicago: University of Chicago Press.

Lee, S. (2000). Contrastive rhetorical study on Korean and English research paper introductions. *Pan-Pacific Association of Applied Linguistics, 4*(2), 316–336.

Miao, D. (2003, March 24). Personal communication.

————. (2005, March 28). Personal communication.

Monterey Institute of International Studies. (2007). *President's welcome message.* Retrieved July 15, 2007, from http://www.miis.edu/president.html?catid=143

Najjar, H. Y. (1990). *Arabic as a research language: The case of the agricultural sciences.* Unpublished doctoral dissertation, University of Michigan, Ann Arbor.

Namsaraev, V. (1997). Hedging in Russian scientific writing within the field of sociology. In R. Markkanen & H. Schroder (Eds.), *Hedging and discourse* (pp. 64–82). Berlin: Walter de Gruyter.

Nattinger, J. R., & DeCarrico, J. S. (1992). *Lexical phrases and language teaching.* Oxford: Oxford University Press.

O'Keefe, A., McCarthy, M., & Carter, R. (2007). *From corpus to classroom: Language use and language teaching.* Cambridge: Cambridge University Press.

Ortega, L. (1999). Rethinking foreign language education: Political dimensions of the profession. In K. Davis (Ed.), *Foreign language teaching and language minority education* (pp. 21–39). Honolulu: University of Hawai'i Press.

Ortiz, I. (2004). Preface. In A. Johns & M. Sipp (Eds.), *Diversity in college classrooms: practices for today's campuses* (pp. vii–xii). Ann Arbor: University of Michigan Press.

Phillipson, R. (2005, September). *English, a cuckoo in the European higher education nest of languages?* Paper presented at the Bi- and Multilingual Higher Education Conference, Helsinki, Finland.

Powers, E. (2007). Foreign graduate applications up again. *Inside Higher Ed.* Retrieved July 17, 2007, from http://www.insidehighered.com/layout/set/print/news/2007/04/16/grad

Pritchard, C. (2005). Aiming to increase NNSs' participation in discussions with NSs'. [Electronic version]. *TESOL IEPIS Newsletter, 25*(2). Retrieved November 1, 2007, from http://www.tesol.org/s_tesol/sec_issue.asp?nid=3063&iid=4047&sid=1

Ricento, T. K., & Hornberger, N. H. (1996). Unpeeling the onion: Language planning and policy and the ELT professional. *TESOL Quarterly, 30*(3), 401–428.

Ronald, K. (1988). On the outside looking in: Students' analyses of professional discourse communities. *Rhetoric Review, 7*, 130–149.

Rybak-Akimova, E. (2005, March 9). Personal communication.

Salager-Meyer, F., Angelas, M., Ariza, A., & Zambrano, N. (2003). The scimitar, the dagger, and the glove: Intercultural differences in the rhetoric or criticism in Spanish, French, and English medical discourse (1930–1995). *English for Specific Purposes, 22*, 223–247.

Schneider, M., & Friedenberg, J. (2001). Sheltering suicide: A collaborative approach to sheltering complex content for native and nonnative English speakers in a university setting. In J. Crandall & D. Kaufman (Eds.), *Case studies in content-based instruction* (pp. 155–168). Alexandria, VA: TESOL.

Song, B. (2006). Content-based ESL instruction: Long-term effects and outcomes. *English for Specific Purposes, 25*, 420–437.

Swales, J. (1990). *Genre analysis: English in academic and research settings.* New York: Cambridge University Press.

Swales, J., & Feak, C. (2004). *Academic writing for graduate students: Essential tasks and skills* (2nd ed.). Ann Arbor: University of Michigan Press.

Tikoo, M. (1996). English in Asian bilingual education: From hatred to harmony. *Journal of Multilingual and Multicultural Development, 17*, 2–4.

Tinto, V. (1987). *Leaving college: Rethinking the causes and cures of student attrition.* Chicago: University of Chicago Press.

———. (1997). Classrooms as communities: Exploring the educational character of student persistence. *Journal of Higher Education, 68*(6), 599–623.

Tinto, V., Goodsell Love, A., & Russo, P. (1993). Building community. *Liberal Education, 79*(4), 16–21.

Trice, A. (2001, November). Faculty perceptions of graduate international students: The benefits and challenges. Paper presented at the meeting of the Association for the Study of Higher Education, Richmond, VA (ERIC Document Reproduction Service No. ED457816).

Tudor, I. (2005). *The challenges of the Bologna process for higher education language teaching in Europe.* Retrieved December 17, 2007, from http://userpage.fuberlin.de/~enlu/downloads/Bologna_ENLU_OK.rtf

University of Helsinki (2005). *Bi- and multilingual universities: Challenges and future prospects.* Retrieved December 17, 20007, from http://www.palmenia.helsinki.fi/congress/bilingual2005/

University of Maastricht (2006). *Integrating content and language in higher education.* Retrieved December 17, 2007, from http://www.unimaas.nl/iclhe/

Vassileva, I. (2001). Commitment and detachment in English and Bulgarian academic writing. *English for Specific Purposes, 20*, 83–102.

Ventola, E. (1997). Modalization: Probability—An exploration into its role in academic writing. In A. Duszak (Ed.), *Culture and styles of academic discourse* (pp. 157–179). Berlin: Mouton de Gruyter.

Wiley, T., & Lukes, M. (1996). English-only and standard English ideologies in the U.S. *TESOL Quarterly, 30* (3), 511–536.

Wray, A. (2005). Idiomaticity in an L2: Linguistic processing as a predictor of success. In B. Bevin (Ed.), *IATEFL 2005 Cardiff Conference Selections* (pp. 53–60). Canterbury, UK: IATEFL.

Yakhontova, T. (1998). *Selling or telling? Towards the issue of cultural variation in research genres.* Manuscript submitted for publication.

——. (2001). Textbooks, contexts, and learners. *English for Specific Purposes, 20,* 397–415.

Yeh, H., & Yang, S. (2003, April). Listen to their voices: Expectations and experiences of Asian graduate students. Paper presented at the meeting of the American Educational Research Association, Chicago, IL (ERIC Document Reproduction Service No. ED479385).

7

Social Support

As noted in chapter 2, many of the issues that affect domestic students entering college also impact international students. However, the effects are almost always amplified for international students. The need for social support is an excellent case in point. Universities across the United States recognize that part of their educational purpose is to create a college environment that encourages positive student growth both academically and socially (Evans, Forney, & Guido-DiBrito, 1998). As early as 1937, the American Council on Education declared in its landmark, "Student Personnel Point of View," the need for the higher education community to "guide the whole person" to reach his or her full potential in society (American Council on Education, 1994, p. 67).

Universities devote considerable time and resources to providing services and activities that meet students' social needs. Nevertheless, providing social support for international students is a challenge since they come from diverse backgrounds, have few (if any) personal contacts when they arrive, and experience cultural and linguistic barriers. These factors make it difficult for international students to develop relationships. Without assistance, they can become socially isolated from their peers and the surrounding campus. Contributors to this chapter present programming ideas designed to help international students build strong social ties on their new campuses and in the surrounding community.

Students reaching out to other students is a common theme in the first two contributions. Millie Audas describes the University of Oklahoma Cousins program, designed to nurture friendships between international and domestic students. While the impetus behind the program is to help international students feel welcomed and involved in campus life and in local culture, the experience has proved to be enriching for both domestic and international students. The Ambassador Program, directed by Anjali Pai Hallett at the University of Utah, similarly helps new international students transition into university life by pairing them with currently enrolled students. Each newly arriving international student is greeted by a student with whom he or she has been in e-mail contact for nearly two months prior to arrival. This program eases transitional issues for new students by helping them establish friendships and assisting with practical issues such as finding housing, enrolling in classes, and adjusting to the community.

Not only do international students need to adapt to a new campus and academic culture, but they must also become part of a community. Udo Fluck from the University of Montana describes how the Missoula International Friendship Program has taken the initiative to help international students feel welcome in the community. When international students arrive at the airport, they are welcomed, and throughout their first year, helped by community members.

The chapter concludes with a description of two programs at the University of Florida. Aleksandra Nesic first describes programming provided for almost invisible international sojourners—students' spouses. Although many international students bring their spouses with them to the United States, little is done to help these individuals transition to their new environment. Aleksandra raises awareness of issues that students' spouses face and offers solutions that can be easily adapted to other universities. Finally, Chun-Chung Choi and Debra Anderson describe the Global Coffee House, an idea that originated with international students who expressed the need for a place to meet and socialize with domestic students. The authors suggest that such a program can be low-budget and low-maintenance but highly effective in connecting culturally diverse students.

One has only to go as far as a bulletin board in the student center of any campus in the country to see how central social functions and services are in the lives of college students. The possibilities seem endless to students who are aware of them, but the potential for social support and inclusion is nonexistent to international students who are unaware of available opportunities. Formal programming ideas are contributed in this chapter to increase international students' awareness of available social supports and services.

OU Cousins Program

Millie Audas

RATIONALE

When a departing international student told University of Oklahoma (OU) President David Boren and his wife that his only regrets were that he lacked friendships with American students and that he never saw an Oklahoma ranch, the idea of OU Cousins was born.

The mission of the OU Cousins program is to promote and nurture friendships between international and American students. Such friendships deeply enrich the college experience of both groups of students. They not only help international students adjust to new surroundings, but add an international element to the OU experience for American students. The ultimate goal of the program is to help international and domestic students recognize their commonalities and enjoy a wider perspective of the world.

President Boren considers OU Cousins to be "one of the most important new initiatives to be undertaken on this campus in recent years." He notes, "This program makes a major contribution to the University by greatly enhancing the educational experience that all our students receive by having more interchange between American and international students" (Boren, 2008).

DESCRIPTION OF THE INSTITUTION AND STUDENTS

The University of Oklahoma is a doctoral degree-granting research university in Norman, Oklahoma, serving the educational, cultural, economic,

183

and health care needs of the state, region, and nation. OU has 29,931 students, including 1,526 international students from almost one hundred countries. China and India are the most represented, with two hundred and 140 students respectively. OU boasts of 174 signed, reciprocal exchange agreements and programs that reach sixty-six different countries. Approximately seven hundred American and international students participate each year in reciprocal study-abroad exchange opportunities.

PROGRAM DESCRIPTION

The University of Oklahoma has a full range of programs designed to enrich the international student experience. These include an international leadership class and the International Circle of Friends—a forum for international women to discuss the cultural issues they face as students in the United States. However, the focus of this best practice description is the extremely successful OU Cousins program.

OU Cousins is a model for campuses that want to promote the socialization of international students. Approximately eight hundred students—two Americans to every international student—participate in each year. In addition to the Norman campus, the OU Health Sciences Center in Oklahoma City and the Schusterman Center at the OU campus in Tulsa have active Cousins programs.

Each year, the program recruits American and international students through e-mail, campus newspaper advertisements, presentations at international student orientation, and online through Facebook. Word of mouth and strong support of campus organizations like fraternities and sororities are powerful recruitment tools.

Students register for OU Cousins on their website (oucousins.ou.edu), where they complete a questionnaire that facilitates good matches between students based on common majors, languages spoken, living arrangements, and hobbies, or on mutual interests. This provides the program with the ability to match students with a "cousin" most similar to them. No cross-gender matches occur because they may not be considered appropriate in some cultures. Students can also join the program at any point during the academic year and a match will be made at that time.

A matching party and an ice cream social kick off the year's activities, which are completely funded by the university. Other activities include:

- Homecoming parade (Cousins march in the parade with international flags)
- International Bazaar (Food, handicrafts, and other cultural items are sold here as a fundraiser for international student organizations)

- Traditional Thanksgiving meal (Organized for international students by the OU Center for Student Life)
- Campus holiday lighting event (American winter traditions, such as holiday carols and tree and menorah lighting)
- OU basketball games (Certain OU games with free tickets for international students and their OU cousins)
- Eve of Nations (University-wide event with performances by most of OU's twenty-seven international cultural organizations)
- President's Associates Dinner (Features national and international speakers)
- End-of-year traditional Western Party and Barbecue (Event at a local ranch with live country music and square dance lessons)

In addition to these events, which are all optional, students are encouraged to meet as friends outside of the program to study, shop, and socialize.

The program is led by the Cousins Advisory Board, which consists of twelve to fifteen international and American students, who have all been previous program participants. The board plans and executes all Cousins activities, provides oversight for potential program revisions, and organizes the student matching program. The involvement of the advisory board has dramatically strengthened the program.

Staff support, including a program director and a student assistant, is funded by the university. The staff oversee the viability and success of matches. If a match is not working well, the staff quickly communicate with both parties and create new matches if necessary.

EVALUATION

The University of Oklahoma conducts an annual evaluation to continually improve the program. The evaluation includes a learning outcome survey, which measures satisfaction with the matching process, events, and Cousins friendships. The survey also asks all participants about their willingness to renew their involvement in the program. Table 7.1 lists results from the first annual advisory board survey. Responses are shown in order of most learned to least learned. These results are typical of subsequent advisory board surveys.

In addition to the survey, participants are sent an e-mail asking for further feedback. Members of the advisory board also participate in a final focus group session to evaluate the year's events. Through this process, the board compiles a collection of success stories, including firsthand accounts of visits to the American Cousins' homes for the holidays, shopping excursions, and trips to see the sights of Oklahoma. These stories

Table 7.1.   Results from the First Annual Advisory Board Survey

Question	Average Score
Rate these items in terms of your OU Cousins experience	1 (least learned) to 5 (most learned)
Ability to communicate with diverse people	4.83
Desire to enhance/create "community" at OU	4.67
Knowledge/appreciation of other cultures	4.50
Clarified view of the world	4.33
Better awareness of my own culture	4.33
Creating meaningful personal relationships	4.33
Appreciating diversity	4.33
Eliminating stereotypes	4.33
Ability to share/articulate personal belief	4.17
Leadership development	4.17
Event planning/participation	4.00
University programs/policies	3.33
Knowledge/use of another language	3.17
Awareness of global policies/social situations	3.17

illustrate in the students' own words the breadth and depth of their friendships.

As director of OU's Education Abroad and International Student Services, I have witnessed these student success stories unfold year after year. The same skills that are obtained studying abroad can be gained on the university campus when relationships between international and American students are formed. In fact, members of OU Cousins exhibit tolerance and celebration of differences; the ability to put themselves in another person's position; and respect for each other's cultures, values, and beliefs. Through this opportunity, participants view other countries and peoples with compassion, respect, and care. The hope for a more secure and peaceful world is recognized through the experience of OU Cousins.

The following testimonies were collected as part of the program's e-mail invitation to share experiences related to the Cousins program. One was written by Kenah Nyanat of Malaysia, who made OU history as the first international student to become president of the University of Oklahoma Student Association, and the other was written by Lauren A. Ballinger, an American student who has been an active OU Cousin.

From Kenah Nyanat:

My first OU Cousins match was with Dan, who was from a small town in Oklahoma and had never lived abroad. Hence, I really enjoyed sharing the many experiences abroad I had from growing up in the many different countries and cultures, and even my journey to the United States. As an international student, being able to share my journey with an American is truly monumental in connecting with new friends and developing deeper relationships, as we yearned to share.

We cooked dishes from our home countries, played American games, attended American sporting games like football and basketball, American musicals and dance performances, and cultural nights hosted by International Organizations. Our cultural sharing resulted in Dan choosing to study abroad in Sweden for one year. When Dan returned, I was able to learn of his interesting life experience abroad[,] resulting in an understanding of each other and our cultures that still continues to enrich our friendship.

The second year, I was paired with Ben from Amarillo, Texas. I had the opportunity to visit his hometown and my first Texas State Fair, where I also watched my first rodeo. I really enjoyed getting to know an American family and it was a unique opportunity to share my cultural values with Ben and his family.

Through this program, I have not only experienced the American culture and learned from our exchanges, but I have gained lifelong friendships that I will treasure as I graduate and move forward in life.

From Lauren A. Ballinger:

Last year, my OU Cousin Marie-Anne was from Nice, France. I was very glad to meet her, especially as I am a French major and planned on studying abroad. We hung out together on the weekends making crêpes with other French exchange students, or going to dance parties when there were no Cousins events.

With a few trips to Wal-Mart in a car full of French exchange students, I was able to practice speaking and listening to the French language for several hours at a time. She taught me how to make French variations on pasta dishes, and I taught her the Texas two-step. At the end-of-the-year OU Cousins Barbeque at a ranch, I showed Marie-Anne the Southwestern traditions that I was used to growing up.

Because of Marie-Anne and the other French students I met last year, I already have friends waiting for me when I study abroad in France next semester. I even have an offer for someone to pick me up at the airport when I arrive. OU Cousins is a wonderful program, and I wouldn't have met Marie-Anne or any of my wonderful French friends without it.

APPLICABILITY TO OTHER INSTITUTIONS

The success of OU Cousins is apparent. The program's accomplishments should not be limited to the University of Oklahoma. In fact, the university regularly communicates with peer institutions interested in establishing similar programs. Both Oklahoma State University and the University of Kansas have followed OU's lead. The Oklahoma State University group, modeled directly after the OU program, was named "Cowboy Cousins" in honor of the OSU mascot. It currently serves hundreds of international and domestic students on the various OSU campuses. The University of Kansas "Global Partners" program was reorganized several years ago into its current form, patterned after the OU program. Both the OSU and KU programs are engineered specifically to enrich both the international and domestic student populations through mutual experience and cultural understanding. With modifications applied to local contexts, OU Cousins could be an important part of many campus internationalization efforts.

The University of Oklahoma strongly believes in developing a sense of community, and nowhere is that sense more powerful than when the university builds bridges that promote international understanding. The success of the OU Cousins program has been strongly influenced by the philosophical and financial support of the university administration. With a strong campus focus on internationalization and with successive classes of students willing to learn about the world beyond their hometowns, the future remains bright for OU Cousins.

University of Utah's Ambassador Program

Anjali Pai Hallett

RATIONALE

Those who have traveled alone outside of their country know how frightening it can be when their language is useless and the most basic tasks seem foreign. Being unable to communicate well and not knowing where to turn for help is common for international students new to the United States. These students require support as they confront unfamiliar situations.

To alleviate the stress that often occurs in these situations and to further develop a sense of belonging to the campus community, programs that go beyond new student orientation should be developed. Their purpose should be to support international students' academic, cultural, and social adjustment.

For these reasons, the Ambassador Program was developed at the University of Utah. The program's goal is to provide a team of well-trained role models to assist new international students. Ambassadors provide consistent cultural, social, and academic support prior to international students' arrival and during their transition into university life.

DESCRIPTION OF THE INSTITUTION AND STUDENTS

The University of Utah, often referred to as the "U," is the flagship institution in the State of Utah with an enrollment of approximately 28,500 students. The university strives to help students "excel . . . . preserve academic freedom, promote diversity and equal opportunity, and respect individual beliefs" (Mission Statement, 2006). It also promotes "rigorous interdisciplinary inquiry, international involvement, and social responsibility" (Mission Statement, 2006). With approximately 1,800 international students and five hundred visiting scholars, including their dependents, the international student and scholar population is a significant portion of the student body.

The U's International Center assists international students with immigration and sponsors cross-cultural initiatives, such as the Ambassador Program, to provide students with a global perspective. Contact with peers from diverse backgrounds and cultures fosters understanding and promotes a sense of community. In this way, the program supports the institution's mission and offers a positive intercultural experience for students.

PROGRAM DESCRIPTION

Each year, the U admits nearly 550 international students from over 110 countries. When these students enter the United States and a new campus culture, they have already been in contact with current students, known as ambassadors, who are assigned as peer mentors to provide friendship and an instant network of support. Ambassadors are international students who have been on campus at least one semester or are returning study abroad students wishing to stay connected to a previous international experience. These highly dedicated student volunteers come from all academic departments with two features in common: they have prior international experience and a strong desire to help new international students.

The Ambassador Program is managed by the International Center's associate director and a program coordinator. The coordinator assigns each ambassador eight to ten international students whom they must contact via e-mail prior to the students' arrival. Most ambassadors have e-mail exchanges with their partners for several months before the students arrive on campus. In this early correspondence, ambassadors explain that they will meet their students face-to-face at an international student orientation. After the ambassadors and new international students have already exchanged ideas and developed a friendship through e-mail, this first meeting is a wonderful thing.

RECRUITMENT AND TRAINING

Ambassadors are primarily recruited by means of the International Center's website (www.sa.utah.edu/inter/iss/ambassador), the international student electronic mailing list, and the Study Abroad Office. The program is thriving; consequently, many ambassadors are recruited by word of mouth. Additionally, the coordinator attends predeparture orientations for study abroad programs and describes the Ambassador Program to participants as a way to keep their international experience alive and ease their transition back to the United States. Recruitment also occurs at study abroad fairs, on the website, and through the electronic mailing list for study abroad students.

Ambassadors are required to attend a training session, after recruitment and prior to interacting with their assigned international students. The training is conducted by International Center staff and consists of a cross-cultural exercise adapted from *Understanding Cultural Viewpoints*, a Peace Corps training exercise. The training encourages the ambassadors to reflect on their values and perceptions to develop a deeper understanding of other cultural perspectives. It includes a primer on intercultural communication and an overview of the challenging visa process faced by many international students.

Finally, ambassadors are given eight topics to discuss at new student orientation, where they interact with their students for one and a half hours. The topics include how to obtain a student ID card, register for classes, buy textbooks, get around Salt Lake City and use public transportation, open a bank account, obtain a cell phone, and locate off-campus venues for entertainment and relaxation. Ambassadors are given additional information on how to stay involved with their students throughout the year.

PROGRAMMING

The first meeting between the ambassadors and international students occurs at orientation several days before the fall semester begins. This orientation is structured so that university administrators address issues such as immigration, safety, and health insurance. Ambassadors then discuss the eight key topics mentioned earlier and take students on a campus tour. An information fair, where students can gather materials about campus organizations, academic support, and campus activities follows. The orientation ends with a lunch, allowing the ambassadors and students to socialize and further develop their friendships.

In addition to international student orientation, the International Center offers cross-cultural programs that allow ambassadors and international students to interact. Each Friday, the International Student Council hosts an International Café for the international community on campus. This program aims to build community within the university (each week the activity is sponsored by a different college department) and offers a cross-cultural experience for students, faculty, and staff. The International Center also sponsors monthly activities (such as hikes, movies, and shopping excursions) and encourages ambassadors to attend and invite their international students. Many international students find this to be a meaningful way to develop their friendships and practice speaking English.

International students can be seen with their ambassadors and other peers at a variety of university activities; some are informal gatherings while others are planned with the specific purpose of helping the students adjust to their new surroundings. Below is a list of programs offered to international students and ambassadors:

- The International Center's Language Exchange program allows domestic students to practice their second language and also teach English to nonnative English speakers. Many ambassadors join this program.
- The Union Programming Council and the International Student Council organize an annual campus-wide International Night. Both international students and ambassadors plan and participate in the event.
- The International Center and various academic departments organize International Week, which includes panel discussions with international students.
- The "Go Global" floor in the residence halls develops a cross-cultural program each month that includes activities for new students and Ambassadors.
- The Cross Culture Club takes students on monthly trips to Utah sites and invites international students and their ambassadors.
- The International Student Council uses the student electronic mailing list to send students a weekly events guide that outlines events on campus and in Salt Lake City (e.g., football games, art and cultural events).

EVALUATION

Data collected at international student orientation over a five-year period demonstrates that over 95 percent of students strongly agreed with the statement, "My ambassador was helpful and familiarized me with the campus." The following testimonials, from two international students who became ambassadors after participating in the program, indicate the benefits of the program. Mohammed is from Pakistan and his ambassador was from the Netherlands. Prem is from India; his ambassador was from the United States.

From Mohammed, master's student in mathematics:

For numerous international students[,] traveling abroad is the first experience. It is a sudden transition from one culture to another let alone housing, academic issues. Barb, a Modern Dance Master's Student, was my ambassador. She made this transition not only smooth but also enjoyable. Even before I arrived at the U.S., she e-mailed me about the potential problems [that] I might face. She also helped me [with] renting an apartment, finding a roommate, buying and carrying necessary stuff require[d] in the beginning.

Barb invited me to her birthday party and it was a remarkable event. There were almost fifty international students with different majors, which provided a truly international experience. That, too, before the orientation day. Since then I am volunteering myself to be an ambassador for every orientation.

From Prem, master's student in mechanical engineering:

The initial day I stepped in the U (i.e., the day of the orientation), I was shaking with fear of the unexpected and also feeling totally at sea . . . . I knew not what to do and how to go about the wide range of possibilities and problems which engulfed me . . . . Problems like my registration for classes, getting around the massive campus, getting a phone to speak with, opening an account to deposit my money and so on . . . . I was rescued by a humble soul, my ambassador.

He took me to the different places via foot and showed me the various important places. He showed me how to register for the courses and the places to get my initial paperwork done at the U. He made me aware of the various events that happen [around] the U and [. . .] Salt Lake. I was totally overwhelmed by the help and support I received. I found he had managed to calm my nerves down. Thanks to the International Center for the brilliant idea of having something like an ambassador program.

APPLICABILITY TO OTHER INSTITUTIONS

The U's Ambassador Program is an adaptable and useful approach to assisting new international students. It is easily implemented primarily because it operates on a small budget and can be largely administered by students, who perform many duties of a program coordinator. Ambassadors who are international students themselves serve as volunteers without incentives since they have a strong desire to help others as they were helped. The Ambassador Program and similar programs develop a community of support and friendship for new international students and create lasting cross-cultural experiences for participants.

Social Support for International Students Through a Community Friendship Program

Udo Fluck

RATIONALE

Every year, approximately 170 new international students arrive in Missoula to attend The University of Montana (UM). The duration of their stay ranges from a single semester to four years, with a majority visiting a foreign country for the first time. For many, their experience at UM is their first extended absence from family, friends, and a known support system. Like international students at other universities, these students face uncertainties in almost every aspect of their lives. Over twenty years ago, community members recognized this and established the Missoula International Friendship Program (MIFP), which assists incoming international students with their cultural transition.

According to the official charge of the organization, "The mission of the Missoula International Friendship Program is to promote global awareness, understanding, friendship, and intercultural learning between international students and scholars at The University of Montana and the greater Missoula community" (MIFP Mission, 2008). MIFP assists international students in their transition and in benefitting from their time in the United States. It provides opportunities for social and cultural interaction among Missoula community members, international students, and international scholars by sponsoring activities and gatherings throughout the year.

DESCRIPTION OF THE INSTITUTION AND STUDENTS

The University of Montana is a public institution located in Missoula, a town of more than seventy-three thousand. The university is ranked seventeenth in the nation and is fifth among public universities in producing Rhodes Scholars. UM alumni are the sixth largest group of Peace Corps volunteers. On average, the university has a total enrollment of fourteen thousand, which includes about two thousand graduate students and 550 international students from sixty to seventy countries. The campus community also includes sixteen international student associations and nationality clubs (Undergraduate Admissions, 2008).

UM offers a highly developed support system through the Office of Foreign Student and Scholar Services. This office "assumes responsibility for the general welfare of foreign students at UM from admission to graduation and practical training" (FSSS Greetings, 2008). It works closely with UM's International Student Association and a variety of campus administrative centers and services. Support for international students is typical on many U.S. campuses, but UM's organized involvement (since 1988) with the Missoula community through MIFP is unique. MIFP is described next with a particular focus on the Community Friendship Program (CFP).

PROGRAM DESCRIPTION

Community hospitality groups for international students exist in many cities across the country, but MIFP's twenty years of activity is noteworthy. It began in 1986 when four individuals discussed the idea of forming an interest group for foreign student activities and services in the Missoula community. Between 1986 and 1988, this informal group of four grew to ten members. In 1988, the group became a structured organization with officers selected from outside the university.

One of MIFP's great assets is the board of directors, which is responsible for planning and, to a large degree, executing the annual program. The officers include an elected president, a treasurer, a recording secretary, and a corresponding secretary. The current board consists of eight executive officers and two ex-officio members from the Office of Foreign Student and Scholar Services. The board has ninety-minute monthly meetings during the academic year to discuss and organize upcoming events and finalize the details of specific activities. In May or June of each year, the board has a retreat to set the calendar for the coming year. The organization has become more aggressive in fundraising and publicity. Funds raised now support the majority of organizational expenses, although volunteers continue to absorb the bulk of the expenses for social events.

Providing a support system for international students begins when they step off the airplane at the Missoula International Airport. MIFP representatives greet students and hand them a welcome bag minutes after they have landed. The bag contains a welcome message, eating utensils and plates, fresh fruit, a granola bar, and fruit juice. Air travel is the primary way for international students to arrive in Missoula, with the majority of international flights arriving after 10:00 p.m. Being able to enjoy these snacks when campus facilities are closed is a pleasant and memorable introduction to the campus and community.

At least one MIFP-sponsored activity is offered every month. The program traditionally hosts a welcome dinner at the beginning of each semester. Fall semester events include an ice cream social in September. A highlight is a reception hosted by the UM president, typically in October. International Week in November features an evening lecture and discussion that focuses on culture, global awareness, or similar topics, and is available to students, faculty, staff, and the Missoula community. Fall semester closes with a holiday party in December.

Spring semester provides a similar airport welcome for new international students and a dinner in January. A potluck and Valentine's Day bake sale are among the highlights in February. Every March, MIFP sponsors and participates in the planning and execution of the International Culture and Food Festival at UM, one of the largest international events in Montana. The end of the semester is customarily celebrated with the End-of-Year Barbeque, hosted by MIFP volunteers at the International House, which is close to campus.

While yearly programming is meaningful and well received, one of the most effective ways that MIFP facilitates community–student interaction occurs after students have been on campus a few weeks. MIFP sponsors a community friendship program (CFP) in which a year-long match is arranged between international students and a member of the Missoula community. Over the program's history, matches have doubled from thirty in 1988 to over sixty in 2008. CFP promotes the idea that cultural out-of-classroom experiences accelerate the adaptation process and reduce potential culture shock. Thus, CFP promotes personal balance and academic success for international students at both the undergraduate and graduate levels.

After a match is made by the board, both the community member and the international student receive a letter of introduction based on information that each of them submitted to MIFP. Once the letters are received, the community friend, as the official host, makes the first telephone call. During the school year, the extent of the friendship depends on the time limitations and interests of the community member and the student. Home stays are not part of the program, but the community friend may extend an invitation for an occasional overnight stay.

When the year ends, friendships often continue informally. MIFP encourages participants to maintain friendships, but new community friends are recruited each year as some choose to be inactive for a year or two or relocate. Some members like to host a student from a different country for the next year, or wish to become involved in MIFP in another capacity. However, community friends must be matched with an international student to remain part of the program.

EVALUATION

To determine if MIFP is effective in meeting its goals, a written survey of twenty-eight community friends was conducted in April 2008 (Crafts, Tateyama, & Yoshikawa, 2008). Findings indicated that 35.7 percent of the community friends met with their matches between six to eight times during the year. The survey also indicated that 64.3 percent were very satisfied with MIFP activities, 21.4 percent were satisfied, 10.7 percent were neither satisfied nor dissatisfied, 3.6 percent did not know, and none were dissatisfied. The survey also examined the relationship between the community friends and their matches and discovered that 89.3 percent of the community friends were satisfied. Only 10.7 percent stated that there was either a lack of compatibility with their international match or inactive communication, often caused by the international student being too busy. With English and non-English speakers being matched, language barriers could potentially occur frequently, but 85.7 percent of respondents stated that there were no language hurdles between them and their students.

The survey also inquired about favorite activities that community friends and their matches engaged in. The International Culture and Food Festival was preferred because of the high rate of interaction between students and their community friends. Other activities included, but were not limited to, going to the movies, participating in holiday and outdoor activities, attending sporting events, and shopping. As a result of the diverse activities, 64.3 percent of community friends were so pleased that they stated they would continue in the CFP and apply for an international friend the next year.

International students were also invited to provide feedback about the program by participating in an online survey. Findings supported the success of MIFP, showing that "67.8% of international students were connected with a community friend through MIFP, and 93% of them were satisfied with the experience" (Flaherty, 2008, p. 4).

The results of both surveys and testimonials by program participants have allowed the MIFP board to polish individual aspects of the cultural adaptation activities. A twenty-year learning curve has been a significant advantage in bringing the program to the level of quality it enjoys today.

APPLICABILITY TO OTHER INSTITUTIONS

The success of the MIFP is primarily based on the open-mindedness, generosity, and support of the Missoula community. The structure of the organization can easily be replicated in other communities among institutions of higher learning. The success of the entire program rests with committed members interested in volunteering to organize and facilitate activities that foster cultural understanding.

Expenses are minimal for the basic setup. The nonprofit status of the organization allows for donations from and fundraising among local businesses. Thus, funds can be generated to ease program costs such as renting vehicles for educational sightseeing trips to national monuments, national parks, and museums. In any volunteer organization, the commitment of the people is the biggest asset—this is definitely true with MIFP.

The MIFP provides a unique, interactive, and important aspect to the cultural adaptation process for international students and scholars while attending The University of Montana. CFP offer an important, informal experience that helps students adapt to unfamiliar U.S., local, and academic cultures. The opportunity for learning and growth is beneficial for community members as well. They have a window to the world through their interaction with foreign students.

Social Connections for International Students and Spouses

Aleksandra Nesic, Chun-Chung Choi, Debra Anderson

RATIONALE

Due to financial and cultural benefits of hosting international students, university personnel make strong recruitment efforts to attract them. However, once these students come to the United States, they are confronted with a number of adjustment issues such as finding suitable health care and establishing relationships with new friends, roommates, and academic personnel. Even locating places to eat or shop can be difficult. If not properly addressed, these issues can negatively affect the student's level of satisfaction, attitude toward host nationals, and even academic performance (Heikinheimo & Shute, 1986). Simply put, inadequate social adjustment can significantly diminish an international student's chances of success in the United States.

Furthermore, an important fact that gets overlooked when considering social support issues is that many international students do not take their educational journeys alone. On average, nearly 10 percent of international students in the United States are married, 85 percent of their spouses reside in the United States (Bhandari & Chow, 2007), and many bring their children. Despite international spouses' physical presence in the United States and their significant contribution to the U.S. economy, they are virtually invisible on university campuses and in surrounding communities. Universities typically do not provide information specifically geared for nonstudent spouses. A compelling argument can be made that an international student's success is directly related to how well his or her family adjusts to the new environment.

U.S. higher education institutions that recruit and educate international students must not ignore the social and cultural immersion needs of these students and their families. In response to the sociocultural needs of its substantial international student population, the University of Florida's International Center has developed programming specifically focused on international student spouses and has established a Global Coffee House to help students transition into campus life.

DESCRIPTION OF THE INSTITUTION AND STUDENTS

The University of Florida is a public, land- and sea-grant research university located in Gainesville, Florida. It is the oldest and largest university in the state of Florida, one of the five largest universities in the country, with one of the largest international student populations. With more than fifty thousand students, the university hosts approximately four thousand (421 undergraduate and 3,554 graduate) international students from over 130 countries.

International student affairs at the University of Florida are predominantly managed through the International Center (UFIC), which consists of four units: International Student Services (ISS), Study Abroad Services, Faculty/Scholar Services, and Program Development. International student-related services, such as petitioning for and maintaining visa status, are managed through ISS. Outreach programs that attend to the needs of international students and their spouses are created by the Program Development office staff. The following includes the descriptions of two such programs.

DESCRIPTION OF THE STUDENT SPOUSE PROGRAM

Recognizing the presence of international students and their spouses on campus and in the community, the UFIC staff created programs to make the campus and community more welcoming. Based on conversations they had with spouses of international students and their own creative ideas, the staff provided suggestions for spouse-support programs and services.

Predeparture and Arrival Packet for International Spouses

UFIC sends each matriculated international student a copy of the *International Student Handbook*, which includes information for dependents (the handbook is also available on the center's website). Even though it is useful, the information is often not communicated to the spouse. To address this issue, UFIC staff should mail a predeparture International Spouse Handbook directly to the spouses (or refer them to the link on the website), familiarizing them with the new environment and university services as well as helping them feel recognized and included.

Welcome Orientation for the International Spouses

As UFIC staff interacted with student spouses, many spouses indicated the importance of having an orientation to welcome the families of international students. The UFIC arranged an orientation acting on these suggestions in which spouses were able to meet each other and feel a sense of community. The orientation was organized with the help of spouses who had been in the community for a while. The orientation was successful in several ways. The experienced spouses felt useful as they helped their newly arrived counterparts feel more at ease with the new adjustments. The new spouses were able to associate with others who had experienced similar situations, and were able to establish a support network.

Required E-Mail and International Spouse Electronic Mailing List

International students and their spouses suggested that one of the best ways to disseminate information and reach all students is through an electronic mailing list. UFIC responded by creating an independent mailing list using a free online Yahoo! group and sending e-mail alerts to the spouses about various campus and community events and activities. Through the electronic mailing list, spouses were able to contact and share information. It was well received among those who joined. After the staff initiated it, maintenance was assigned to one of the spouses, who maintained the contact list and additional electronic mailing list functions.

International and Community Spouse Support Group

The UFIC improved its effectiveness in meeting the needs of the spouses by appointing one of its staff members to be an official adviser and contact for the spouses. Over time, this spouse support group has become more self-sustained, since those who organized it have gained confidence in providing leadership and structure. Many spouses have felt great satisfaction and responsibility in being part of the organizational structure. They have worked diligently to expand the group and reach out to other spouses. The group has had a positive impact on new spouses by welcoming them and providing them with information and a place to belong.

Additional Suggestions for Community Involvement

One of the best aspects of the program is the connection of spouses with the community. The Rotary Connections program, initiated by the Rotary Club and the spouses, provides each member of the Rotary Club the opportunity to interact with one or more international students and their spouses. In doing so, both club members and international students and their spouses learn about each other's cultures. Spouses who join the program are thrilled to be included. This innovative program is recognized by the National Association of Student Personnel Administrators (NASPA) as one of the best practices in international student programming.

EVALUATION

While no formal evaluations have been conducted, feedback provided by the spouses during the events and in meetings has suggested that the needs of students' spouses are real and need attention. Their feedback confirms the notion that without some kind of programming, international spouses do not receive enough support from the university, and as a result are marginalized, even isolated. The spouses indicated that this isolation is even more intense when they do not speak English; or, even if they do, they have few opportunities to communicate with others. Many international spouses have very little interaction with local community members or students on campus.

However, what has been encouraging is that the programming implemented by the UFIC has met many of the needs of the spouses. Spouses are often content, being provided the opportunity to connect with each other and meet Americans through the Rotary Connections program. Community members who participate in this outreach program also express a great deal of excitement to be able to share their culture and learn about other cultures in the process. Formal evaluation is needed, however, to address the programs' effects on spouses' initial adjustment and transition, as well as the effects on the academic achievement of the husband or wife who is in school.

APPLICABILITY TO OTHER INSTITUTIONS

This support initiative could be implemented at institutions that host any number of international students. The key to success is having a person associated with the institution—with UF it was a staff member from the International Center—to serve as a contact for the spouses. This adds stability to the relationships between the spouses and the university, and provides access to needed resources. This staff member should be knowledgeable about social and cultural adjustment issues and about the needs of international students' spouses.

The UF programs help to fulfill the need to integrate international spouses on campus and in the community, but the commitment to maintaining the support network should be a permanent part of any international center. Sustainability of a program is a challenge that must be considered in initial planning stages. The UF program proved a success among international spouses and was recognized at NAFSA and NASPA conferences where attendees expressed interest in implementing similar programs on their campuses.

DESCRIPTION OF THE GLOBAL COFFEE HOUSE PROGRAM

After considerable discourse with international students, the staff at the UFIC felt that international students needed assistance with their social adjustment to campus life. One of the most consistent ideas expressed by international students was the need for a gathering place where they could interact in an informal social environment. As Furnham and Bochner (1982) note, international students need to build relationships with both conationals and host nationals. In response to this need, the UFIC staff created, with support from a Title VI grant, the first University of Florida International Coffee House. The aim was to maximize cross-cultural learning by integrating U.S. students with international students.

The first of three coffee house sessions was scheduled on a trial basis. The grant covered costs for the coffee, tea, and cookies, which cost $200 for each session. Staff from UFIC reserved a lounge at no cost in the student union. The room was large enough for students to mingle but had the feel of a living room, and seating was appropriate for cozy conversations.

International students and American students who had studied abroad were e-mailed an invitation to the International Coffee House. To ensure a smooth start, the UFIC staff also attended. The first coffee house attracted only about forty students, but was deemed a success based on participant response. Students immediately gravitated to each other, introduced themselves, and even remained after the designated closing hour. Operating hours were from 7:00 to 8:30 p.m., but at 9:00 p.m., the staff had to start escorting students out of the room.

The students were excited for and appreciated the opportunity to leave their labs, study halls, and the library and come to a central location for a break and to meet new people. Each subsequent coffee house that semester saw an increase in attendance. Several student groups contacted the staff at

UFIC with suggestions for possible activities that could take place in the coffee house. One idea, a discussion group centered on a specific topic, was taken under consideration and later implemented.

Feedback from international students during the first semester was so positive that staff decided to support a coffee house every week. Two challenges arose, however. First, American students did not participate in significant numbers, and second, international students enjoyed the interaction with each other in the relaxed social atmosphere so much that incorporating a formal time for a discussion topic was difficult. Response to the first issue was to change the name from International Coffee House to Global Coffee House, creating a more inclusive atmosphere. Many domestic students thought it was a coffee house for internationals only.

To address the second concern, staff and faculty from other departments were invited to participate, sponsor, and provide alternative activities. Rather than having discussions about specific topics, which could be controlled and formal, departments developed activities to test each person's knowledge of other countries and global issues, providing small gifts. This created the opportunity not only for students to interact, but for faculty and staff to participate. It also resolved the funding issues since the Title VI grant that covered the costs of the original three coffee house sessions had expired. The participating departments provided funding for food and drinks.

Coffee houses were off to a good start. During spring and fall semesters the average attendance was seventy-five to 150 students. Because of this initial success, UFIC hired personnel to oversee the program after the first trial semester. However, university-wide budget cuts made it impossible for UFIC staff to continue this. Even supporting departments were unable to provide the level of support needed for the coffee house program to continue. Despite its early success, the coffee house program seemed doomed. However, one unit on campus interested in international student issues, the Counseling Center (CC), became an advocate by supporting two gatherings a semester with staff and funding. In addition, the program director of the student union agreed to incorporate the coffee houses into a preexisting, highly successful student activity, Gator Nights. Gator Nights is a late-night program offering free first-run movies, entertainment, and cultural events for University of Florida students and their guests. The director of Gator Nights not only agreed to make the coffee houses part of its lineup of Friday night activities but to provide financial support and secure a location in the student union.

The coffee houses are regaining momentum after the setbacks from budget cuts, and evolving to meet student and institutional needs. They are now located in a restaurant in the student union, and various student groups associated with the Volunteer International Student Association

(VISA) come each Friday to share their cultures and plan activities. They bring printed material, posters, artifacts, and music from their countries, and several groups have even taught their traditional dances.

EVALUATION

To get a sense of the impact of coffee houses, international graduate students who had attended at least one coffee house during the first two years of operation were recruited for a focus group. Participants were asked to respond to the following questions:

- Describe your experiences attending the Global Coffee House.
- What (if anything) would you change about the event?
- Why do you attend the Global Coffee House?
- How often do you attend the Global Coffee House?

Responses were analyzed for themes with the aim of improving future coffee houses. First, participants were appreciative of the program. They reported feeling lonely and isolated and saw this event as a main social venue: "This is where I got to see them [friends] every week. I'm so thankful the university is doing this." Most participants indicated that they initiated friendships with people from all over the world through this event: "We go to the restaurant (or movie) together after this. It became something I look forward to every Friday." Participants also reported that they wished there were more American students attending the event routinely: "I wish there are more American students here. It's been hard to make friends with Americans." Another participant said, "I wish they could come routinely and not as an assignment or a one-time club activity." Some participants reported that they disliked the restaurant tables because they hindered individuals from chatting with others. "I like to stand and talk. It's easier for me to get to know people. I can't break into a group when people are sitting around a table." As for food, most focus group participants seemed to agree that they would not mind if there was no food. Coffee and tea with pleasant conversation were sufficient.

While data were collected from a limited number of participants and their input was subjective, their ideas have provided a baseline from which modifications can be made. For instance, we have a sense that these gatherings follow the Three Social Network Model (Furnham & Bochner, 1982) of building relationships with conationals and host nationals. We have also learned that effort and planning are needed to facilitate the bonding of international and American students. Encouraging interested

American students to participate benefits both domestic and international students. Finally, creating activities for the coffee house is not as desirable as creating a comfortable environment that allows easy social interaction. Again, these insights are preliminary and will require more thorough evaluation, but response to the global coffee houses is positive.

APPLICABILITY TO OTHER INSTITUTIONS

The Global Coffee House program requires few human or financial resources. Funding and resources could be generated from service units (e.g., the international center, the counseling center, or the Dean of Students' office); academic units that host large numbers of international students (e.g., colleges of business or engineering); religious organizations; or business entities (e.g., restaurants, car dealers, fast food restaurants). Global coffee houses have applicability to most institutions regardless of the number of international students hosted. The need for social support is not limited by size.

REFERENCES

American Council on Education. (1994). The student personnel point of view. In A. L. Rentz (Ed.), *Student affairs: A profession's heritage* (American College Personnel Association Media Publication No. 40, 2nd ed., pp. 108–123). Lanham, MD: University Press of America (Original work published 1937).

Bhandari, R., & Chow, P. (2007). *Open doors: Report on international educational exchange*. New York: Institute of International Education.

Boren, D. L. (2008, January). Personal communication.

Crafts, T., McCann, C., Tateyama, E., & Yoshikawa, Y. (2008). *Community members' opinions regarding MIFP*. Unpublished survey, University of Montana, Missoula.

Evans, N. J., Forney, D. S., & Guido-DiBrito, F. (1998). *Student development in college: Theory, research, and practice*. San Francisco: Jossey-Bass.

Flaherty, B. (2008). *Foreign student survey and assessment*. Unpublished survey, University of Montana, Missoula.

FSSS Greetings. (2008). University of Montana, Office of Foreign Student & Scholar Services. Retrieved June 19, 2008, from http://life.umt.edu/fsss

Furnham, A., & Bochner, S. (1982). Social difficulty in a foreign culture: An empirical analysis of culture shock. In S. Bochner (Ed.), *Cultures in contact: Studies in cross-cultural interaction* (pp. 161–198). Oxford: Pergamon.

Heikinheimo, P. S., & Shute, J. C. (1986). The adaptation of foreign students: Student views and institutional implications. *Journal of College Student Personnel, 27*(5), 399–406.

MIFP Mission Statement. (2008). University of Montana Missoula International Friendship Program. Retrieved June 19, 2008, from http://www.mifp.org

Mission Statement. (2006). University of Utah. Retrieved December 3, 2008, from http://www.admin.utah.edu/president/mission.html

UM by the Numbers. (2008). University of Montana Enrollment Services. Retrieved June 20, 2008, from http://admissions.umt.edu/numbers.html

Undergraduate Admissions. (2008). University of Montana, Enrollment Services. Retrieved June 20, 2008, from http://admissions.umt.edu/

8

Intercultural Adjustment
and Learning

Intercultural adjustment is a central challenge for international students in the United States. How institutions support students in this area helps determine the success of their transition to the new environment. Given the educational benefits of admitting international students in terms of intercultural learning (e.g., see NAFSA 2003, 2006), institutions must consider how to structure opportunities for varying cultural groups to form associations and experience diverse perspectives. Related to this, training must occur so that the individuals involved will be able to effectively manage and benefit from these interactions. For international sojourners, interaction with host country nationals supports the acquisition of needed language skills and the development of cultural knowledge and skills (Chapdelaine & Alexitch, 2004; Furnham & Bochner, 1986). Related to chapter 7 where we focused on social support programming, we next examine ways in which social support can be designed to promote intercultural learning. Additionally, we see how elements of social interaction and cultural learning are integrated with academic success.

In this chapter, we highlight exemplary programs from institutions that recognize the wisdom of supporting intercultural learning and have implemented successful programs for both graduate and undergraduate students to accomplish this goal. We begin the chapter with a contribution from Darla Deardorff, who argues that all students (not only international students) must develop intercultural competence. Based on findings from her research, she shares illustrative examples of programs that are designed to result in intercultural competence. We then turn to two program descriptions related to supporting international graduate student teaching assistants. The first, by Michael Smithee and Stacy Lane Tice, relates the success of a long-standing teaching fellows program at Syracuse University in which new international teaching assistants undergo a three-tiered training program involving cultural, pedagogical, and disciplinary components with the assistance of more seasoned teaching assistants. The second, by Lynne O'Connell, Michael Panichas, and Suzanne Barrett, describes the use of undergraduate guides to help international teaching assistants at Boston College adjust to the cultural, linguistic, and pedagogical components of teaching U.S. undergraduate students.

The remaining three contributions focus separately on extending intercultural learning into the residence halls and community, global leadership training, and support for a specific group of international students. Sheila Schulte explains how the Georgia Institute of Technology promotes intercultural learning through an on-campus living-learning program in the residence halls and through a program in which international students tutor elementary students in the community. Recognizing the need for formal training in global leadership, the University of Georgia offers a Global Leadership Institute in which U.S. and international students not only focus on acquiring knowledge about leadership, but also develop intercultural skills through their interactions with each other as explained by Leigh Poole. Finally, Melissa Rigas discusses adjustment challenges for Saudi students as they prepare to meet academic expectations in U.S. higher education. ELS Language Centers Teaneck has created a specialized language program and assessment measures to address the cultural and academic adjustment needs of the Saudi student population.

The program descriptions in this chapter present a sample of innovative approaches spanning pre-university, undergraduate, and graduate levels of study. They demonstrate how institutions are actively engaged in understanding the needs of international students and supporting intercultural adjustment not only to create a positive transition for international students, but to extend intercultural learning opportunities to other students, faculty and staff, and the community.

Connecting International and Domestic Students

Darla K. Deardorff

RATIONALE

International students on American college campuses are a greatly underutilized resource in the educational process. Given the small percentage of U.S. students who study overseas, it becomes crucial for institutions to maximize available curricular and cocurricular resources, from international students and scholars to international faculty to service learning opportunities in the community—something that has been referred to as "internationalization at home" (Nilsson, 2003). This integrated approach can help institutions develop comprehensive programming that goes beyond providing social experiences to creating intercultural learning opportunities for all students. Placing the programming within the context of comprehensive institutional internationalization efforts through an integrated "internationalization at home" approach can benefit both students and the institution.

Intercultural competence, broadly defined as "effective and appropriate communication and behavior in intercultural situations," consists of specific attitudes, knowledge, and skills that impact effectiveness and appropriateness (Deardorff, 2006). In my research study documenting consensus among leading intercultural experts on the specific elements of intercultural competence, some interesting findings emerged that impact programming. The importance of being able to understand and see the world from others' perspectives was the only element that all the experts agreed on. To that end, it becomes important for programs, when possible, to address multiple world views and comparative perspectives. Second, the

211

study demonstrated that, like the contact hypothesis theory (Allport, 1954), mere contact with those from other cultures is not sufficient; in fact, Putnam's (2007) Harvard study demonstrated that greater diversity of a community led to greater distrust. Thus, adequately preparing students—both international and domestic—for interactions with each other is crucial. Such preparation should extend beyond a requisite orientation to one that addresses key intercultural skills and knowledge.

A third finding of my study addressed the role of language in intercultural competence. There was no consensus among experts about language, with some stating that language alone does not make one interculturally competent. So, while language is often cited as a barrier to integration of international and domestic students, programs like intramural sports can address other aspects of intercultural competence beyond language.

A fourth finding was the importance of attitude (specifically openness, respect, and curiosity) to the acquisition of intercultural knowledge and skills. As Bok (2006) states, "Since undergraduates learn so much from one another, the presence of many young people from different countries could be a valuable resource in opening minds to other values, traditions, and perspectives" (p. 238). Programs that challenge students' assumptions can have an impact on changing students' attitudes toward those who are culturally different.

The overall intercultural competence model developed from this research can serve as a framework for developing programs that address specific learning goals related to intercultural competence development. Rather than presenting a specific institutional best practice, the following contribution explores how varying types of institutions can implement and evaluate such programming and provides illustrative examples.

DESCRIPTION OF THE INSTITUTION

Institutions of all types—from community colleges to large research universities—can benefit from connecting international and domestic students in meaningful ways. On larger campuses, specific ethnic student groups or clubs are often available, which, while providing invaluable support to those from that culture, can lead to obvious barriers to those students interacting with others. Even on smaller campuses, an international student club or housing situation can quickly lead to the "ghettoization" of international students. It is also important to work with first-generation ethnic students, an often-overlooked population. These are students who were born in the United States, but whose parents are originally from another country; such students can often be excellent resources since they are often more fully integrated into campus life than are international students.

In his book, *Our Underachieving Colleges*, Bok (2006) points out that few colleges have succeeded fully in integrating international students into campus life. Integration is certainly not a new topic and numerous articles and studies have been written about integrating international students (e.g., see Chen, 1999; Hanami, 2007; Heikenheimo & Shute, 1986; Trice, 2004; Yang, Teraoka, Eichenfield, & Audas, 1994). The literature suggests the importance of an institutional commitment to intentionally integrating students into the fabric of campus life—both in and out of the classroom—within the context of the institution's mission and implementation of a comprehensive internationalization plan. This institutional commitment is reflected at all levels, from administrator, faculty, and academic advisor efforts to staff support.

PROGRAM DESCRIPTION

There appears to be an increased interest in developing programs that bring domestic and international students together. Traditional programs have included conversation clubs, language partners, speakers' bureaus, and friendship programs. Recent innovative programs often partner international offices with other units on campus. For example, at North Carolina State University, the international office in conjunction with the Center for Student Leadership, Ethics, and Public Service developed the International Students and Scholars Engaged in Reaching Out and Volunteering (ISSERV) program (see www.ncsu.edu/oisss/programs/isserv.htm). Through this program, international students and scholars are encouraged to volunteer in the community on a regular basis and, in that way, interact with Americans more meaningfully. In addition, domestic and international students and scholars are encouraged to participate together in ISSERV service trips over the fall and spring breaks, and in the process of serving together, they often build lasting relationships.

Another example at the same university is the Departmental Ambassador program in which current students are designated and trained as ambassadors and then work with international students in their departments to help those students become more integrated into the formal and informal opportunities within the department (see www.ncsu.edu/oisss/resources/dptamb.htm).

Study abroad offices may partner with international offices in their speakers' bureau programs in which an American and an international student/scholar are sent out in pairs to give cultural presentations. In some cases, a school in the community may "adopt" these students and build a long-term relationship with them over the period of the school year, so that the interaction goes beyond a one-time presentation to include multiple presentations and even a joint project with local school children. At Duke University, students took the initiative to create a "house course" that is facilitated by students and brings together American and international students for cultural learning in the classroom, with some required community engagement assignments.

At the University of Wisconsin, Madison, the international office created the Building Relationships in Diverse Global Environments (BRIDGE) program (see iss.wisc.edu/bridge/). The BRIDGE program partners international students who are new to UW, Madison with currently enrolled American students to participate in one-on-one and group activities. Group activities include field trips around the state. According to Stromborn (2007), BRIDGE partners commit to meeting at least seven times during the semester and to recording their experiences and activities in a journal, which program administrators use to check student progress. Stromborn (2007) quotes May Lee Moua-Vue, the ISS adviser and BRIDGE program coordinator as saying, "'The goals of the BRIDGE program are to expose international students to U.S. culture and the UW, Madison community; to expose American students to the world and to the experiences of international students; and to play a part in internationalizing our campus.'" The structured, intentional nature of this program seeks to cultivate lasting relationships. The journal component allows for reflection in what is being learned and facilitates the development of intercultural competence over the course of the program.

Other possible programs to develop include those that address teamwork within diversity, leadership, and those that focus on substantive issues that benefit from multiple perspectives. In these programs, collaborating and developing partnerships are central to integrating domestic and international students/scholars on campus. There is a great need for programs to be developed that would do the following:

- Provide adequate preparation for domestic/international student interaction.
- Have specific learning goals for all participants.
- Encourage meaningful domestic/international interactions through relationship-building opportunities.
- Have an integrated approach to evaluating the program on an ongoing basis.

EVALUATION

In evaluating the success of programs designed to bring together American and international students and scholars to develop their intercultural competence and achieve greater integration of these populations on campus, it is important to use sound evaluation principles. The starting point is the mission and goals of the program, including participant learning goals. These goals then determine the tools and methods used in evaluation, which would ideally be an integrated, intentional, and ongoing part of the program. Often, when evaluation is done at all, satisfaction surveys are the most prevalent tool used. These surveys can be modified to yield necessary data needed to determine whether program goals are met. Other evaluation methods could include observation or focus groups. Regardless of the evaluation tools and methods, program administrators need to have a plan for using the data collected—for program improvement, participant feedback, advocacy, and communicating with key stakeholders. Administrators should collect only the data that will actually be used in a variety of ways.

APPLICABILITY TO OTHER INSTITUTIONS

Maximizing international student or scholar presence on U.S. campuses can be done successfully through intentional programming regardless of institutional size or type. There are challenges to overcome, including individual barriers (e.g., language, culture, time, motivation) as well as institutional ones. While it is difficult to address some of the individual barriers, institutions can hone their commitment to the integration of students on their campuses and the development of students' intercultural competence through top-level administrative support and by ensuring that the necessary infrastructure is in place to develop and implement such programs. Initiating and facilitating partnerships on campus as well as with the community can play a key role in the success of these programs. Intentionally integrating international scholars and students and domestic students will ultimately enhance student learning on our campuses and increase institutions' capacity to prepare global-ready graduates.

The Teaching Fellow Program of the Syracuse University Graduate School

Michael B. Smithee and Stacey Lane Tice

RATIONALE

In the late 1970s and early 1980s, international students who served as teaching assistants at Syracuse University and in universities nationwide were being severely criticized, primarily for their weak English language and communication skills. Public and private universities came under fire from state legislatures, parents, and students due to issues such as the quality of teaching, dependence on foreigners, and the learning outcomes of students.

In response to growing criticism of teaching assistants in general and international teaching assistants in particular, a variety of assessments and meetings were conducted at Syracuse University with faculty, current teaching assistants, and undergraduate students. Findings indicated that the teaching assistants exhibited a variety of language and speaking patterns, assumed classroom roles that were culturally different from their students, and lacked a well-rounded knowledge of pedagogy. As a result, academic departments, individual faculty, administrators, and the international office staff gained a sense of what improvements were needed in training teaching assistants.

Rather than attack the issue piecemeal, two key administrators established a steering committee to develop a model and a plan for implementation. The committee gathered data regarding practices from other institutions, attended a national conference on teaching assistants, and sought faculty input. The results led to the development of an approach accepted by all academic departments for a mandatory university-wide teaching assistant program. A major component of the program was the use of successful graduate students, to be known as *teaching fellows*, who were seasoned in the art of teaching to serve as mentors and role models for new teaching assistants.

Administrators realized that both financially and instructionally, utilization of experienced teaching assistants overseen by faculty teachers would be sufficient for the establishment of the program (Hiiemae, Lambert, & Hayes, 1991). Thus, the concept of teaching fellows as peer educators was introduced to meet the needs of the university community program.

DESCRIPTION OF THE INSTITUTION AND STUDENTS

Syracuse University was officially chartered in 1870 as a private, coeducational research institution offering bachelor's through doctoral degrees. It is located in Syracuse, New York, the geographic center of the state and approximately 250 miles northwest of New York City. Students represent fifty states and more than ninety foreign countries. The total enrollment is approximately nineteen thousand students, with 9 percent from foreign countries. Currently, of the nearly four thousand full-time and two thousand part-time graduate and law students, approximately 1,900 are international students, and of these, approximately 450 hold teaching assistantships. The enrollment of international students is largest in engineering and computer science, management, information studies, and public administration. Over 70 percent of the international students are from Asia, with the next highest geographic region being Europe, at 9.4 percent. English proficiency levels for both graduate and undergraduate international students have steadily increased over the past twenty years.

PROGRAM DESCRIPTION

The teaching assistant program seeks to improve excellence in undergraduate teaching as well as prepare both international and domestic teaching assistants and fellows for their future roles in academe. The program consists of three basic segments arranged in blocks: international (four days), generic pedagogical (five days), and academic discipline (three days). Teaching fellows are instrumental in the first two segments, while individual academic departments provide orientation to discipline-specific instructional approaches.

International Segment

The international segment assists new international teaching assistants with their transition to the United States and the university. The teaching fellows assist the adjustment and orientation of newly appointed international teaching assistants who have been living in the United States and are continuing their graduate work, or who are newly arrived. The former group may include students seasoned in the culture and rules of the United States, but who need more instruction in pedagogical skills and academic responsibilities, while the latter group would need more intensive mentoring on adjustments to the culture and the academic system, as well as training relating to pedagogical skills and the American academic environment.

Topics in the international segment of the training include immigration arrival verification and documentation collection, employment eligibility verification, purchasing health insurance, Social Security number applications, and payroll sign-up. In addition, campus tours and hospitality in the form of welcoming receptions and dinners, seminars, small-group discussions, and opportunities for one-on-one interaction among participants on subjects such as personal cultural awareness, culture shock, the structure of the American university, teaching duties, and the role of the teaching assistant are included.

Generic Pedagogical Segment

In this segment, the international teaching assistants join with the new domestic teaching assistants to focus on pedagogical issues, such as the improvement of teaching skills through micro-teaching and problem-solving exercises, and the delivery of key topics associated with the instructional process (i.e., effective lecturing, the first class, using media, and time management). Also, time is devoted to discussions of ethics, plagiarism, and cheating, as well as the characteristics of Syracuse University students, university rules, structure, and support programs.

Training goes beyond the international segment in exploring pedagogy. In the micro-teaching exercise, each teaching assistant is required to conduct a videotaped classroom presentation of five to seven minutes. The primary purpose of the exercise is to build confidence and begin an ongoing process of reflection about teaching. Only the teaching fellow and the teaching assistants view the videotape. During the workshops, time is spent preparing the fellows to provide constructive feedback to the new assistants. A document entitled *Using Video to Improve Instruction: Sample Criteria for Providing Feedback* (VanGulick & Lynch, 1996) was developed for this purpose.

For international teaching assistants, providing feedback is most critical. The categories include feedback about oral presentation skills, techniques to maintain interest, organization and preparation, attention to students, and use of media. In addition, small-group activities provide new domestic and international teaching assistants the opportunity to discuss issues related to pedagogy and success strategies for succeeding as scholars in their graduate studies and teachers in diverse classrooms. Typical American behaviors are identified for international students to help them develop coping strategies for classroom management.

The Academic Discipline Segment

Since this segment is organized and conducted by each academic department specifically for their teaching assistants, teaching fellows are not directly involved with this training (Syracuse University, 2008).

Preparation of Teaching Fellows

Preparation for the teaching fellows begins after their selection in March and culminates just prior to the arrival of new international teaching assistants in August. With regard to the issues of intercultural adjustment and learning, the preparation includes (a) an in-depth review of the international population in the United States and on the Syracuse campus; (b) issues of international student adjustment, such as culture shock, classroom behavior, approaches to academic life, and socializing; (c) likely difficulties international students (including international teaching assistants) may encounter during their first and subsequent semesters, such as the culturally laden approaches such students may use to resolve difficulties; and (d) legal limitations international students face (i.e., deadlines, employment, travel, course hour requirements, etc.). The fellows are trained to listen to comments and conversations with international teaching assistants and respond appropriately through comments or referral to the teaching assistant program staff, academic department, or Center for International Services regarding any issue raised.

The teaching fellows provide mentoring and guidance to the new international teaching assistants by their individual interactions in a variety of settings external to the training agenda. For example, in the international segment, teaching fellows are assigned to groups of five to seven assistants to provide them with individual and small-group attention on adjustment issues, as well as help in accomplishing the many tasks required prior to the beginning of the next segment. In the generic pedagogical segment, international and domestic teaching assistants are combined into groups of ten to twelve, led by a teaching fellow, to focus on the topics mentioned earlier.

EVALUATION

In the early years of the program, extensive evaluation that included feedback from participants, faculty mentors, administrators in academic departments, and undergraduate students indicated that the program was successful and should be continued (Diamond, 1989; Rogler & Gray, 1989). Evaluations have been conducted annually since 1987. These evaluations are both formative and summative. The teaching fellows were instrumental in obtaining feedback from participants through formative evaluation. Summative evaluations show that new international teaching assistants rate the performance of the fellows consistently high. For the past five years, the average mean of teaching fellow performance has been 4.8 on a 5-point scale (1 = not, 3 = somewhat, 5 = very) on the following variables: led small group effectively (4.7); communicated effectively (4.7); encouraged discussion (4.8); was receptive to alternate points of view (4.8); and provided helpful feedback (4.8). In all, the small-group sessions are among the highest rated component of the orientation program with microteaching having been the highest-rated session annually from 1987–2007 with a mean rating of 4.4 for being interesting and informative.

Nearly three hundred new teaching assistants regularly attend the orientation program, and the majority of comments about teaching fellows included on the participant evaluation form are positive. Several sample quotes follow. "Was really wonderful at engaging the group. Positive, enthusiastic, intelligent and open-minded. Open to students/teaching assistants and their thoughts." "Passion for teaching shone through, as did her remarkable sensitivity to the complexities of teaching in the kind of diverse university we are in. In three hundred fold I am extremely grateful to her for her efforts." "Was excellent! He was a great discussion leader, good at involving everyone, positive but also good with constructive criticism."

APPLICABILITY TO OTHER INSTITUTIONS

This program is eminently applicable to other institutions. However, we must mention that Syracuse University "has put its money where its mouth is" in developing an all-university program that meets the students' needs as well as those of academic departments. Because the program is required, there is no option to not participate. A major program element is the attention given to international teaching assistants. Thus, any institution that would like to implement such a program must be willing to invest in the future of their teaching fellows. The University of South Florida and Binghamton University modeled significant portions of their programs after Syracuse University. In the early years of teaching assistant program development (1975–1989), the University of Washington and University of California at Berkeley used experienced teaching assistants to help mentor junior colleagues.

The teaching fellow program meets several needs: training for the newly arriving international teaching assistant, well-trained and qualified teachers for the institution's undergraduate population, highly skilled teachers and researchers for the academic department, and experience and skill development for the fellows themselves, both domestic and international. The program is recommended as an example of excellence in providing for international student adjustment.

Undergraduate Guide Program for International Teaching Assistants in Chemistry at Boston College: A Description and Assessment

Lynne A. O'Connell, Michael A. Panichas, and Suzanne M. Barrett

RATIONALE

Many students begin working as teaching assistants as soon as they arrive in graduate school. In the physical sciences, this often means serving as laboratory instructors in the first semester. When these students are international and recent arrivals in the United States, they sometimes have problems with spoken English, especially with student slang. In addition, international teaching assistants (ITAs) are very likely to lack experience with undergraduate culture in the United States and may simply not know what to expect from American students in a lab setting (Tanner, Selfe, & Wiegand, 1993). While these problems tend to work themselves out over time as the ITA learns colloquial English and becomes more familiar with American culture, an entire semester can go by in which both the ITAs and their students are frustrated by communication difficulties (Damron, 2003; Gravios, 2005). Consequently, the undergraduate lab students may miss important classroom material. Some schools have discovered that undergraduates can play a valuable role in helping ITAs in such situations (Sarkisian & Maurer, 1998). This article describes the Undergraduate Guide program at Boston College, which recruits undergraduate students to help ease the transition for the ITAs into teaching, while benefiting student learning in the laboratory classroom.

DESCRIPTION OF THE INSTITUTION AND STUDENTS

Boston College (BC) is a Jesuit, Catholic university located in Chestnut Hill, Massachusetts, a suburb of Boston. BC has over fourteen thousand students, one-third of whom are graduate students. Approximately 10 percent of the graduate students are international. In fall 2004, seventeen of the thirty-nine new graduate students in the chemistry department were international, including thirteen from China, two from Korea, one from Japan, and one from India. Among the fifteen ITAs who participated in the Undergraduate Guide program, the average TOEFL score was about 10 percent above the required passing score of 550. Like most first-year graduate students, they would be supported as full-time teaching assistants and would serve as laboratory instructors, regardless of their fluency in English.

PROGRAM DESCRIPTION

While teaching is an excellent experience for the ITAs, the lab director knew that communication problems between ITAs and undergraduate students would arise. In the past, students in some lab sections had approached the director early in the semester asking to be transferred to a different section because they could not understand their instructor. (This is a common situation nationwide; e.g., see Gravios, 2005). The director had also learned from a focus group with ITAs in the previous year that they found Americans spoke very rapidly, pronounced words differently than the ITAs had been taught, and used unfamiliar expressions. Seventeen was an unusually large number of new ITAs for the department, raising the concern that communication problems would be more numerous and perhaps lead to more student requests to change sections or complaints from parents that their student's lab instructor did not speak proper English.

To improve the laboratory classroom experience for both the ITAs and their students, the directors of the chemistry labs and the campus learning center decided to implement the Undergraduate Guide program. For the duration of the fall semester, one undergraduate guide was paired with each ITA. The ITAs taught one lab period per week (usually three to four hours) while the guide attended the lab period for the first hour to help the ITA if communication with a student became problematic. Since the role of the guides was primarily to help with communication, not with course content, guides were instructed to make sure that students perceived the ITA as their teacher—with the guide acting as an assistant—and to refer student questions to the ITA as often as possible. Each guide also met with the ITA for an hour each week outside of lab to discuss what happened during the lab period and to answer the ITA's questions about English language, including slang expressions and American culture.

Since it was important that the undergraduate guides be excellent students who would understand the subject matter of the lab, only senior chemistry and biochemistry majors with good GPAs and personal recommendations were chosen. The guides were paid an hourly stipend through the learning center's tutoring budget (less than $200 per guide, which was the only program expense for the semester). They attended an orientation at the start of the semester to meet with their ITAs, participate in some ice breakers, and learn about the logistics of the program. Although they received a stipend, most guides seemed genuinely motivated by their interest in getting to know an international graduate student and in helping to improve laboratory instruction. Their commitment to the program resulted in no problems with follow-through on attendance, meetings, or other related duties.

EVALUATION

To assess how well the program had met its goals, we gathered feedback from the three groups involved: the undergraduate guides, the ITAs, and the students in the labs. The ITAs and guides completed written surveys and participated in separate focus groups in the middle of the fall semester. The lab students completed written surveys at the end of the fall semester.

Findings for Perceptions of the ITAs and Guides

The findings from the written surveys given to the ITAs and guides indicate that a large majority of both groups perceived the presence of the guides in the classroom as useful for both the students and the ITAs. However, the two groups differed in their perception of the kinds of questions that the guides would answer for the students. Most guides said they answered "many" questions about lab techniques, while most ITAs said the guides answered "some." Likewise, most guides said they answered "some" questions about chemical principles and theories, while most ITAs said the guides answered "few." Perhaps these differences arose because the ITAs were not always aware of the kinds or number of questions the students asked the guides.

The findings also indicate that a large majority of both ITAs and guides found the weekly meetings useful for the ITAs. However, the two groups again seemed to differ in their perception of what was discussed during the meetings. The majority of both groups agreed that they discussed events that occurred during the lab period. As for other topics, both groups responded about equally regarding how much of their discussion focused on English expressions and BC students; however, compared to the ITAs, the guides perceived that more of their discussion focused on American culture.

Compared to the findings from the written surveys, the focus group discussions yielded more detailed descriptions of what was actually happening in the labs and in the weekly meetings between ITAs and the guides. Both groups reported on the value of the guides' presence during the ten-minute introductory prelab talk given by the ITA at the start of the lab period. This talk is an important aspect of laboratory instruction for which the guides were able to give feedback to the ITA during the weekly meeting. Some guides mentioned giving specific advice, such as to face the students rather than the blackboard when speaking and to speak louder. One guide said she wrote down words and phrases during the lab period that the ITA did not seem to understand, and then explained the words later at their weekly meeting. The ITAs said they also welcomed the chance to discuss upcoming experiments with the guides.

Both groups reported some difficulty in finding topics to discuss during the weekly meetings. While the guides explained such things as the premedical program and various aspects of American culture, several said they would like to have more structured discussions, with suggested topics such as sports or politics. Many of the guides were in favor of at least occasional large group meetings with other guides and ITAs, mostly for social interaction.

Finally, both groups were very positive about their experience with the program. When asked if they still needed their guides for the rest of the fall semester, all ITAs said yes. The guides felt the program was valuable not only for the ITAs, but also for themselves as they were gaining insight into another culture and life perspective.

Findings for Perceptions of the Students

From the written surveys given to the students, the findings indicate that by the end of the fall semester, many of the students perceived an improvement in their ITA's language ability, along with their own ability to understand the ITA's lectures and answers to questions. While this result would be anticipated over time, with or without the presence of a guide, it is reassuring to note the students indeed recognized an improvement in the ITA's communication skills.

The findings also indicate that many of the students found the guides helpful in answering questions about lab techniques and chemical principles and theories, but less helpful with questions about course policies. While less than half the students showed a preference for directing questions to the guide rather than the ITA, a majority of students found the guides to be helpful with facilitating communication between themselves and the ITA. Although the Undergraduate Guide program was planned for only the fall semester of the lab course, a large majority of students indicated a preference for having the guides present in the classroom for the spring semester as well.

SUMMARY

Based on the findings from the written surveys and focus groups, we conclude that the Undergraduate Guide program does help to bridge the communication gap between ITAs and their students. Several significant findings were obtained from the assessment data:

- All three groups (ITAs, guides, and students) found the presence of the guides in the laboratory classroom to be useful.
- All three groups perceived that the guides are most helpful in answering students' questions about lab techniques and, to some extent, chemical principles. ITAs and guides differed in their perceptions of the types and number of questions the students asked the guides.
- ITAs and guides found that their meeting outside of the lab classroom was a useful component of the program. The guides were able to give the ITAs specific advice on classroom issues, such as the pre-lab lecture. While a variety of other topics were discussed, there is room for improvement, such as having more structure for these one-on-one discussions and including larger group meetings with the other ITAs and guides.

For a simple innovation that is inexpensive in terms of money and time, the Undergraduate Guide program has been effective in helping both ITAs and their students. The level of satisfaction among students with the guides was high. While a few students did complain to the lab director about lab report grades from specific ITAs, none of the students asked to be moved to a different lab section. With the assessment results pointing to the success of the program, the chemistry department has decided it will be worthwhile to recruit undergraduate guides in the future for the benefit of new ITAs and their students.

APPLICABILITY TO OTHER INSTITUTIONS

The Undergraduate Guide program was designed within the lab course structure to meet the needs of the ITAs and students. In this case, the lab classroom setting readily allowed one-on-one interaction between the guide and both the students and the ITA. Adapting the guide program to another type of classroom setting (or discipline) would require planning for these two kinds of personal interaction. For example, in a lecture classroom setting, it might be awkward for the guide to interject in front of a roomful of students. But if at some point in the class, students are broken into small groups, a guide could help by interacting with each group to clarify materials they did not understand in the ITA's lecture. However, the weekly meetings outside of class between the ITA and guide described here are adaptable to any college course. In a lecture setting, a guide could simply make observations and then discuss with the ITA issues that arose in class, such as language, presentation, and student reaction. In fact, in the focus group with the ITAs prior to implementing the program, it was the outside meeting with the guide that seemed to be the most important component of the program for the ITAs.

Understanding and Adjusting to the United States: Two Initiatives for International Students at Georgia Tech

Sheila K. Schulte

RATIONALE

The strategic plan for Georgia Tech calls on the university community to prepare students for lifelong engagement within an international setting. The plan states the following:

> A Georgia Tech education must impart a greater awareness and appreciation of the broader differences in language, culture, and custom. Even if our graduates never leave home, they should be prepared to work as a part of an international team that collaborates and shares work electronically around the globe. (Georgia Tech, n.d.)

In response, Georgia Tech's Office of International Education (OIE) aims to facilitate programming that will allow international students and scholars to better understand U.S. culture through interaction with American students. Two of these programs, the International House (I-House) and the International Community School (ICS) Tutoring program are outlined in this program description.

Recognizing the need for globally competent leaders, OIE, the Department of Housing and Residence Life, and the Sam Nunn School of International Affairs established the I-House to provide an on-campus living-learning option that addresses internationalization opportunities. OIE was involved in this project from the beginning because of its potential to help internationalize Georgia Tech's campus. Specifically, OIE wanted to promote an environment where international undergraduate students lived with U.S. students and each was able to learn from the other. Anecdotal evidence suggested that international undergraduate students found it difficult to create a community of friends. OIE believed that creating an international community for international undergraduate students would assist them in succeeding at Georgia Tech.

The other programming initiative is the ICS Tutoring program. In 2002, OIE partnered with a new charter school in the metro Atlanta area called the International Community School (ICS) to develop a program for the international student population to learn more about the U.S. system of education by sending a group of Georgia Tech students (international and domestic) to tutor the students of the ICS in their after-school program. According to the ICS website, the school "was strategically designed to bring together refugee, immigrant, and native-born children in an academically challenging and nurturing environment." Because of its international focus, the ICS is an excellent venue for connecting Georgia Tech student tutors (both U.S. students who have studied abroad and international students) and the diverse students at the ICS.

DESCRIPTION OF THE INSTITUTION AND STUDENTS

The Georgia Institute of Technology in Atlanta, Georgia, is the only technological university to be consistently ranked in *U.S. News & World Report*'s listing of America's top ten public universities. Georgia Tech has nearly three thousand student visa holders enrolled, which is approximately 17 percent of the total student population at the institution. Like other institutions, Georgia Tech's international students hail mainly from India, China, and Korea, and the majority of the international students are graduate students. The Office of International Education (OIE) at Georgia Tech has a three-fold purpose: internationalizing the curriculum, assisting students with education abroad programs, and serving the international student and scholar population. I-House and ICS Programs exemplify this purpose.

DESCRIPTION OF I-HOUSE

Located in one of Tech's residence halls, the I-House opened in the fall semester of 2005, currently has forty-eight residents. The residents are all undergraduate students and are a mix of international and U.S. students, many of whom have studied abroad or have had significant international experiences. The overarching goal of the I-House is for students to form a living community with a shared commitment to promote cultural exchange and awareness, contribute to a healthy and dynamic living community, and explore the global dynamics of politics, current events, economics, and culture. A faculty member from the Sam Nunn School of International Affairs is the director of the I-House and receives support from a graduate assistant. The director initiates a range of activities for the I-House to encourage residents to study, experience, and reflect on international issues.

The mission of the I-House goes beyond the building of an isolated community, however, by extending horizontally to build networks with other international organizations and clubs across campus as well as within our city. The I-House accomplishes this goal by the programming that it promotes and facilitates. Each I-House resident must participate in a minimum of eight programs each semester to remain in the I-House. These are divided into categories: I-Service, I-Angle Lectures, I-Culture, I-Dinners, I-Stimuli, and I-Films. One example of an I-Service activity is residents taking a group of refugee children from the ICS to the Georgia Aquarium for a day. The I-House takes advantage of the plethora of international activities on campus and in the Atlanta community and organizes opportunities for I-House residents to attend films, lectures, and performances.

The I-House also facilitates its own programming. One example is the Coffee House, an informal social opportunity open to the entire campus, which takes place every Monday evening in the I-House lounge, and often includes newly arrived international students and scholars. On average, thirty people show up each week to meet new friends, see old friends, and share cross-cultural experiences. This kind of informal interaction makes the I-House a vibrant and successful program. Each I-Dinner focuses on a country or region of the world and students, scholars, and faculty come together over food to discuss current issues about that particular place. It is unusual for undergraduates to have the opportunity to engage with faculty in an informal learning environment, and the I-Dinners are one of the most popular activities of the I-House.

The programming for the I-House is determined by the I-House Steering Committee, which is made up of I-House residents led by a graduate assistant. In this way, the residents themselves determine which activities will be offered and are encouraged to facilitate programs. Planning begins at a retreat held at the start of each semester at an off-campus location. The goal of the retreat is getting new residents integrated into the I-House and discussing plans for the coming semester. An I-House Board, comprising two staff from each of the offices that contribute resources to the I-House (OIE, the Department of Housing and Residence Life, and the Sam Nunn School of International Affairs), meets monthly and is charged with financial oversight and marketing of the program as well as recruitment of residents and future development of the program.

EVALUATION

The board is involved on a continual evaluation process during these monthly meetings to ensure that the goals of the program are met. The shared vision and investment of time and energy is essential to the success of the living-learning community. One new piece of the program that was developed from these meetings was adding an academic component to the I-House. A class for credit will soon be offered for I-House residents and will be taught by the faculty director. The course, entitled "International House Globalization," will cover current international topics and be based in reading and discussion.

Evaluations indicate that the ability to have open discussions and learn from one another is the residents' favorite aspect of their I-House experience. An expansion of the I-House program is being considered because of demand from applicants who are turned away due to a lack of space, and a very thorough survey is planned to gather data to that end.

APPLICABILITY TO OTHER INSTITUTIONS

The process that Georgia Tech used for implementing the I-House could be followed for other campuses interested in replicating such a program. The process starts with gathering faculty, staff, and departments with an interest in creating an internationally focused residential community. A committee of interested parties develops the vision for the I-House and focuses on the contributions that each specific department would make in implementing the program. This will differ from campus to campus depending on institutional structure, mission, and culture, but it is crucial that all of the interested departments are a part of the planning process from the beginning. A proposal should then be written that outlines the goals and direction of the program, and a budget must be developed.

Once all departments agree on the proposal and budget, the programmatic details can be put into place. These details include creating a selection process for the participants, developing a website, marketing the program, selecting the participants, and hiring a graduate assistant. The time line for these details will depend on the institution, but for Georgia Tech the marketing and recruitment efforts start in January. In the beginning, marketing the program included electronic mailing lists, school newspaper advertisements, website promotions, and class presentations, but the program more or less markets itself now, and there are twice as many applicants as space available in the I-House. The cycle for selection of I-House participants happens twice a year.

A key factor in the I-House's success is the commitment of residents, faculty, and staff to the vision of the program. This vision was crafted directly from Georgia Tech's strategic plan, and this connection to the overall mission of the university allows for easy buy-in from departments and provides a clear answer as to why this program is important to our institution.

DESCRIPTION OF ICS TUTORING PROGRAM

The ICS, which opened in 2002, was looking for tutors for their after-school program. This particular program involves foreign language and culture activities, playground time, and time spent on homework assignments. The volunteer coordinator at ICS was very keen to have Georgia Tech students assist elementary-aged ICS students with their homework. OIE wanted to take advantage of this opportunity to include both study abroad and international students as a way for them to get to know one another and work together on a common project, so OIE targeted these students via electronic newsletters, flyers, and e-mail lists.

The ICS volunteer coordinator provided an orientation to introduce ICS and discuss the types of issues that children of refugees face as well as ICS's expectations for the tutors. This orientation happened at Georgia Tech, after which the tutors decided whether they were willing to commit to a semester of tutoring. The orientation information emphasized that tutoring for the entire semester was necessary, since a bond is created from the interaction and mentoring between the ICS student and the Georgia Tech student. Tutors and students met weekly for one hour, which often involved both homework and play. Many of the ICS students were very new to the country, often with limited English skills, and were encountering culture shock. The tutors, many of whom were international students themselves, had gone through the same transition, but at the college level, and so were able to truly empathize with the ICS students.

Acting as tutors allowed the Georgia Tech students time to think about their own cultural adjustment to the United States. It also allowed them to think about how their own elementary education compared to the one provided by ICS. Most of the international student tutors were amazed by the lack of academic rigor in comparison to their own elementary education, and when an international student would make a comment along those lines, it provided a good way to begin a conversation among the tutors that helped them learn from each other about elementary education around the world. Many of the Georgia Tech tutors who are international students volunteered for the project because it was their chance to interact with children and to better understand a U.S. elementary school environment. Having international students as tutors was an excellent way for the

ICS students to have role models they could relate to on a cultural level. Thus, the time spent by tutors and ICS students was beneficial to both groups.

Over the years, the tutors have worked with a variety of age groups, ranging from first graders to fourth graders, depending on the needs of ICS. The Georgia Tech students travel to the school once a week for one hour of tutoring with the students. At the end of their hour, the tutors are asked to write about their experience in a journal that is kept and read by the volunteer coordinator. Any issues, questions, or problems are directed to the volunteer coordinator. At the end of each semester, OIE sponsors a celebration with the children at ICS to say goodbye. One example of such an event was taking digital photos of each tutor and student, and then together they created a frame for the photo for the student to keep as a remembrance.

Georgia Tech supports the tutors as a part of the tutoring program in several ways. Georgia Tech specifically chose ICS because of its special mission, not because of its proximity. The school is located in a suburb of Atlanta and travel time from Georgia Tech to ICS is about forty-five minutes one way. OIE has provided transportation support for the tutors since the inception of the program, but that support has followed a couple of different methods, and since the number of tutors has ranged from eight to twenty-two, the transportation costs fluctuate based on the numbers involved.

At first, OIE provided a van with a staff driver for the tutors. The OIE staff member who drove was also a tutor and provided a very direct connection between the ICS and Georgia Tech. Also, the staff member could use the travel time back to Tech to lead an informal discussion among the tutors about what happened with their students and to encourage tutors to share suggestions with each other about how to handle difficult situations. OIE has also allowed the students to go to the school with their own transportation; although this option gave the tutors more flexibility, it resulted in less cohesiveness as a group, since individuals traveling alone missed the discussions that happened during the travel time. OIE now provides train tickets for the tutors to take the subway to the school.

The other main way that OIE provides resources to the tutoring program is through staff support. Again, this has come in a variety of ways, from an International Student Advisor going weekly with the tutors to having a tutor be the student leader in charge of logistics and communication for the group. When a student leader was in charge, that student would meet bimonthly with an International Student Advisor in OIE to give updates and keep the lines of communication open. This was a great opportunity for a Georgia Tech student to develop leadership skills, and it was very beneficial to OIE since it replaced a staff member with a competent peer leader for the tutors. Overall, the resources needed to maintain the program are small in comparison with the impact of the program. Here is what one of the past student leaders of the tutors, a student from the United States, had to say about her involvement:

> Upon initially arriving at ICS, "Where are you from?" was the first thing I was asked. Unlike most cases, confirming my status as a local seemed like a bit of a letdown. However, I was amazed to learn of the many diverse cultural backgrounds the students had come from, and more remarkable was just how readily students embraced these differences in each other as if nothing were more natural. Just as readily as students welcome persons of all types of backgrounds, Georgia Tech tutors were met with willingness and eagerness to learn, something I found highly unexpected when the alternatives include playing outside and gabbing with friends. Being met with this kind of enthusiasm, I felt valued as a tutor and confident that, with such highly motivated students, I could contribute to their progress in academics. As weeks passed, I saw that principles I had tried to teach them were being retained and exercises that were initially challenging and sometimes frustrating were being completed with confidence and ease after just the small amount of time I spent with them each week. One could see the sense of achievement the students felt by observing their reaction when told they had gotten the right answer, affirming the efforts of the tutor and the students.

EVALUATION

The evaluations that OIE has used are qualitative and ask for feedback on how to improve the program for the next year. The structure of the tutoring has changed over time due to tutor feedback and has included more information from the teacher on each student's learning needs as well as more social time in the beginning for the Georgia Tech student to get to know the ICS student so that they are comfortable with one another. The evaluation is also an opportunity for the Georgia Tech students to reflect on their experience volunteering. One Georgia Tech international undergraduate student who participated as a tutor wrote the following:

> The fact that a place like ICS exists really reinforced the refugee situation in America for me . . . in developing countries such as India, there is a notion that the U.S. is all glitter, with high-rise buildings, and technologies. A place like ICS shows one of the challenges (like integrating such diverse nationalities) that the U.S. faces. On a more personal level, I felt 'useful' or rather appreciated for my services in my immediate community when tutoring at ICS. As an international student, it is very easy to feel like a stranger, and at ICS, the community is very welcoming and all the tutors are really appreciated by the children and teachers alike.

APPLICABILITY TO OTHER INSTITUTIONS

OIE was very deliberate in choosing the ICS for the tutoring program due to its cultural diversity and mission, but this program could be replicated in any elementary school. Our main goal was to assist Tech's international students in understanding the school system in the United States, and this could happen in any setting, as long as the school is supportive of the tutors. Regardless of the setting, one recommendation would be to have a regular contact person at the school for communication and logistics. Also, it would be useful to find out the specific needs of the school and the structure of the tutoring sessions. Another recommendation is to ensure that there is an orientation to tutoring and the school to set expectations and address any questions or concerns. Other issues to take into consideration are the cost of transportation, materials costs for end-of-semester celebrations, program staffing, marketing, and recruitment of new tutors.

Once these details are in place, maintenance of the program is quite easy. The program is cyclical in nature and begins with the recruitment and orientation of the tutors. This leads to the weekly tutoring sessions. The program finishes with a celebration at the end of each semester and evaluations by the tutors.

CONCLUSION

These programs are just two of the ways that Georgia Tech tries to integrate international students into campus life. Both of these programs have an impact not only on the international students but also on the U.S. students involved in the I-House and the ICS Tutoring program. Bringing international and American students together for a common cause or activity allows both groups to learn from one another. These interactions build greater awareness and appreciation of cultural differences and, therefore, help to meet the strategic goals of the university.

The University of Georgia's Global Leadership Institute

Leigh Poole

RATIONALE

Among institutions of higher education in the United States, there is increasing pressure for all students to gain global, international, and/or intercultural experiences (Love & Estanek, 2004). However, few opportunities exist for international and U.S. students to gain formal leadership experience in an intercultural and global context. In fact, many traditional on-campus student leadership roles do not incorporate or recognize global leadership styles. Often, student leadership roles are based on U.S. cultural patterns and values similar to those articulated by Stewart and Bennett (1991), including being action oriented and pragmatic. A lack of intercultural and international leadership experiences may impact students' abilities to successfully interact with individuals from other countries, as is often required by today's global workforce (Bikson, Treverton, Moini, & Lindstrom, 2003; Hodge, 2000; Gesteland, 1999). International students may find it particularly challenging to adapt to leadership roles within U.S. higher education institutions due to language and cultural barriers and U.S. leadership styles.

Individuals who study outside their home countries (i.e., international students who study in the United States or U.S. students studying abroad) often find it difficult to make friends, navigate new cultural rules, and adjust to their new lives in the host country (Hodge, 2000; Pederson, 1995). International and U.S. students who participate in study abroad opportunities often receive little formalized training to prepare them to interact with individuals who have cultural backgrounds different from their own. Intercultural training can serve as a mechanism to assist international students with cultural adjustment while helping teach and train U.S. students how to successfully interact with other cultures. Additionally, by providing structured, educational opportunities for both groups to interact beyond the classroom setting, international and U.S. students can gain valuable global leadership experience while working to understand their differences and similarities.

Based on the lack of student leadership opportunities that incorporate intentional, formalized education and training in an intercultural context for both international and U.S. students, the International Student Life Office (ISL) created the Global Leadership Institute at the University of Georgia (UGA) in 2007. The purpose of the Institute is to provide opportunities for international and U.S. students at UGA to learn about global leadership styles and develop intercultural leadership skills together. Through this program, international and U.S. students (a) receive formalized education and training relating to issues of global import, (b) have an opportunity to interact closely with one another, and (c) learn skills that may assist them with cultural adjustment while studying in another country.

DESCRIPTION OF THE INSTITUTION AND STUDENTS

Founded in 1785, the University of Georgia (UGA) is the United States' first state-chartered university. A comprehensive land-grant and sea-grant institution, UGA offers seventy-two baccalaureate, master's, doctoral, and professional degrees in more than 371 fields. Overall enrollment includes more than thirty-three thousand students from over 130 different countries. About 8,500 (or 25 percent) of the total number of students are enrolled in graduate and professional degree programs while roughly twenty-five thousand are pursuing undergraduate degrees. International student enrollment includes approximately 1,300 foreign students, which is approximately 4 percent of the overall student population.

More than 1,400 UGA undergraduate students are involved in some form of international education each year, while many participate in the more than ninety study-abroad and student exchange programs that UGA conducts in countries around the world. Nationally, UGA ranks second in the number of students who travel on short-term study abroad programs, eighth in the number of students studying abroad, and ninth among the top twenty research universities in the number of students studying abroad. Projected rates for study abroad include 25 percent of undergraduates having an international experience by the year 2010. UGA also has international campuses located in England, Italy, and Costa Rica.

PROGRAM DESCRIPTION

The inaugural Global Leadership Institute consisted of four interactive workshops. The seminars included two hours of instruction per session and incorporated topics such as global leadership, international service learning, cross cultural competencies and intercultural training, and an internationally related career seminar. The topics were selected by providing various student leaders as well as potentially interested participants with an assessment instrument to determine which topics were the most compelling (as well as which ones they would most likely attend).

The seminars were open to the entire UGA student body and occurred approximately two weeks apart from each other. They began in mid-October around midterms and concluded before the Thanksgiving break in November. Each workshop was held during the early evening (from 6 p.m. to 8 p.m.) and was conducted by either a professor or full-time staff member. The lead facilitators for the series were referred to as institute faculty in the advertising and promotional materials due to their level of expertise in the topic they would be teaching. Presenters were selected based on their presentation skills and ability to engage participants, as well as their areas of professional expertise and interest. Institute faculty members were responsible for the actual content of their individual sessions and were encouraged to be interactive as well as incorporate experiential learning into their seminars.

The first seminar focused on an exploration of international and U.S. students' understanding of global leadership. The faculty member facilitated a discussion that helped participants define their personal concept of global leadership and challenged students' perceptions of what characteristics make a "good" global leader. Students were asked to participate in experiential exercises to help them gain a clearer understanding of various types and examples of global leadership. They were also encouraged to actively share their personal experiences and thoughts throughout the session.

The second workshop moved students' attention beyond global leadership to the concept of global service learning. The faculty member for this particular workshop focused on the importance of civic engagement while also sharing information about how students could participate in local and international service learning opportunities that had global impact. Projects highlighted included service opportunities in Tanzania and Thailand as well as local projects working with Mexican immigrants and an online global textbook project that serves faculty and students who do not have ready access to books and academic materials.

The third seminar provided an opportunity for students to learn more about various cultural nuances and explore their personal world views. The session was highly interactive and included numerous cross-cultural exercises to challenge students' understanding of both themselves and each other. Specifically, one exercise required reading a form from right to left (instead of left to right) while another required both international and U.S. students to articulate cultural proverbs and connect their meanings to various cultural values. Students were also encouraged to share personal experiences of learning about customs and traditions outside their own personal and cultural norms.

The fourth and final seminar focused on career-related opportunities for both international and U.S. students. The faculty member led interactive exercises that included a discussion of how best to articulate international experiences such as study abroad and intercultural training (including the Global Leadership Institute). Students were exposed to various online resources for finding jobs in the United States and internationally and were also provided a general overview of the services offered through UGA's career center.

Because the program was created after budgets had been allocated, little funding was available. International Student Life staff worked to creatively facilitate the inaugural Global Leadership Institute during the fall 2007 semester. Working with a graduate student intern who had assisted the previous semester with gathering assessment information for the program, ISL was able to keep costs to a minimum while offering a quality program. Advertising consisted of a brochure created in house and then photocopied in black and white on colored paper.

Information about the seminars went out to students attending current office programs; student leaders (who were already connected to the international office); websites and student postings on online social networking pages; as well as through free, electronic advertising including the university master calendar (where campus events are posted); flyers to language departments and international affairs majors; electronic mailing list announcements; e-mail messages; and the on-campus Blue Card program, which permits students within one of the largest colleges on campus to qualify for early registration if they attend a certain number of previously approved cultural events during the course of a semester.

To further encourage attendance as well as provide students with something tangible to take with them after having attended the seminars, ISL created a noncredit certificate as an incentive for the institute. Students who attended three of the four seminars received a certificate of completion for the Global Leadership Institute. The certificate was signed by both the director of International Student Life as well as the director of Intercultural Affairs at UGA.

The ISL office made reservations for the rooms (free of charge for offices on campus) and provided advertising, a laptop for presenters as needed, and a projection system for each workshop. The projection system and a few costs associated with photocopying for flyers were the only financial obligations for the institute. Attendance was taken through the Blue Card program as well as with sign-in sheets at the start and conclusion of each program (for latecomers). Staff collected names and e-mail addresses for each participant to track students who wanted to complete the certificate program, to send e-mail reminders of upcoming workshops, and to send out evaluations at the conclusion of the semester. Student participants were informed about future seminars verbally at the end of each institute session and an overall evaluation of the program was sent out at the end of the semester to gain feedback from the participants.

EVALUATION

With the assistance of a graduate student intern who worked with the ISL office for two semesters, ISL was able to complete a comprehensive internal evaluation process to assist with the creation of the Global Leadership Institute. During the first semester the intern completed individual interviews with international and U.S. student leaders to determine their level of interest in such a program as well as assess areas in which they would like additional training and instruction. Additionally, surveys were given out at various programs and events sponsored by ISL to obtain quantitative data concerning the types of seminars, length of time, and topics of interest for students with international interests. The graduate intern also conducted informational interviews during the first semester with various professional staff members around campus to determine what types of leadership activities, programs, training opportunities, and services were currently being offered.

The conclusion was that a majority (if not all) of the opportunities available were heavily based on U.S. cultural values with no programs supporting international/global leadership. Based on this information, there was clear support for the creation of a program of this type to help expand international and U.S. students' leadership skills beyond the types of opportunities previously available. Additionally, the graduate intern spent time with student leadership from the thirty international and multinational student organizations advised by ISL to determine their level of interest in this program. The findings from this qualitative data were that the international organizations were strongly supportive of the creation of the Institute not only for the international student leaders, but for the U.S. students as well.

After the initial assessment plan was completed and the actual program had been implemented, the graduate intern created online evaluations for the program workshops through free online software programs. The participants were separated into two groups (students interested in completing the certificate program and students not interested in completing the certificate program). Each participant was invited to complete the appropriate online survey prior to the end of the semester. Feedback from the original assessment as well as the overall program evaluation was used in the implementation of sessions as well as to make improvements for future seminars. Due to the timing of the seminars (during midterm exams), ISL originally expected five to fifteen students to participate in the first seminar, which focused on global leadership. The first workshop had more than seventy student participants. Subsequent workshops included fifty-four students for the service-learning seminar, twenty-five students for cross-cultural competencies and intercultural training, and thirty students for the internationally focused career seminar. For each seminar, there was a mixture of U.S. and international students as well as undergraduate and graduate students.

The data collected from the participants for the pilot program centered on having the ability to contact them in the future rather than on quantitative data regarding specific numbers of international and U.S. students. Out of the total attendance of 179 students for all four seminars, twenty students completed the certificate program. Several of those who did not complete the certificate requirements requested future seminars the following semester so that they would be able to receive a certificate. Based on the unexpectedly high response to this program and the numerous requests for future seminars, ISL plans to both continue and expand the Global Leadership Institute in the future. Specific quantitative information concerning the breakdown of international and U.S. students participating in the program as well as receiving certificates will be collected during future seminars.

APPLICABILITY TO OTHER INSTITUTIONS

This program can be modified in a number of ways to fit a variety of institutions and budgets. The Global Leadership Institute can be incorporated into orientation programs for international students to help them prepare for their assimilation into U.S. culture. It could also be added to the core general education requirements of an institution. The institute could be used as part of introductory or semester-long orientation courses to help build an international component into the student experience and provide all students with an international or intercultural experience. The institute could become a certificate program, with the certificate being offered either formally through the college or university registrar or informally through an office or department or professor for that particular program or course.

Additionally, the institute could be a series of short seminars, a one- or two-day workshop (Kohls & Knight, 1994), an entire course for one semester or an extended course for two semesters depending on the campus needs. The institute could be focused on creating connections between international students and other subpopulations within an institution—such as commuter students, honors students, and student leaders—or even among members of the general student body. Individual institutions could also determine whether or not to have a process for students to apply for the program. Topics for the seminars (or class sessions) could vary from global leadership to providing international and U.S. students with formalized research opportunities to explore an aspect of another country that is important to the purposes of the course. This program could also be tied to service learning or volunteer opportunities in the local community for cities and towns that have significant international populations.

One important aspect to remember is that the institute can be very inexpensive. At UGA, the ISL office completed this program initially with little funding by using resources and outlets that were already in place and readily available. Before starting this program formally, it was vital to understand the campus culture and climate (as well as the services currently being offered by other departments) to mold and shape the Global Leadership Institute in a manner that would work for the international and U.S. students at the University of Georgia. Ultimately, ISL has been extremely pleased by the positive response generated by student participants and is considering expanding the program in a variety of ways (including several of those enumerated previously in this section).

ACKNOWLEDGMENT

A special thank you is extended to Abe Saunders for his invaluable assistance with the inaugural Global Leadership Institute at the University of Georgia.

Saudi Students at ELS Language Centers/Teaneck

Melissa Rigas

RATIONALE

The specific target group of this best practice description is the Saudi student population at ELS Language Centers, a proprietary, for-profit English language school in Teaneck, New Jersey. Saudi students experience difficulties with respect to American educational culture within the larger context of American culture in general. My intentions have been to understand the cultural source of their challenges and then to assist them by constructing parallel but culturally cognizant programs and assessment paths. The objectives that have been set must comply with both ELS's standards and American post-secondary educational methods. By taking these students out of the mainstream and teaching them how to approach the mandatory material using alternative programs and assessment, they are better prepared to learn what is needed at ELS and hence, are better able to succeed in the future in the American universities that they will attend.

DESCRIPTION OF THE INSTITUTION AND STUDENTS

At ELS Language Centers/Teaneck, we welcome an average of 150 international students per session for intensive English language instruction. Since each session lasts for just four weeks, literally hundreds of students come through our doors each year. It must also be noted that the percentage of continuing students is high and the mean stay is approximately six months.

Students have the choice of attending six (intensive) or four (semi-intensive) classes a day; however, if they elect the six-course program, they attend what we call skills enhancement courses in the afternoon, and it is often in these classes where they have the opportunity to develop skills that they lack. All students do a core curriculum in the four morning classes—two structure and speaking practice courses (SSP), one reading and writing course, and one multimedia or presentation skills course.

The King of Saudi Arabia generously offered scholarships in 2005 to his people to pursue their post-secondary education in America; these full scholarships included the cost of English language instruction in addition to four years of undergraduate study or two years of graduate study. ELS Language Centers procured many of the contracts for English language instruction, and Teaneck began to see large enrollments of Saudi students starting in January of 2006. The Saudi Cultural Mission, in conjunction with the Saudi Ministry for Education, prepared a list of approved postsecondary institutions as well as majors that the students could choose. ELS Teaneck's host institution, Fairleigh Dickinson University, is on this list. Consequently, we receive a fair number of the Saudi students each session. After one year, this has translated into a student population that is 40 percent Saudi Arabian, 50 percent Asian, and 10 percent other nationalities. It should be noted that the Saudi students study at ELS on average for one year and all those who will go on to study at the university must be enrolled in the intensive program.

The Issues

Teachers noted that many of the Saudi students had difficulty adapting to American educational standards. This caused somewhat of a crisis in the classroom because there was a wide gap between them and the other students. The Saudi culture is oral, and hence it comes as no surprise that the Saudi students are more at ease with oral communication skills than the Asians. However, their grammar, reading, and writing skills lag far behind those of their Asian classmates. Saudi students often feel that spending six hours in school is ample studying time, and their general concept of time is diametrically opposed to North American punctuality. In addition, many of them have difficulties with test taking in general and the final test, which is standardized, is a source of extreme anxiety. Failing the test could mean failing the level of English language instruction altogether. This leads to negotiating for a higher grade—something unimaginable in U.S. culture and, thus, a further source of frustration.

Because of the glaring weaknesses that Saudi students exhibit in reading, writing, grammar, and spelling, they are at a disadvantage at ELS because these issues make it very difficult for them to adapt to our curriculum and to American assessment techniques. The ramifications of this are serious because they will be encountering more difficult learning tasks when they move on to American universities. In addition, assessment will be brutal in as much as university professors will not make allowances because the student happens to be Saudi; they will be treated as any other student. The Saudi students have come to ELS with expectations of not only learning the language but also of being prepared for their postsecondary studies. This is the foundation of our mission statement and their repetitive failures illustrated the urgency with which we had to act if we were to uphold the quality education that our reputation is based on.

Educational systems vary from country to country because of the differences that exist in each country's cultural norms and values. For our Saudi students to be successful within an American educational environment, more particularly at ELS Language Centers, assessing our program and student needs is crucial at all phases: in planning, implementation, and review.

PROGRAM DESCRIPTION

The task at hand was therefore to find out exactly what programs and assessments we could apply to Saudi students to ascertain the probability of their readiness for and eventual success in an American educational experience. One thing was clear—irrespective of the solutions that I implemented, these students had to be ready for the American higher educational system by the time they left ELS. The task at hand was no easy one, but I was ready for and motivated by the challenge.

Our Saudi students were having setbacks with standardized tests, essay writing, and research papers. Was it because they did not study enough? That was clearly one of the problems, but it was one that could be easily remedied. More importantly, their shortcomings in structure, note taking, reading quickly, understanding what they read, and critical thinking so that they could write argumentatively, were at the core of the assessment issues.

An additional problem is based on the fact that neither ELS's curriculum nor our methods of assessment can be radically altered to accommodate one particular group of students in one particular center. It would certainly put our accreditation (ACCET) in question as well as the homogeneity of our program espoused by forty-nine centers in the United States. In any case, to do so would be counterproductive, as these students will be encountering more of the same when they leave our institution to go on to college. This left the individual centers to determine how to instruct the Saudis so that they could succeed within our program and the U.S. higher education system.

The Globetrotters

To address these issues, I created a special class named the globetrotters. It was composed of Saudi students from different levels—intermediate to advanced—and hence did not follow any one book. The teaching and content of the classes addressed the specific needs of the students in question. Their core curriculum comprised six classes instead of four: two classes of reading and writing skills, two classes of oral communication and listening skills, and two classes of structure and test-taking skills. This strengthened their handwriting, spelling, writing and reading speed, grammar, and organization of ideas. Additionally they visited actual university classes so that they could observe what awaited them in the future.

After participating in this specialized curriculum and strengthening their language skills, students had a choice to remain in this special class or move back into the mainstream. The goal, of course, was for them to get back into mainstream classes as quickly as possible, and I wanted this special class to be an option only for the beginner to intermediate levels and the lower advanced levels. The issues with the Saudi students had to be resolved before they reached the highest advanced level, where they were confronted with a standardized exam that had to be passed in order for them to move into the college-preparation levels.

Writing Portfolios

Of the four basic language skills (reading, writing, listening, and speaking), our Saudi students experience the majority of their difficulties in reading and writing. This is understandable because, as I have stated previously, their culture is an oral one and in addition, their alphabet bears no resemblance to English. Furthermore, the Arabic language reads from right to left (and not left to right as in English). All of these factors contribute to the challenge of Saudi students being able to get through texts in timed situations and understand what they have read without the clock running out. One alternative program and assessment technique that I eventually hope to incorporate in our program, which would span all twelve levels, is the use of writing portfolios.

More qualitative than quantitative, a writing portfolio would afford the Saudi students the time they needed to assimilate a new alphabet and the manner in which we approach writing in American education. What is more, it would also provide them with the means to compare past with present work and therefore allow them to see a genuine progression because the portfolio would follow the students from level to level in the program. This progression would provide motivation and would, in addition, teach such necessary skills as self-assessment and reflection, which would in turn foster critical thinking and skills of analysis (Nicholson, n.d.), skills that are crucial to success in the American post-secondary classroom. It would ultimately permit the students to partake in learner-centered rather than teacher-directed education, and this is an important concept, especially when one considers the collectivist nature of Saudi culture versus the overwhelming individualist reality present in American culture and education.

EVALUATION

Globetrotters was a huge success, and every student passed the midterms and their level's final proficiency test that is given to all ELS students. Even if they did not get top scores on the final test, this was progress since they were previously failing altogether. However, at the inception of the globe-trotter program, some Saudi students who had reached the higher levels were in great need of tailor-made classes. They were, in fact, the reason the globetrotter classes were created. Since they have now graduated from the highest level and thus, ELS's program, we have been able to isolate the problems more successfully at the lower levels.

The globetrotters course does not take place every session, but it will continue as needed, as will private tutoring for those Saudi students who have special needs and cannot be integrated into a group. What is more, after-school workshops will continue twice a week, since they have not only been popular, but also efficient in providing reinforcement in structure and study time.

In essence, the alternatives have opened up a greater understanding of Saudi culture, of the areas where these students are consistently having difficulties and of how they learn best. As time progresses, I am quite certain that other possibilities will be implemented. One thing is certain; it is a step-by-step process that needs to be addressed from the onset, and if this is done, we have demonstrated that Saudi students can be successful and well prepared for what follows.

APPLICABILITY TO OTHER INSTITUTIONS

Rose and Leahy (1997) underscore that "too little attention has been paid to the problems of cultural bias that permeate the assessment process" (p. 99). This issue manifested itself in the nonlearning and subsequent failures that our Saudi students encountered with increasing frequency. One thing is certain: alternative programs, such as the globetrotters program, must be implemented before Saudi students—or any other international students— enter American universities.

I realize that not all international students will have the good fortune to be enrolled in an intensive English program like ELS before the onset of their American university studies. This leaves room for the colleges and universities themselves to step up to the task at hand. Most postsecondary institutions that accept international students require an English-language placement test prior to enrollment and may require subsequent English language courses for those students in need. The number of these courses that a particular student must take depends on the student's initial level. It is possible to use the university's language placement test not only as a gauge for level, but also as a diagnostic tool for identifying particular problems associated with certain educational cultures. According to the results of these culturally diagnostic tests, parallel classes could be created to remedy the real difficulties instead of trying to impart knowledge using methods that the students simply do not understand because those methods are based in a North American system of values and norms.

Although all of the elements that I have proposed in this plan are not yet a reality, the ones that are in use have proved to be an immense success. By continuing to attend to what the Saudi students are bringing with them as far as culture and educational norms and values are concerned, we at ELS can concentrate on learning itself. This has created and will continue to strengthen the symbiotic relationship of learner–teacher give and take and will lead these students to the exact point where they need to be in any American educational setting.

REFERENCES

Bikson, T. K., Treverton, G. F., Moini, J., & Lindstrom, G. (2003). *New challenges for international leadership: Lessons from organizations with global missions.* Santa Monica, CA: RAND.

Bok, D. (2006). *Our underachieving colleges: A candid look at how much students learn and why they should be learning more.* Princeton, NJ: Princeton University Press.

Chapdelaine, R. F., & Alexitch, L. R. (2004). Social skills difficulty: Model of culture shock for international graduate students. *Journal of College Student Development, 45*(2), 167–184.

Chen, C. P. (1999). Common stressors among international college students: Research and counseling implications. *Journal of College Counseling, 2,* 49–65.

Damron, J. (2003). What's the problem? A new perspective on ITA communication. *Journal of Graduate Teaching Assistant Development, 9*(2), 81–86.

Deardorff, D. K. (2006). The identification and assessment of intercultural competence as a student outcome of internationalization. *Journal of Studies in International Education, 10,* 241–266.

Diamond, R. M. (1989). *Designing and improving courses and curricula in higher education: A systematic approach.* San Francisco: Jossey-Bass.

Furnham, A., & Bochner, S. (1986). *Culture shock.* New York: Methuen.

Georgia Tech (n.d.). *Georgia Institute of Technology strategic plan.* Retrieved December 2, 2008, from http://www.gatech.edu/president/strategicplan.html

Gesteland, R. R. (1999). *Cross-cultural business behavior: Marketing, negotiating, and managing across cultures.* Copenhagen: Copenhagen Business School Press.

Gravios, H. (2005, April 8). Teach impediment. *Chronicle of Higher Education,* p. A10.

Hanami, P. (2007). 5 steps to student integration. *IIE Networker.* Retrieved March 21, 2008, from http://www.iienetwork.org/?p=79986

Heikenheimo, P. S., & Shute, J. C. M. (1986). The adaptation of foreign students: Student views and institutional implications. *Journal of College Student Personnel, 27,* 399–406.

Hiiemae, K., Lambert, L., & Hayes, D. (1991). How to establish and run a comprehensive teaching assistant training program. In J. D. Nyquist, R. D. Abbott, D. H. Wulff, & J. Sprague (Eds.), *Preparing the professoriate of tomorrow to teach* (pp. 123–134). Dubuque, IA: Kendall Hunt.

Hodge, S. (2000). *Global smarts: The art of communicating and deal making anywhere in the world.* New York: Wiley.

Kohls, L. R., & Knight, J. M. (1994). *Developing intercultural awareness: A cross-cultural training handbook* (2nd ed.). Yarmouth, ME: Intercultural.

Love, P., & Estanek, S. M. (2004). *Rethinking student affairs practice.* San Francisco: Jossey-Bass.

NAFSA: Association of International Educators (2003, January). *In America's interest: Welcoming international students.* Retrieved July 4, 2006, from http://www.nafsa.org/_/Document/_/in_america_s_interest.pdf

———. (2006, June). *Restoring U.S. competitiveness for international students and scholars.* Retrieved July 4, 2006, from http://www.nafsa.org/_/Document/_/restoring_u.s.pdf

Nicholson, B. L. (n.d.). Course portfolio. In M. W. Galbraith (Ed.), *Adult learning methods: A guide for effective instruction* (3rd ed.) (pp. 321–340). Malabar, FL: Krieger.

Nilsson, B. (2003). Internationalisation at home from a Swedish perspective: The case of Malmö. *Journal of Studies in International Education, 7*(1), 27–40.

Pederson, P. (1995). *The five stages of culture shock: Critical incidents around the world.* Westport, CT: Greenwood.

Putnam, R. D. (2007). E pluribus unum: Diversity and community in the twenty-first century. *Scandinavian Political Studies, 30*(2), 137–174.

Rogler, D. K., & Gray, P. J. (1989). *The Syracuse University teaching assistant orientation program: An evaluation report.* Syracuse, NY: Syracuse University, Center for Instructional Development.

Rose, A. D., & Leahy, M. A. (1997). Assessment themes and issues. In A. D. Rose & M. A. Leahy (Eds.), *Assessing adult learning in diverse settings: Current issues and approaches* (pp. 97–100). San Francisco: Jossey-Bass.

Sarkisian, E., & Maurer, V. (1998). International TA training and beyond: Out of the program and into the classroom. In M. Marincovich, J. Prostko, & F. Stout (Eds.),

The Professional Development of Graduate Teaching Assistants (pp. 163–180). Bolton, MA: Anker.

Smithee, M. B. (1990). *Factors related to the development and implementation of a university-wide teaching assistant program*. Unpublished doctoral dissertation, Syracuse University, Syracuse.

Stewart, E. C., & Bennett, M. J. (1991). *American cultural patterns: A cross-cultural perspective* (Rev. ed.). Yarmouth, ME: Intercultural.

Stromborn, A. (2007). Program partners international and American students to enhance learning. Retrieved March 21, 2008, from http://www.news.wisc.edu/13660

Syracuse University. (2008). All-university teaching assistant orientation. Retrieved January 10, 2008, from http://gradschpdprograms.syr.edu/programs/tap_orientation.php

Tanner, M. W., Selfe, S., & Wiegand, D. (1993). The balanced equation to training chemistry ITAs. *Innovative Higher Education, 17*(3), 165–181.

Trice, A. G. (2004). Mixing it up: International graduate students' social interactions with American students. *Journal of College Student Development, 45*(6), 671–687. Retrieved April 4, 2008, from http://findarticles.com/p/articles/mi_qa3752/is_200411/ai_n9472311/

VanGulick, B., & Lynch, M. (1996). Using video to improve instruction: Sample criteria for providing feedback. In L. Lambert, S. L. Tice, & P. H. Featherstone (Eds.), *University teaching: A guide for graduate students* (pp. 88–94). Syracuse, NY: Syracuse University Press.

Yang, B., Teraoka, M., Eichenfield, G. A., & Audas, M. C. (1994). Meaningful relationships between Asian international and U.S. college students: A descriptive study. *College Student Journal, 28*, 108–115.

9

Immigration and Legal Issues

An understanding of immigration and related legal issues is critical for institutions of higher education that enroll international students as well as for the students themselves. These issues have become even more important in recent years due to the tightening of immigration policies affecting international students and scholars. Some claim that these policies have been a deterrent to the growth of international student enrollments in the United States (Brumfiel, 2004; NAFSA, 2006; Smith, 2005) although reforms are seeking to streamline the visa process (Redden, 2008). Other complications for international students in the United States are employment restrictions and lack of opportunity to immigrate after graduation. The nation's competitors have more liberal policies in this regard, some giving immigration priority to graduated international students (Birrell, 2006). Immigration compliance is regularly cited as a major adjustment factor for international students (Meyer, 2001; Sarkodie-Mensah, 1998). As such, expertise in immigration matters is a priority for higher education institutions.

Regardless of the current stance of the nation on immigration practices related to international students, institutions have a clear role. They must not only understand and strictly follow these policies themselves, but also ensure that the students they admit understand and abide by the policies. In this chapter, we focus on five descriptions of best practices related to immigration and legal issues. First, William Stock of Klasko, Rulon, Stock, and Seltzer, LLP, provides an overview of current legal issues affecting institutions of higher education by sketching a historical foundation to the current state of affairs. He explains the partnership between institutions and the government and discusses how an institution must balance the regulatory side of maintaining compliance for enrolling international students with assisting students in maintaining status and successfully completing their educational programs.

We then turn to a contribution by Bernadette Guimberteau, University of California at Berkeley, who raises awareness of issues affecting Fulbright Scholars in the United States. Although the program provides an excellent opportunity for international exchange and learning, immigration restrictions related to unemployment upon return home, blocked visa status, and funding mistakes can present serious complications to those accepting these prestigious scholarships. In contrast, Victoria Donoghue illustrates how the City University of New York advocates for and assists the immigration of foreign scientists who come to the United States to study. In so doing, the institution encourages scientific research and the exchange of knowledge and strengthens the nation's reputation as a leader in this area.

The final two contributions in this chapter provide practical suggestions for helping students navigate immigration regulations. Adria Baker addresses the need for ongoing regulatory training for international students beginning before they arrive on campus until they complete their studies and prepare to return home. She examines how institutions can address students' needs at various points in time with a variety of programming ideas and activities proven successful at Rice University. Elizabeth Risa presents an innovative approach to foreign student casework developed at the University of Pittsburgh. Rather than having immigration advisors specialize in a particular visa category, this model entails cross-training so that advisors can be assigned to a particular academic area and serve the various immigration needs of students in that area. She details how the program was implemented, including advisor training.

Immigration regulations for international students apply to all types of higher education institutions and affect their ability to recruit, enroll, and retain foreign students. As institutions partner with the government to maintain these regulations, they are not only responsible for ensuring that they are following appropriate policies, but also that students understand and abide by these policies. The examples of best practices that follow demonstrate the broad experience of institutions in this area. From providing an overview of essential information to demonstrating how institutions can assist students and scholars with immigration both during and after their time as a student, these descriptions offer the best of creative thinking from experts in the field.

School Sponsorship of International Students: Regulatory Compliance Perspectives

William A. Stock

RATIONALE

While the value of international education and exchange has long been recognized in the United States, the welcome extended has always been tempered by a regulatory regime that controls which students are allowed to enter the country, regulates the conditions under which they are allowed to stay, and enforces the requirement that they depart when they terminate their studies. The relationship between institutions of higher education and the government has always been a partnership, but the issues of most importance to each have changed with world events.

This best practice description reviews the perspective of the government agency that regulates foreign student affairs and the commitments an institution makes when accepting permission to enroll foreign students, and provides recommendations for assisting students to maintain their student status.

Background Perspectives of Higher Education Institutions and the Government

It is helpful, when considering the relationship between institutions of higher education and the government, to understand that the initial step of an important government function has long been delegated to institutions: the determination of who is and who is not entitled to enter the United States. While consular officials and immigration officers make the final decision about whether to admit a student, they rely heavily on an institution's admission determinations that a student is both academically and financially qualified to pursue a given course of study. Furthermore, students are admitted to the United States to pursue a course of study; their presence at and progress through the institution's academic program serves as the touchstone of their lawful presence in the United States.

It is also helpful, at the outset, to note that concerns about the ability of immigration authorities to monitor the academic progress of international students are not new. Tracking foreign students became an issue when the former Immigration and Naturalization Service (INS) could not provide definitive information to President Carter about the number and status of Iranian students in the United States after the fall of the Shah, and became more acute after the 1993 World Trade Center bombing and the 1996 CIA shootings, in which at least some of the individuals involved were out-of-status students.

While better information exchange about these students might not have prevented the attacks, their occurrence did focus Congress' attention on the issue of how INS would be able to know if a student fell out of status. In the creation of the Department of Homeland Security (DHS), the decision was made to give responsibility for school and student affairs within DHS to the bureau of Immigration and Customs Enforcement (ICE). ICE was charged with the apprehension, detention, and removal of all immigrants in the United States in violation of law as its primary mission. This perspective has caused tension between ICE and its partner institutions, which tend to see international education in terms of promoting mutual educational exchange and citizen diplomacy.

ICE has implemented a Web-based system to provide the exchange of near real-time information about students. This system is known as SEVIS, the Student and Exchange Visitor Information System. SEVIS provides a centralized database, maintained by ICE, into which institutions record information about the students they admit and their academic status. The database, in turn, can be accessed by any government agency dealing with a person claiming to be admitted to a school in the United States, whether a consular officer considering a student visa application from overseas, a Customs and Border Protection inspector interviewing a student visa holder at an airport, or an ICE agent inside the United States. Through SEVIS, ICE can also review a student's entire history of regulatory compliance, and can view an institution's handling of its students over time, allowing it to detect patterns that may point to the need for closer review of the school's practices.

PROGRAM DESCRIPTION

Maintaining a successful international education program involves a balance between following the regulations and providing the government with timely information on the compliance side, and assisting the institution's students to maintain their student status and complete their academic programs, on the education side. The following sections outline the two perspectives an institution must balance for a successful program.

Institutional Requirements for Enrolling Foreign Students

The regulations impose numerous requirements on institutions wishing to sponsor foreign nationals for student visas (see Title 8 of the Code of Federal Regulations in Sections 214.2(f) and 214.3, available online in the "Laws and Regulations" section of www.uscis.gov.) These requirements are meant to ensure that only bona fide academic or vocational programs are able to sponsor foreign students, and to ensure that institutions choosing to sponsor international students make sufficient resources available to both assist the students and ensure that all required reporting is done.

Only accredited schools with the facilities to actually perform instruction may be approved to admit nonimmigrant students. In addition, applying for such permission requires an institution to demonstrate that it has the ability and commitment to meet regulatory requirements in the following areas.

Recordkeeping

Approved institutions must record the admission of students and their current home address (both physical address and mailing address) in the SEVIS system. Each quarter or semester, the school must update the SEVIS system with the student's current registration status, and notify SEVIS of any termination of the student from registration. Even after graduation, the school must track its students if they elect to pursue postgraduation work in student status through practical training work authorization.

Entry Document Issuance

Approved institutions must ensure that they only issue the documents necessary for students to apply for student visas to individuals accepted for admission to their schools. This admission process must ensure that accepted students are both academically and financially qualified to attend the school and complete their programs of study. Schools must issue entry documents from within the United States and admission decisions must be made through the school's regular admissions office.

Appointment and Support of DSOs

Approved institutions must agree to appoint only U.S. citizens and lawful permanent residents to the position of designated school official (DSO), who acts for the school and interfaces between the SEVIS system and the institution's students. The institution must ensure that the DSO has enough training and supervision to ensure that the institution complies with the regulations. The DSO must be familiar enough with the regulations to be able to assist students in maintaining status, changing immigration status, and traveling in and out of the United States. In addition, it is ultimately the institution's responsibility to ensure that enough DSOs are appointed so that the SEVIS system is updated in a timely manner.

Consequences of Failure to Comply

Should an institution fail to comply with the regulations for correctly admitting students, recording their status in the SEVIS system, or providing educational programs, ICE can withdraw its designation as an approved school. The regulations provide that an institution's ceasing of operations or changing in ownership is grounds for automatic termination of designation (in the case of change of ownership, the new owners must apply for re-designation within sixty days of the change to preserve their designation). The regulations also provide that any violation of the regulations or loss of accreditation status is grounds for termination of designation on notice.

If ICE determines that one or more regulations may have been violated, they will notify the institution of their intention to withdraw designation. The institution then has the opportunity to respond with documentation supporting their compliance or, if appropriate, their change in practices. An interview is held between the ICE school compliance branch and the school's representatives, after which the school compliance branch will issue a letter indicating what, if any, action it will take. The school compliance branch also has the option of proceeding more informally, notifying the school officials of practices that, if unchanged, would lead to a Notice of Intent to Withdraw Designation.

While the SEVIS reporting requirements may seem to be more onerous than prior requirements, it should be noted that the SEVIS system merely automates data interchange that was already provided for in the regulations. Because the system was paper-based, however, it was very resource intensive, and frequently out of date. SEVIS has provided for real-time updating of student's status, increasing the stakes for students who fall out of status by failing to report to the school that admitted them or by failing to maintain a full course of study.

Institutional Roles in Assisting Foreign
Students with Regulatory Compliance

Institution administrators, and particularly DSOs, may feel that they have been deputized by ICE to aid in immigration enforcement. Institutions do have an important role in providing information to immigration authorities that will allow immigration agencies to detect and remove out-of-status students. They also have an equally important role, however, in ensuring that students understand the rules with which they must comply, and in assisting students to avoid running afoul of the regulations.

One important way in which institutions must assist their students to maintain compliance is to provide continuous training. While an initial orientation to the regulations and pre-arrival information about the school and maintenance of immigration status is required by the regulations, institutions are well advised to continuously remind students of their responsibility for compliance with regulatory requirements.

Another important way in which institutions should assist students is providing individualized counseling during their studies. The regulations provide many opportunities to deal with students' needs in advance of a problem with their status, and students must have an office to which they can go and have their problems dealt with on an individual basis in a confidential atmosphere. Institutional officers must be prepared to walk a delicate line, making all assistance available through the regulations open to students while not going so far as to assist a student beyond what the regulations allow. A few examples may serve to illustrate this balance.

The regulations generally provide that a student must attend a "full course of study," for example, twelve semester hours at an undergraduate college. They also provide, however, that a student may drop below that course load with pre-authorization from the DSO: in the case of "initial difficulties" with English or U.S. teaching methods, in the case of improper course level placement, or if medical conditions prevent a student from registering for a full or partial course of study. Faced with a student wishing to drop below a full course of study, therefore, the DSO must be able to work with the student to document that one or more of the exceptions to the full course of study requirements applies, while not crossing the line into creating a reason where none exists.

Regulations provide other safety valves as well. While a student is normally expected to meet his or her expenses without resorting to employment in the United States, for example, the regulations do provide for routine on-campus employment authorization, and for emergency hardship employment authorization in those cases where a student's financial situation changes dramatically (for example, a currency devaluation that makes the overseas family's financial support worth less). By seeking input from a DSO, the student in financial difficulties can be apprised of ways to supplement his or her income without resorting to illegal employment.

Similarly, DSOs can play a role even where the student has already fallen out of status. The regulations provide for reinstatement to student status in those situations where the student has failed to maintain status but has not worked without authorization. DSOs can use the opportunity presented by a student's reinstatement application to diagnose the underlying problems that caused the failure to maintain status. In the case of academic difficulties, the DSO may need to suggest that the student transfer to another school where deficiencies in the student's preparation can be remedied. In the case of personal difficulties, the student can be pointed to other resources through which those difficulties can be addressed.

EVALUATION

Institutions should periodically assess their compliance with the regulations and the success of their admissions and international student counseling operations. Regulatory compliance can best be assessed by an audit of the institution's decision-making processes and outcomes by its experienced foreign student advisors or, if an institution does not have that capacity in-house, by an outside regulatory compliance auditor such as a law firm familiar with international student operations. The success of an institution's admission, orientation, and educational/counseling programs for international students can best be accomplished by outcomes measurement, looking at a number of statistics (in addition to four-year graduation rates and similar outcomes measurements applicable to all students):

- the number of admitted students whose visa applications are rejected (the higher the percentage, the stricter the screening of applicants by the admissions office should be),
- the number of admitted students whose SEVIS records must be terminated for nonenrollment (the higher the percentage, the more support should be provided to students to overcome the issues causing them to fall out of status), and
- the number of students whose SEVIS records must be transferred to other schools (an exit interview can reveal whether students are going to less or more challenging institutions, and focus a school's admissions better).

CONCLUSION

Institutions involved in international education need to understand the commitment they have made to assist the U.S. government in properly balancing public diplomacy efforts with controls to ensure that foreign students engage in the studies for which they are admitted. At the same time, they should realize the critical role they play in ensuring that students have the tools needed to comply with the regulations, and support their students' efforts to maintain student status.

All institutions must determine how they are going to resource both the compliance and international education components of their programs, and strike a balance that is appropriate to their institutional culture and international education goals. By adequately resourcing their international offices to perform both compliance and educational/counseling activities, they will not only ensure their institutional compliance with the regulations, but also the success of their international education program.

Understanding the Fulbright Experience: Immigration Issues

Bernadette Guimberteau

RATIONALE

The Fulbright program was created in 1946 as a foreign policy tool for the United States. Under its umbrella, the Foreign Fulbright Fellows program offers scholarships that allow accomplished foreign students to study in American colleges and universities. When these students later return to their home countries, often to positions of leadership, they bring with them a greater understanding of and empathy for the United States.

The Fulbright program has benefited countless foreign students. However, its immigration requirements, compounded by certain conditions for their enforcement, create problems for the students. The goal of this contribution is to bring these issues to light.

DESCRIPTION OF THE STUDENTS AND THE INSTITUTIONS

About 3,200 foreign Fulbright students currently study at American universities, mostly at the graduate level, throughout the United States. Each year brings about 1,800 new fellows. In 2005/2006, students came from 132 countries in Europe and Eurasia (40 percent), the Western Hemisphere (22 percent), Near East and South Asia (20 percent), East Asia and Pacific (12 percent), and Africa (6 percent). They were enrolled in all fifty states, as master's (57 percent), Ph.D (24 percent), and bachelor's degree (1 percent) students, or as nondegree visitors and visiting researchers (18 percent). They studied in forty fields, including education (13 percent), engineering (9 percent), business administration (8 percent), law (6 percent), and economics (5 percent) (U.S. Department of State, n.d.).

Fulbright awards vary in size and duration. Certain students are funded for the expected duration of their program of study, which can take up to several years, as in the case of a Ph.D; others are funded with some grants as small as the price of round-trip airfare.

PROGRAM DESCRIPTION

The Fulbright program is administered by the U.S. Department of State's Bureau of Educational and Cultural Affairs, nonprofit partner organizations in the United States, and binational commissions in foreign countries. It is governed by strict immigration regulations, as outlined below.

Description of Immigration Requirements

In exchange for their awards, grantees must accept the following two conditions:

Blocked Visa Status

Once they are in the United States, international Fulbright students cannot change their nonimmigrant status or acquire legal permanent status. Even if they marry U.S. citizens, Fulbright students are not allowed to file for permanent residency. They enter the United States as Exchange Visitors (J-1 visa) and remain Exchange Visitors.

Two-year Home Residency Requirement

At the end of their programs, grantees must spend two years in their home country to bring back their experiences from the United States and to contribute their talent. This requirement is dictated by Section 212(e) of the Immigration and Nationality Act of 1952. Fulbright students are precluded from changing their status to that of H (Temporary Workers), L (Intracompany Transferees), or K (Fiancé[e] of U.S. Citizen), or to immigrant or legal permanent status until the two-year return (home residency requirement) has been satisfied or waived.

Waivers of Immigration Requirements

Blocked visa status cannot be waived. Only the two-year residency requirement may be waived. Unfortunately, these waivers are restricted and extremely difficult to obtain. For Fulbright students to remove the home residency requirement, they must obtain a "no objection" statement from the Fulbright Commission in their home country, a second no objection statement from their government (e.g., their embassy in the United States), and a waiver from the Department of State. The possibility of obtaining a waiver from the Department of State is very limited. A no objection waiver exists, but is not usually enough to remove the two-year home residency requirement of Fulbright grantees. This requirement may be waived only under the following conditions:

- Persecution upon return to the student's country.
- Extraordinary hardship on a United States citizen or legal permanent resident spouse or child resulting from the Fulbright student's return.
- A government agency requesting a waiver based on national interest (e.g., if the international student were a nuclear physicist whose project benefits U. S. defense).

Most international Fulbright students do not fit into these narrow categories. Even for those few students who do, waivers of return (i.e., home residency requirement) are notoriously difficult to obtain.

EVALUATION

Published works such as books (e.g., Arndt & Rubin, 1993) and surveys (e.g., SRI International, 2005) report that foreign Fulbright students claim a high degree of satisfaction with the program. Students emphasize the benefits associated with international exchange (e.g., discovery of a new culture and new friends), the prestige they acquired as a Fulbright student, and the professional opportunities that, as a result, opened up for them. These evaluations conclude that the Fulbright program is a sweeping success.

Issues with Interpretation of Existing Data

The above studies involve empirical problems. Books tend to describe Fulbright scholars' experiences without attempting to triangulate their data with other sources. The personal stories are interesting, but the general conclusions drawn from them may not be warranted. Surveys require caution as well (e.g., see Groves, Dillman, Eltinge, & Little, 2002). Participants do not respond, either because they cannot be located or because they do not return their questionnaires, making potentially critical data inaccessible. Those who do respond may produce answers that they believe are expected, due to a desirability bias (Goodwin, 2008). In the 2005 survey cited earlier, 65 percent of the students did not respond. Did some of them have problems with the Fulbright program? Are some of the remaining students' favorable responses caused by a desirability bias? Both possibilities must be ruled out before we can conclude unreservedly that the Fulbright program is a major success.

Difficulties Caused by the Enforcement of Immigration Requirements

The above studies leave crucial questions unanswered because they fail to include immigration issues in their assessments. How are immigration rules enforced and how is a student's life affected? Some researchers claim that questions about processes, such as these, are best examined through case study research (Yin, 2003). What follows is a report of key findings gathered using the case study approach (Guimberteau, 1996). Twenty cases were selected because of immigration problems they experienced (criterion sampling) and analyzed in depth. To generalize the immigration-related issues they presented, three other sources of data were obtained: a second sample of cases satisfying the criterion, international student advisors, and immigration lawyers who are expert in Fulbright waivers.

The study reveals that foreign Fulbright students are subject to blocked visa status and the home residency requirement even under difficult circumstances. These include unemployment upon return, funding mistakes, hardships associated with blocked visa status and home residency, and missing statements in the Fulbright contract concerning conditions of enforcement.

Unemployment upon Return

The two-year home residency requirement applies even if students cannot find a job to contribute their skills in their home country, and will potentially remain unemployed during the two years they are required to remain in their home country.

Funding Mistakes

Blocked visa status and the home residency requirement apply even if students receive less funding than was originally promised for their awards as a result of management errors, and even if students experience hardships because of these funding errors.

Hardships Related to Blocked Visa Status and Home Residency

Blocked visa status and home residency apply even if students experience serious hardships as a result of them. Students cannot leave the Fulbright program to remove these hardships even by reimbursing their award. Their only recourse is to apply for one of the waivers mentioned earlier, which are very difficult to obtain.

Missing Conditions in the "Conditions of Award"
Section of the Fulbright Contract

Blocked visa status and the home residency requirement apply even though the problematic conditions of unemployment upon return, funding mistakes, and hardships associated with blocked visa status and home residency may not be stated in the contract. For the contract to be fair, these factors need to be specified clearly and explained so that students can give their informed consent. However, conditions of enforcement of Section 212(e) of the Immigration and Nationality Act of 1952 take precedence over what is or is not stated in the Fulbright contract.

The above situations are not tied to specific cases, but reveal broad problems. For example, the unemployment problems reflect changing economic situations not taken into account in the immigration requirements of the Fulbright program. The fact that return (i.e., home residency requirement) is enforced anyway (Ware, Bedient, & Stelljes, 2005) creates a difficult situation for foreign Fulbright grantees:

> As an adviser to over 2,000 scholars a year that came to UC Berkeley, I was consistently confronted with Fulbright recipients who said they regretted having accepted the award because of their lack of understanding of what the 2-year requirement would mean to their careers. The problems, they stated, were a lack of jobs in the home country to which they would be forced to return and the fact that they could not meet the requirement in another country such as a country that is also a member of the EU for many of the Europeans or a country that was offering jobs where Fulbright also exists. (Law, 2007)

APPLICABILITY TO OTHER INSTITUTIONS

Higher education administrators involved with international education should be aware of the issues discussed here for several reasons. Foreign Fulbright students are enrolled all over the United States. Their host institutions need to clearly understand the conditions that affect them to inform and advise them properly. These host institutions are also uniquely positioned to help improve international exchange programs by raising awareness of immigration requirements and improving assessment methods of the programs.

Survey data, when used to evaluate the success of the programs, should be interpreted with caution. Case study research provides valuable insights concerning general problems, such as those involving enforcement of immigration requirements.

The Fulbright program has a generous spirit at its core, and includes many benefits for its students. Problems arising from its immigration requirements, however, can create genuine hardship. Careful evaluations of international exchange programs, such as the Fulbright program, are needed for an accurate representation of their strengths and weaknesses. Better assessment means a stronger position to compete with other nations, such as Australia and the United Kingdom, for foreign students. It is important to acknowledge the problems that exist in the program so that they can be addressed and solved. The information presented here hopes to move the Fulbright program in that direction.

A Program to Promote Scientific Research at the City University of New York

Victoria Donoghue

RATIONALE

There can be little doubt that during the last half of the twentieth century, the United States has been a leader in scientific research. Amazing scientific discoveries have been made in disciplines such as physics, chemistry, and medicine. And American universities have played a huge role in placing the United States in the forefront. University labs have been, and continue to be, filled with talented and ambitious young scientists, whose commitment has been the force behind scientific advancement.

The high quality of scientific research in the United States has made this country a magnet for foreign scientists. They come to the United States because they want to be a part of its vibrant scientific community, and they bring with them their desire to contribute to scientific progress. This, of course, is beneficial to universities, especially at a time when American students are increasingly pursuing careers in business and law instead of science, and the pool of American scientists is diminishing. For universities, foreign national scientists are often the key to continued research.

While foreign scientists are drawn to the United States, they face a web of complicated immigration laws and regulations that can be daunting, to say the least. Universities that invest in programs that assist foreign scientists in this area, and generally provide a climate that is hospitable toward foreigners, can reap the benefits. This has certainly been true for the City University of New York (CUNY).

DESCRIPTION OF THE STUDENTS AND INSTITUTION

The Research Foundation of the City University of New York (RFCUNY), the entity that administers the $360 million in grants that come into the CUNY system annually, has long recognized that its scientific research endeavors and its international community of researchers are among its greatest assets. Accordingly, it has endeavored to attract and retain these scientists by providing a range of immigration services and, perhaps more importantly, a caring environment for its foreign born employees.

PROGRAM DESCRIPTION

The following two examples illustrate how RFCUNY's immigration support programs have fostered the mutually beneficial relationship that exists between CUNY and its foreign scientists:

Dr. Vishnu discovered his love for science while he was an undergraduate student in his native India. Drawn to organic chemistry in particular, he went on to earn his Ph.D in that field at the world-renowned Indian Institute for Science. Upon completing his Ph.D studies, Dr. Vishnu looked for a postdoctoral fellowship position that would give him the opportunity to make an impact in the burgeoning discipline of green chemistry. Having grown up in southern India, a region rich in plant-based resources, he was fascinated with the possibility of transitioning from dwindling petroleum-based feedstock to renewable plant-based feedstock. After reading the publications of Dr. Henri, a CUNY professor with international recognition in the field of green chemistry, Dr. Vishnu reached out to him and eventually landed a research position. As a young man committed to science, Dr. Vishnu believed that the United States had a wealth of outstanding scientific minds and state of the art facilities; he welcomed the opportunity to immerse himself in that world.

Of course, Dr. Vishnu needed a visa to live and work in the United States. RFCUNY was ready to provide assistance. Recognizing the value of having scientists like Dr. Vishnu in its academic community, RFCUNY has provided in-house training (facilitated by an immigration attorney) to its human resources staff in the area of employment-based immigration. This training includes step-by-step instructions on preparing the employer support letters and immigration forms needed to petition the United States Citizenship and Immigration Service ("USCIS"), as well as an overview of the green card options available to employees.

RFCUNY also encourages regular attendance at continuing education seminars, given by providers such as the Practicing Law Institute, the New York City Bar Association, and private law firms, that keep the human resources staff up-to-date on this ever-changing area of the law. The staff understands the legal challenges facing foreign nationals and is always available to answer questions and give advice. If a question goes beyond their knowledge, they consult with immigration attorneys to get answers. In accordance with RFCUNY's pro-immigration policy, the foundation regularly obtains H-1B status (the immigration status that permits a foreign national to work in a professional, or specialty, occupation and enables that person to obtain the actual visa from an American embassy abroad) on behalf of its foreign nationals, and guides these individuals through the complicated process of either adjusting their immigration status in the United States or applying for a visa at the American embassy post in their home country.

RFCUNY's willingness to assist Dr. Vishnu has born fruit. The work of Drs. Vishnu and Henri has shown that agricultural or plant-based feedstock can serve as the building blocks for a wide array of products now made from petrochemical feedstock. Their work in the City University lab has resulted in numerous publications in leading scientific journals, presentations at national and international scientific conferences, and wide recognition from news and media organizations. This attention has been beneficial to CUNY as an institution involved in scientific research and to Dr. Vishnu, who is establishing himself in the world of science.

Because H-1B visas limit the length of time that a foreign national may remain in the United States, Dr. Vishnu will need to get a green card if he is to remain in the country and continue this cutting-edge research. Again, RFCUNY's immigration program is providing assistance in this area. While RFCUNY does not provide the complicated legal services necessary to get a green card, its human resources staff, who are knowledgeable about immigration, recognized that Dr. Vishnu was either an "outstanding researcher" or an "extraordinary ability alien" within the meaning of immigration law, and recommended that he seek legal counsel.

Dr. Vishnu already knew something about the outstanding researcher category because he had attended one of the many seminars on immigration presented by RFCUNY. As Dr. Vishnu and his attorney work toward getting his green card, RFCUNY will assist in the process by serving as a resource to the attorney, reviewing the petition, and signing off on the employer support letter that will be submitted to the United States Citizenship and Immigration Services.

Although Dr. Zarruq's area of research is much different from the area pursued by Dr. Vishnu, she was drawn to the United States for similar reasons. Dr. Zarruq earned her medical degree and completed a two-year internship in her native Morocco. But her real interest was in research, particularly in the field of neuroscience, and she felt that she would find the best opportunities in the United States. While attending an international neuroscience conference, she met Dr. Laroui, a CUNY professor conducting research into Fragile X Syndrome, a leading genetic cause of mental retardation and autism. His research had produced a drug therapy that had shown promise in laboratory mice, but needed to be moved to clinical trials. This stage of the research would require the assistance of a medical doctor. Dr. Laroui offered this position to Dr. Zarruq. She gladly accepted; this was exactly the opportunity she had been hoping for.

This collaboration has also been successful. Drs. Zarruq and Laroui are now working on presenting the results of their research to the neuroscience community, and having those results published. Preliminary reports on their research have already been well received. It goes without saying that the development of an innovative drug therapy for autism will be a boost for CUNY's standing in the realm of scientific research.

As it had done for Dr. Vishnu, RFCUNY obtained a visa for Dr. Zarruq. But Dr. Zarruq will have to obtain a green card to remain in the United States and continue her work with Dr. Laroui. RFCUNY's human resources staff recognized that Dr. Zarruq might be a good candidate for obtaining a green card through a "National Interest Waiver" on the grounds that the goal of finding a drug therapy for autism is in the national interest. As in Dr. Vishnu's case, RFCUNY will assist Dr. Zarruq and her attorney in getting through the legal process.

APPLICABILITY TO OTHER INSTITUTIONS

RFCUNY's success in retaining foreign scientists in their research projects has more than justified the costs of providing their support initiatives. Following RFCUNY's blueprint, any academic institution could implement a similar program. Essentially, it involves a commitment on the part of management to creating an immigration-friendly environment, and training the human resources staff about the employment of foreign nationals.

Fostering scientific research is in the best tradition of academic institutions, and providing research opportunities to dedicated scientists from other parts of the world is in the best tradition of America's leadership role in raising the quality of life through scientific research.

*The names of the scientists discussed in this article are fictitious.

The Life Cycle of F-1 Regulatory Training: Partnering with International Students

Adria L. Baker

RATIONALE

International students (F-1 visa holders) are required to maintain legal immigration status while studying in the United States. The consequences for not maintaining visa status range from losing immigration benefits to being deported and barred from returning to the country for up to ten years or more. International students cannot manage their visa status alone, however. Since August of 2003, institutions that enroll F-1 international students must comply with Student & Exchange Visitor Information System (SEVIS) requirements. SEVIS is monitored by the Immigration & Customs Enforcement agency, which is under the Department of Homeland Security (DHS). Although students are responsible for their immigration status, maintaining this status can be achieved only through a true partnership between the institution, which is in compliance with SEVIS standards and reporting, and the student, who is following all F-1 regulations.

Given that international students need different types of immigration information during their time at the university, regulatory training must be ongoing. The following discussion offers best practice suggestions for disseminating F-1 visa information to students throughout the admission and enrollment periods including (a) prearrival, (b) arrival, (c) the first year, (d) the middle years, and (e) the final year.

DESCRIPTION OF THE STUDENTS AND THE INSTITUTION

Rice University is a small, highly selective private research university in the heart of Houston, Texas. Bachelor's, master's, and doctoral degrees are offered in many disciplines. Internationalization of the university is a key priority, which has been clearly outlined and publicized through the institution's mission statement called "A Vision for the Second Century" (Rice University, 2007).

The international student body consists of more than 16 percent of the overall student population. Although the majority of the international students are at the graduate level, Rice University has articulated in its mission statement a commitment to increase the undergraduate international student population. Therefore, regulatory training needs to appropriately adjust to the needs of foreign undergraduates as well as graduates.

PROGRAM DESCRIPTION

The life cycle of immigration information for international students, and the institution's responsibility to train students regarding F-1 regulations, begins well before the students arrive on campus.

Pre-Arrival

A university's regulatory commitment to international students often begins even before they are admitted and receive their initial I-20 (the document certifying they have been accepted to the university and which they submit to apply for an F-1 visa). Pre-arrival information can be the first opportunity for the sponsoring institution to provide materials related to the students' visa status, and the shared compliance relationship between the school and the student. Rice University's pre-arrival information, included in the initial I-20 mailing, includes instructions about applying for the F-1 visa entry stamp at a nearby U.S. consulate or embassy. Clarification as to the difference between the *visa stamp*, which serves as a "key" to enter the United States, and *visa status*, which refers to the visa regulations one must adhere to while living in the country, occurs in the pre-arrival stage, and is reinforced verbally in an initial orientation upon arrival.

Pre-arrival information also offers a checklist of documents that admitted international students need to be successful in their visa application and interview. The list provides instructions for making the SEVIS I-901 fee payment (see www.fmjfee.com). Other required documents include the visa application, financial documentation, proof of nonimmigrant intent, English language proficiency, and payment of visa and SEVIS fees. The best means for information dissemination in this stage includes an arrival booklet with key visa information, arrival expectations, and an online resource link for incoming students, all of which are included in the personalized welcome letter that accompanies the initial I-20 mailing.

Arrival

Newly arrived international students often struggle with various cultural and linguistic challenges in their first days and weeks in the United States. To assist with this challenge, Rice University compiled key information from handouts and past newsletter articles to create a handbook with resources on getting settled and acculturated to the new environment and maintaining immigration status. The handbook also serves as a reference for future needs. Written resources such as this are an effective way for the university's Designated School Official (DSO) to train new students about maintaining their legal immigration status and the purpose of D/S—Duration of Status (the length of time allowed for completion of their studies).

Additionally, it is essential that the institution present a formal orientation program within the first few days of the international student's arrival. Rice University invites key speakers from the university to insure that newly arriving international students are given instructions about initial bureaucratic processes (e.g., getting a state ID card, registration, fee payment), cultural adjustment, and regulatory requirements.

Often, however, new international students have difficulty remembering these details due to language and cultural differences, information overload, and confusion as to procedures in the new environment. Therefore, the information should not only be presented orally, but also be available in easily understandable and readable formats including brochures, instructional handouts, and online materials. Although the information is available only in English, care is taken to ensure that the language is accessible to second language speakers. Students will be less likely to have immigration problems later if they can refer to F-1 regulations periodically in written materials. Examples of key concepts for training related to maintaining F-1 status include reporting address changes to the DSO within ten days, maintaining a full-course of study, making normal academic progress to complete the course of study in the allotted time, obtaining proper work authorization, and keeping information on the I-20 current.

The First Year

In the first academic year, students should be offered a wide array of training options. Immigration attorneys usually welcome an invitation to speak to international students about immigration laws. Our continuing orientation programs for first-year students are well-attended and provide an excellent opportunity to focus on topics necessary for adjustment as well as immigration compliance. Rice's biannual newsletter, *Rice World* (Rice University, 2008), provides specifics about unique international student needs, including reminders such as working with the DSO prior to dropping below a full course load, and updating SEVIS records with major changes (e.g., financial sponsorship, local address, and travel outside the United States).

In an effort to be accessible to the students, we meet with them by appointment or on a walk-in basis. We also hold roundtable discussions and offer a special speaker series on specific topics, which include on and off-campus employment authorization and visa issuance. As always, plenty of written and online resources that include regulations and links to key informational and governmental websites are critical. Other online and written training materials that provide checklists, FAQs (frequently asked questions), and flowcharts of procedures are advertised in *Rice World*, and referred to when answering calls and responding to student questions via e-mail or telephone.

The Middle Years

Special occasions, such as annual International Education Week (IEW), offer creative opportunities for outreach and training to remind international students (as well as the university community) that unlike their American classmates, international students are required to adhere to two levels of compliance: academic expectations *and* immigration regulations. At times, the two levels of responsibility can collide and be challenging for students and their host institutions, thus the need to reinforce the importance of the partnership relationship. During IEW, Rice invites guest speakers, offers special roundtable discussions, and writes articles for the campus newsletter to highlight the fact that international students are a unique asset for our campuses.

These special events can also provide opportunities for reminders of the immigration benefits international students may have if they maintain their status. An example is gaining work experience through an internship (utilizing curricular or optional practical training), or working on or off campus. Group e-mail reminders of deadlines and procedures, online Web information, and workshops can also help educate students of their eligibility for benefits.

The Final Year

Students approaching graduation should receive multiple reminders of immigration benefits that require prior DSO approval such as dropping below a full-time credit load in their last semester, post-completion optional practical training (OPT), changing educational levels such as moving from a bachelor's to a master's degree, or transferring to another school. By this time in their academic career, our students are well aware of the international office services, are able to find the procedures online, and feel comfortable meeting with a DSO by making an appointment or dropping by. The international advisor often needs to work in partnership with a student's academic department for some processes such as clarification of final graduation day in reference to their thesis defense, or extension of their stay in the event that their research needs more time for completion.

In sum, the partnership between the school and the international student is mandatory. The institution is responsible for maintaining proper and timely tracking, reporting, and record keeping as required by the DHS, as well as offering appropriate training. The student must comply with all F-1 regulations. The international office should keep up-to-date resource information on their website, provide timely group e-mail reminders, publish useful newsletters, and offer continued immigration training to prepare their students. In turn, students must take the proper steps to respond, read, inquire, and keep abreast of the information that is presented to reap F-1 benefits, as a result of maintaining his or her status.

EVALUATION

To ensure that our compliance partnership is effective, we have conducted various assessments. One is simply asking the students short, direct, survey questions about effectiveness by e-mails or an evaluation sheet at the end of a program. Although we can get great feedback from the students, caution is suggested when reviewing the results as the students who are happy with a given program are more likely to respond than those who feel the contrary. Furthermore, in our office, we monitor attendance levels. Students "vote with their feet." If there is a downward shift in attendance at a training event, we follow up by requesting feedback as to the best times, dates, and topics of interest.

Additionally, our university conducted an internal audit of the international office, where an analysis of each immigration process and training program was reviewed. The audit served as one method of assessment as to how we can best maintain our F-1 compliance, and proved to be a helpful benchmarking event for our school.

Our visa-managing system is also useful for evaluating our processes. It provides a quantitative way to evaluate the number of students staying in status and taking advantage of their immigration benefits (as a result of our training). The system has a notes feature, allowing us to analyze who is visiting the advisors and the purpose of their visit. For example, we reviewed the results as to how many students came to our office for practical training advisement and processing, and also determined the peak time of year for these types of requests. This provides us with greater insight as to when we should send out reminders and provide roundtable trainings on this topic. The visa-managing system also assists us with data to enable us to analyze the high-volume time of the year for processing initial I-20s. This gives us clues as to the best time to review and update our website arrival information, and helps us prioritize our responsibilities in the office.

APPLICABILITY TO OTHER INSTITUTIONS

All institutions of higher education that sponsor international (F-1) students must follow the same laws and regulations. However, given the great variety of academic programs, the manner in which rules are applied varies from institution to institution. Even so, the training opportunities mentioned here can be adopted by all institutions, so that they might successfully complete the partnership between the host institution and its international students.

One function of our visa-managing system in particular that may be replicated by other schools includes the ability to record information as to the purpose of an international student's visit to an international advisor. An electronic system for inputting and monitoring notes of meetings with the students can be established whether or not the school has a sophisticated visa-tracking system. The school can analyze the results periodically to assess principal needs, if students are maintaining their status, if they are taking advantage of the benefits, and what times during the year and students' academic tenure are most appropriate for compliance and benefits training.

By partnering with the student and continually evaluating needs, practices, and procedures, institutions can provide a welcoming and supportive host environment.

Holistic Visa-Status Advising: The Pitt Model of Advising Foreign Students and Scholars

Elizabeth Risa

RATIONALE

Research indicates that international students succeed when there are specialized services to assist them (Wilson, 2007). In the post-9/11 environment, universities have developed different approaches to advising foreign students and managing the associated paperwork. Today, advising foreign students often involves more than face time with students, and foreign student advisors are challenged to find unique ways to manage complex and time-consuming cases while maintaining accessibility. The Office of International Services (OIS) at the University of Pittsburgh has adopted a unique model of casework management that allows foreign student advisors to have a comprehensive approach to students' needs with insight into long-term options.

Loveland, Johnson, and Leibach (2006) identify three basic models of foreign student advising and case management for offices that serve international students and scholars: specialist, assignment, and no model. Originally, the OIS followed the specialist model where an advisor or group of advisors is assigned an area of responsibility by visa category: F-1 Student, J-1 Research Scholar, H1-B1 Temporary Worker, and so on. This model allows a foreign student advisor to become an expert in a particular visa category and allows advisors to accommodate the special needs of their particular group. However, in our context, maintaining quality service when the visa category specialist was on extended leave or vacation was challenging, and inequities in workload were not conducive to a team approach. Ultimately, the specialist model did not support continuity of service for our long-term clients: students who transitioned into postdoctoral positions or faculty and staff that transitioned from temporary to permanent positions.

With these challenges in mind, OIS initiated a new approach to managing casework associated with advising foreign students and scholars. In the fall of 2004, the OIS immigration team transitioned to the assignment model (what we call the Pitt model) of workflow management. With this approach, academic units within the university, rather than visa categories, were assigned to an OIS staff member, who was then responsible for all visa categories for his or her assigned units. The rationale behind this transition in case management was to provide redundant coverage of each visa category and a broader scope of expertise to our clients. Redundant coverage was necessary to continue services to individuals in a particular visa category when that visa category specialist was on extended vacation or leave. Having a model with redundancies alleviated the concerns of our internal clients in terms of processing requests during the visa category specialist's absence.

DESCRIPTION OF THE STUDENTS AND INSTITUTION

The University of Pittsburgh serves approximately thirty-two thousand students, including more than nine thousand graduate students, in the sixteen schools at the Pittsburgh campus and the four regional campuses. The OIS, a department of the Division of Student Affairs, is located on the main Oakland campus and has the responsibility for all international students, faculty, and staff who study or work in each of these campuses. Our overall population of internationals is approximately 2,900, of which 1,800 are students. Of the 1,800 students, over 90 percent are graduate students. The remainder of our international population consists mostly of J-1 Research Scholars/Professors and H1-B1 Temporary Workers in a Specialty Occupation.

PROGRAM DESCRIPTION

The Office of International Services had previously assigned one individual to all J scholar casework, another to all working visa casework (i.e., H1-B1 Temporary Worker, O-1 Alien of Extraordinary Ability, and Permanent Residents), and two individuals to F-1 student visas. To implement the new model, each in-house visa category specialist developed a training regimen for their particular visa category to present to the OIS team. After the internal training session, casework for the new visa category was phased in for the newly trained advisors, and the former category specialists served as peer reviewers of the new type of casework for a period of time. This review process was carried out over a semester, with full implementation of the new advising model the following semester.

Implementation of the Pitt model has fundamentally changed how we approach our work with international students and scholars as well as how we support and recruit individuals to our immigration services team. To assist with the latter, we developed a training model for new employees that allows them to add one visa category at a time into their caseloads, developed a series of internal tools to support advisors in managing a spectrum of visa category caseloads, and looked to nontraditional outside resources such as the American Immigration Lawyer's Association, to broaden our professional skill sets.

We also approach hiring for our team differently than most international offices. Originally our training model was aggressive, taking a new hire with little or no experience in immigration advising and training him or her to processing complex casework such as O-1 Alien of Extraordinary Ability and the Outstanding Researcher/Professor category of permanent residency in six short weeks. We have since reevaluated the effectiveness of this model and determined that this schedule attempts to add too much too soon. We have redesigned our process to allow for ample time to acclimate to the environment, establish relationships with our internal clientele, develop confidence, and gain poise with complex immigration cases. Our plan is to adopt a graduated approach, phasing in increasingly complex visa category cases over the course of a full year.

Our training model and internal tools go hand in hand. We developed a series of internal checklists for each visa category and for certain specialized services. The checklists have multiple functions: (1) they help seasoned immigration specialists keep casework organized, (2) they serve as a final reference before submitting a petition to the United States Citizenship and Immigration Service (USCIS) for adjudication or processing a document in-house, and (3) they serve as training tools when integrating new immigration specialists into the team.

Professionally, we have utilized the services and resources of NAFSA: The Association of International Educators, as many offices that serve international students and scholars do. We have also utilized the training tools of the American Immigration Lawyers Association, particularly for our employment-based visa categories.

Just as we have had to rethink our approach to advising, we also had to restructure our approach to recruiting and hiring for our immigration services team. Originally the position required a bachelor's degree with a master's degree preferred; it has since been reclassified to require a master's degree. While advising experience is never overlooked in the selection process, it is only one of many criteria we look for in the selection process. For example, self-motivated, lifelong learners with international experience are preferred over those with perhaps more experience in advising.

The Office of International Services has also implemented an internal support system in terms of an annual professional development budget, which advisors can use to participate in activities that serve their individual interests and contribute to the expertise of the overall team. For example, some members of the team have participated in professional development opportunities such as Web seminars and conferences presented by the American Immigration Lawyers Association in addition to participating in the NAFSA organization.

EVALUATION

The OIS mounted a comprehensive internal evaluation of its new advising system that included a satisfaction survey and focus groups. Participation in an online survey was offered to a random sample of students, scholars, and internal contacts within each academic unit, which resulted in 735 visits to the survey site and 307 completed surveys. When questioned about the professional knowledge of OIS staff members, 79 percent of survey respondents indicated that they were satisfied or very satisfied and 76 percent of respondents indicated they were satisfied or very satisfied with the range of nonimmigrant services offered by OIS. Our internal contacts also indicated in the focus group that they appreciated having one person to contact for all of their concerns.

Informal evaluative indicators of OIS's success include anecdotal feedback from our students, who indicate that they appreciate the expertise our office has to offer. In fact, our office is often called upon by students from other local colleges and universities for advice that may be beyond the area of expertise of their advisors. Often students and scholars will consult with an OIS immigration specialist in addition to consulting with an attorney to get a broader spectrum of advice. Our internal contacts also consult with us when recruiting international faculty and staff, calling on our specialists to verify immigration documents presented to the tuition eligibility, payroll, and human resource offices.

APPLICABILITY TO OTHER INSTITUTIONS

The Pitt model of foreign student advising would work well at institutions with similar demographics that have an environment where each individual school or department functions somewhat autonomously from the central administration. Institutions considering this model might want to consider impact factors prior to making the switch such as workload impact on personnel in terms of casework.

When Pitt made the transition, the casework for the individuals who handled F and J visas increased, while the casework for the individual who handled H casework decreased. Traffic at the centralized office area could also be affected if the office opens service to more individuals with varied visa types. Casework for visa types beyond the student cadre of visas may call for additional resource allocations, and a fee may be warranted to recoup expenditures outside of the scope of the office (i.e., if the office is located within the Division of Student Affairs, yet handles casework for nonstudents, for example). Also, internal political factors may dictate how certain cases should be handled, and institutions would be wise to consider this when making transitions, particularly where faculty and staff are concerned.

CONCLUSION

Students appreciate breadth of knowledge in terms of discussing employment options after graduation, beyond the benefits of their student status. The ability to discuss both J-1 Research Scholar scenarios as well as H1-B1 possibilities for postdoctoral positions is especially helpful to our graduate students. Even though the student visa categories are classified as nonimmigrant categories by the DHS, the practical reality is that many students look to stay and work in the United States beyond their programs of study. Students are dually motivated by experience in their field of study and financial considerations and often turn to their foreign student advisor for assistance in planning their long-term stay.

REFERENCES

Arndt, R. T., & Rubin, D. L. (Eds.) (1993. The Fulbright difference, 1948–1992. New Brunswick, NJ: Transaction.

Birrell, B. (2006). Implications of low English standards among overseas students at Australian universities. *People and Place, 14*(4), 53–64.

Brumfiel, G. (2004). Security restrictions lead foreign students to snub U.S. universities. *Nature, 43*(16), 231.

Goodwin, J. C. (2008). *Research in psychology: Methods and design* (5th ed.). New York: Wiley.

Groves, R. M., Dillman, D. A., Eltinge, J. L, & Little, R. J. A. (Eds.) (2002). Survey nonresponse. Chichester: Wiley.

Guimberteau, B. (1996, December). Two-year residency requirement. Research report submitted to the U.S. Senate, Committee on the Judiciary.

Law, G. (2007, October 10). Personal communication.

Loveland, E., Johnson, A., & Leibach, E. (2006). Providing better service: A case study. *International Educator, 15*(3), 68–71.

Meyer, J. D. (2001). A conceptual framework for comprehensive international student orientation programs. *International Education, 31*(1), 56–78.

NAFSA Association of International Educators. (2006, June). Restoring U.S. competitiveness for international students and scholars. Retrieved July 4, 2006, from http://www.nafsa.org/_/Document/_/restoring_u.s.pdf

Redden, E. (2008, February 8). Any advice about visas? Retrieved February 11, 2008, from http://www.insidehighered.com/news/2008/02/08/visas

Rice University. Office of the President. A vision for the second century (V2C). (2007). Retrieved December 13, 2007, from http://www.professor.rice.edu/professor/Vision.asp

———. (2008). Office of International Students & Scholars. Rice world. Retrieved January 20, 2008, from http://www.ruf.rice.edu/~ois/newsletter.html

Sarkodie-Mensah, K. (1998). International students in the U.S.: Trends, cultural adjustments, and solutions for a better experience. *International Library Education, 39*(3), 214–222.

Smith, M. F. (2005). Visa reform. *Academe, 91*(3), 79.

SRI International, Center for Science, Technology, and Economic Development. (2005, June). Outcome assessment of the Visiting Fulbright Student Program. Retrieved November 20, 2007, from http://www.sri.com/policy/csted/reports/international/documents/Visiting percent20Student.pdf

U.S. Department of State (n.d.). Foreign Fulbright Program statistics, academic year 2005–2006 (n.d.). Retrieved September 12, 2007, from http://foreign.fulbrightonline.org/resources_program_statistics.html

Ware, D., Bedient, B., & Stelljes, M. (2005, November). 212(e)eek! Overcoming fear of the two-year home residence requirement. Paper presented at the NAFSA Conference, Region III, Colorado Springs, CO.

Wilson, E. (2007). Services contributing to international student success at Northern Alberta Institute of Technology. Unpublished master's thesis, Royal Roads University, Victoria, British Columbia, Canada. ProQuest Digital Dissertations (Publication No. AAT MR28990).

Yin, R. K. (2003). *Case study research: Design and methods.* Thousand Oaks, CA: Sage.

Index

Editors and Contributors

EDITORS

Maureen S. Andrade has extensive experience teaching ESL and TESOL courses, and served as an ESL program administrator and department chair at Brigham Young University Hawaii. She is also a former editor of the *TESL Reporter*. Her professional interests include teaching English for academic purposes, content-based language instruction, program assessment, and adjustment and retention issues for international students. She is a regular presenter at national and international conferences related to her scholarship interests and has published on related topics in academic journals and books.

Norman W. Evans is a faculty member in the linguistics and English language department at Brigham Young University. He has spent much of his career working with international students in a variety of capacities as an English language teacher, writing center coordinator, ESL program administrator, and TESOL teacher trainer. His research interests include international student adjustment, the scholarship of teaching and learning (specifically the impact cultural differences have on teaching and learning), writing in a second language, and ESL program administration.

CONTRIBUTORS

Debra Anderson is coordinator for International Student Services at the University of Florida where she has received the superior accomplishment award for administrators/professionals for outstanding service to international students and the university.

Millie Audas is director of Education Abroad and International Student Services at the University of Oklahoma. As a faculty member in the OU College of Education, Dr. Audas's research interests are in comparative higher education systems and education organizational behavior. She developed 174 university reciprocal partnerships in sixty-six nations worldwide and accepted, for The University of Oklahoma, the Paul Simon Award for Internationalization. She has served as Region III Chair of NAFSA and received the Outstanding Service Award in International Education. She can be contacted at maudas@ou.edu.

Marcia Babbitt is professor of English and chair of the Department of English at Kingsborough Community College. She was director of the Intensive ESL Learning Community program and taught in that program for many years. She is currently codirector of the Opening Doors Learning Community program. Marcia received her Ph.D in linguistics from the CUNY Graduate Center. Marcia can be contacted at mbabbitt@kbcc.cuny.edu.

Adria L. Baker is executive director of Rice University's Office of International Students and Scholars. She has served as chair of Region III for NAFSA, and received outstanding service awards in international education as a result of her leadership in advocacy efforts. Her experience as a Rotary fellow at the University of Costa Rica has influenced her many presentations at national and regional conferences on issues affecting international visitors to the United States. She may be contacted at abaker@rice.edu.

Suzanne Barrett is the director of the Connors Family Learning Center at Boston College. She may be contacted at barretsc@bc.edu.

Kelley Calvert is assistant professor in the English for Academic and Professional Purposes program at the Monterey Institute of International Studies. She may be contacted at kelley.calvert@miis.edu.

Bridget E. Canty is associate director of the University of Houston's Office of International Admissions. Her leadership in the field of international education includes serving as chair of the Council on Ethical Practices for NAFSA: Association of International Educators, as subcommittee chair for the mayor of Houston, and on the Task Force for International Visitors.

Diana B. Carlin was dean of the graduate school and international programs at the University of Kansas from 2000–2007 and Dean-in-Residence and director of International Outreach for the Council of Graduate Schools from 2007–2008. She is active in NAFSA: Association of International Educators and chaired its task force on the Bologna Process. She is currently a professor of communication studies at the University of Kansas.

Chun-Chung Choi is clinical assistant professor at the counseling center and an affiliated faculty member at the Department of Psychology at the University of Florida. He has authored or coauthored several book chapters, articles, and the script for a film on cross-cultural issues.

Laurie Cox, is director of International Student Services at the University of Wisconsin, Madison. She has worked with international students at the University of Southern California and Chaminade University in Honolulu prior to coming to the University of Wisconsin, Madison. She may be contacted at cox@odos.wisc.edu.

Cheryl Darrup-Boychuck owns and operates USjournal.com, LLC and its family of seventeen multilingual sites designed to recruit international students for U.S. colleges, universities, and English language programs. She is an active member of NAFSA. She regularly presents sessions about e-recruitment trends and techniques at professional conferences around the world.

Negar Davis is director of global relations and promotion at the Pennsylvania State University. In addition to her administrative responsibilities, she has taught courses in intercultural communication. She has extensive international experiences and a passion for international education. She believes that teaching students about other cultures and peoples will eliminate hostilities and misunderstandings, which will lead to world peace.

Darla K. Deardorff is executive director of the Association of International Education Administrators, a national professional organization based at Duke University, where she teaches cross-cultural courses. She is the past cochair of NAFSA's Knowledge Community on International Students and Scholars. She has spoken and published widely on topics of intercultural competence and international education assessment and is editor of the *SAGE Handbook of Intercultural Competence* (Sage, 2009). She can be reached at d.deardorff@duke.edu.

Victoria Donoghue, Esq., served as the assistant director of human resources for RFCUNY from 2003 to 2007. Currently, Ms. Donoghue is counsel to a national immigration law practice with offices in New York, New Jersey, and Canada. Ms. Donoghue concentrates her immigration practice on handling matters for researchers, scientists, professors, and academic institutions as counsel to Nachman & Associates, P.C. The author can be reached at Victoria_Donoghue@visaserve.com.

Mary Ellen Duncan is president emerita of Howard Community College. Retired after seventeen years in two presidencies, Dr. Duncan is currently serving as a coach for the Achieving the Dream initiative and as a consultant in the areas of fundraising, accountability, assessment (especially the Baldrige model), and international education. She can be contacted at mduncan@howardcc.edu.

Jodi Ebner is the project manager for the Center for Global Education's Project for Learning in the United States (PLUS) at Loyola Marymount University. She might be contacted at jebner1@mlu.edu.

Udo Fluck is senior lecturer at the University of Montana and has been a MIFP Board member since 2005. He can be reached at the Department of Geography, Old Journalism Building 207, The University of Montana, Missoula, MT 59812.

Joan E. Friedenberg is professor in the College of Education at Florida Atlantic University, working in the areas of bilingual education, language policy, and TESOL. She can be contacted at Joan@Illinoisalumni.org.

Bernadette Guimberteau is an expert in research methods for the behavioral sciences and an alumna of the Fulbright program. She is affiliated with the University of California at Berkeley where she earned her Ph.D in education and stayed as a visiting scholar and a psychology instructor for the Behavioral and Health Sciences Division at UC Berkeley Extension. She can be reached at bguimberteau@cal.berkeley.edu.

Anjali Pai Hallett is associate director of the University of Utah's International Center. Anjali lived in Asia for over ten years before coming to the university. She enjoys developing new programs that support international students and increase awareness of international issues on campus.

Heather Housley is director of International Student and Scholar Services at Georgia State University in Atlanta. She has a master's degree in higher education and student affairs from The Ohio State University, and is a former Peace Corps volunteer. Heather can be contacted at www.gsu.edu.isss.

Ravi Kallur has worked for twenty years in international education, during which time he coauthored *PIER Special Report on India*, co-edited *Ethics in International Recruitment*, and authored a publication on India in electronic databases for Global Education by AACRAO. He also established and directed the International Medicine Office at the University of Missouri, Kansas City School of Medicine.

Greg Kessler is assistant professor of computer-assisted language learning in the Department of Linguistics at Ohio University. He can be contacted at kessler@ohio.edu.

Laura Kimoto is instructor of English to speakers of other languages in the English Language Institute at the University of Hawaii at Hilo. She previously served as coordinator of the Intensive English program at Hawaii Community College and instructor of Japanese at the University of Hawaii at Hilo. She can be contacted at laura.kimoto@hawaii.edu.

Ted R. McKown II is director of international student recruitment, admissions, and advising at Kent State University in Kent, Ohio. He has been working in the field of higher education marketing and admissions for sixteen years. He is a member of many organizations including NAFSA: Association of International Educators and AACRAO.

Aleksandra Nesic first came to the United States as an exchange student from Serbia. She has received a best practices award for international community programming while working at the University of Florida. Aleks is currently the Cross-Cultural Programs coordinator at Florida State University.

Lynne A. O'Connell is the director of undergraduate laboratories in the chemistry department at Boston College. Lynne may be contacted at oconnell @bc.edu.

Michael Panchias is the senior laboratory assistant for the undergraduate teaching laboratories in the chemistry department at Boston College. He may be contacted at panchias@bc.edu

Leigh Poole is director of International Student Life and associate director for Intercultural Affairs at the University of Georgia. She can be reached by mail at International Student Life, 210 Memorial Hall, Athens, Georgia 30602 or via the office website at www.uga.edu/isl.

Joe D. Potts is director of International Student and Scholar Services at the University of Kansas. He holds a PhD in the history and philosophy of education and has worked in the PRC and Japan, done consulting in Vietnam, and taught courses in leadership, theory, ethics, and cross-cultural communication. His most recent research focuses on the institutional impact of international students.

Gary Rhodes, director of the Center for Global Education and an affiliated faculty member in the School of Education at Loyola Marymount University.

He has taught graduate level courses on the administration of international programs in U.S. higher education, worked in international higher education at USC, UCLA, and LMU, presented and published widely on these issues, and received Fulbright Specialist Senior Grants to South Africa and India. He may be contacted at grhodes@lmu.edu.

Melissa Rigas is center director of ELS Language Centers in Teaneck, New Jersey. She has lived and taught in Europe and Asia, and is a specialist in cross-cultural communication, cross-cultural management, international corporate cultures, and Asian/Western business cultures. Her professional interests include raising cross-cultural consciousness, transnational education, and the impact of globalization on educational cultures across the world. She can be reached at mrigas@els.edu.

Elizabeth Risa has worked for five years as assistant director of immigration services at the University of Pittsburgh. She can be contacted at betta.risa@gmail.com.

Enid D. Rosenstiel is an academic program specialist in the American Language program at the Ohio State University. She may be contacted at rosenstiel .2@osu.edu.

Sheila K. Schulte is director of International Student and Scholar Services in the Office of International Education at the Georgia Institute of Technology in Atlanta. She has a master's degree in anthropology from the University of Iowa. She has worked with international students and scholars at the University of Iowa, University of Idaho, and Emory University prior to coming to Georgia Tech. Sheila can be contacted at sheila.schulte @oie.gatech.edu.

Tammy J. Silver is director of the International Center at the College of Southern Nevada in Las Vegas. She has previously advised international students and has been an intensive English program instructor and director in Skopje, Macedonia. She can be contacted at tammy.silver@csn.edu.

Michael B. Smithee is retired associate director of the Slutzker Center for International Services at Syracuse University.

William A. Stock, Esq., is a former foreign student advisor and currently a partner in the law firm of Klasko, Rulon, Stock & Seltzer, LLP, where he counsels universities and other employers on immigration law compliance and assists individuals in applying for immigration benefits. He can be reached at wstock@klaskolaw.com.

Christine Jensen Sundstrom is coordinator of the Graduate Writing Support program and a language specialist at the Applied English Center at the University of Kansas. She teaches thesis and dissertation writing and professional writing to international and domestic graduate students and presents workshops for graduate students and faculty members on successful graduate studies and mentoring. Her current research interests include cross-cultural variation in professional genres and teaching and mentoring graduate students. She can be reached at cjensen@ku.edu.

Patricia Szasz is the director of the Intensive English program at the Monterey Institute of International Studies. She has a master's degree in teaching English to speakers of other languages (TESOL) and has taught in the United States and Italy. Her areas of interest include project-based learning, the integration of technology in the language classroom, and language program administration. She may be contacted at patricia.szasz@miis.edu.

Julianne Taaffe is an academic program specialist in the American Language program at the Ohio State University. She may be contacted at taaffe.1@osu.edu.

Laura J. Thomas is an academic program specialist in the American L

anguage program at the Ohio State University. She may be contacted at thomas.19@osu.edu.

Stacey Lane Tice is associate dean of the Graduate School, Syracuse University. For more information, contact Dr. Tice at sltice@syr.edu.

Tara Weiss is assistant professor of English at Kingsborough Community College, where she teaches literature and ESL courses. She has also taught in the Intensive ESL Learning Community program for entering ESL students and currently serves as the associate academic director of ESL in the reading and writing center. She is also the College Now ESL Coordinator at Kingsborough. Tara received her Ph.D in comparative literature from the CUNY Graduate Center. Tara can be contacted at drtara5@earthlink.net.

Francine M. Wilson is assistant director of professional development at Cornell University Office of International Programs, College of Agriculture and Life Sciences. She can be contacted at fj10@cornell.edu.